GLOSSARY OF TERMS
IN
LOGISTICS & SHIPPING

GLOSSARY OF TERMS IN LOGISTICS & SHIPPING

The worlds most comprehensive paper-based logistics & shipping dictionary

First Edition

Paul A.Th. Denneman MSc
Editor

www.theKnowledgeTransfer.com

GLOSSARY OF TERMS IN LOGISTICS & SHIPPING

The worlds most comprehensive paper-based logistics & shipping dictionary

First Edition, 2006

Copyright © 2006 by theKnowledgeTransfer.com
A Mutatis Mutandis, logistic knowledge transfer Company

Al rights reserved. Except for the usual review purposes, no part of this work may be reproduced or transmitted in any form or by any means, electronic or mechanical, including photocopying, recording, or any information retrieval system, without the written permission of the publisher.

www.theKnowledgeTransfer.com
www.eLogistics-TrendwatcH.com

ISBN: 90-78744-01-4 / 978-90-78744-01-6
NUR: 804   BUS 070100

Table of Contents

TABLE OF CONTENTS 5
PREFACE 7
ACKNOWLEDGEMENTS 8
ACRONYMS 9
DEFINITIONS 15
TERMS 159
ABOUT THE EDITOR 183

Preface

The world of Logistics and Shipping has become increasingly global. This means that flows has to be coordinated from and to different continents. Common language in the area of Logistics and Shipping is still the English language, which is full of three-of-more character acronyms, terms and jargon.

In the past I took an example of an article of my news site eLogistics Trendwatch, and noticed that a common English dictionary did not help me to fully understand the meaning of the text. This is all due to the jargon used in our profession. To improve the readability of the news site, I started to collect acronyms, terms and definitions, to finally develop a database, and make it accessible via the Internet. During the trials of the web-based databank, it was regarded as added value when the glossary was made available in a printed format too.

The first tangible result of the process of collecting of acronyms, terms and definitions is now available in book format. The are several entries to use the book. First you can search correct term of an acronym, secondly you can find the correct definition of a given term. For a quick reference, all the terms used in this book are listed as well. Especially for those who are working or studying in the field of Logistics and Shipping, this printed version will be an often used book.

I wish you a pleasant and fruitful exploration and explanation of everything you always wanted to know about shipping and logistics, but possibly were afraid to ask.

Fall 2006,

Paul Denneman

Acknowledgements

Every independent word of this list may be used, reproduced or transmitted in any form or by any means. However the complete list or major parts of it are not free to re-use, reproduce or to be transmitted, because the collection of this information takes a long time.

The acronyms, terms an definitions in this list are based on several sources, like, but not limited to:

- The American Production and Inventory Control Society's (APICS) Dictionary, visit www.apics.org.
- The ABC/M Glossary, Consortium for Advanced Manufacturing, visit www.cam-i.org
- Information Access's Glossary of Data Integration Terminology, visit www.infoaccess.net.
- Maersk Logistics International - Dictionary, visit: www.maersk-logistics.com.
- Manufacturing System's Glossary of Special Terms used in Client/Server Computing, Production Management and Process Automation., visit www.manufacturingsystems.com.
- The Supply-Chain Council's Supply-Chain Operations Reference-model (SCOR), visit www.supply-chain.org.
- The Performance Measurement Group's Supply Chain Metrics Definitions & Calculations, visit www.pmbenchmarking.com.
- The Glossary of terms of Unigroup, international movers, visit www.unigroupworldwide.com

Acronyms

3PL	Third Party Logistics Provider
4PL	Four Party Logistics Provider
A/P	Accounts Payable
ABB	Activity Based Budgeting
ABC	Activity Based Costing
ABM	Activity Based Management
ABP	Activity Based Planning
ACD	Automated Call Distribution
ACE	Automated Commercial Environment
ACH	Automated Clearinghouse
ACSI	American Customer Satisfaction Index
AGVS	Automated Guided Vehicle System
ANSI	American National Standards Institute
APS	Advanced Planning and Scheduling
APS	Advanced Planning Systems
AQ	Any-quantity rate
AQL	Acceptable Quality Level
AS/RS	Automated Storage/Retrieval System
AS2	Applicability Statement 2
ASC	Accredited Standards Committee
ASCII	American Standard Code for Information Interchange
ASN	Advanced Shipping Notice
ASP	Application Service Provider
ASQ	American Society for Quality
ASTD	American Society for Training and Development
ASTM	American Society for Testing and Materials
ATD	Artificial Tween Decks
ATP	Available-to-Promise
ATS	Available to Sell
AVL	Approved Vendor List
AWB	Air Waybill
B2B	Business-to-Business
B2C	Business-to-Consumer
BAF	Bunker Adjustment Factor
BAM	Business Activity Monitoring
BCP	Business Continuity Plan
BMP	Bitmap Image
BOK	Body of knowledge

GLOSSARY OF TERMS IN LOGISTICS & SHIPPING

BOL	Bill of Lading
BOM	Bill of Material
BPM	Business Performance Measurement
BPO	Business Process Outsourcing
BPR	Business Process Reengineering
BTS	Balance to Ship
CAD	Computer Aided Design
CAE	Computer Aided Engineering
CAF	Currency Adjustment Factor
CAM	Computer Aided Manufacturing
CAPP	Computer Aided Process Planning
CBT	Computer Based Training
CFD	Continuous Flow Distribution
CFR	Cost and Freight
CFS	Container Freight Station
CGMP	Current good manufacturing practices
CI	Continuous Improvement
CIF	Cost, Insurance and Freight
CIM	Computer Integrated Manufacturing
CIP	Carriage and Insurance Paid To
CLCA	Closed-loop corrective action
CLM	Council of Logistics Management
CMI	Co-Managed Inventory
CMM	Capability maturity model
CMMS	Computerized Maintenance Management Systems
COA	Certificate of Analysis
COGS	Cost of Goods Sold
COTD	Complete & On-Time Delivery
CPC	Collaborative Product Commerce
CPFR	Collaborative planning, forecasting, and replenishment
CPG	Consumer Packaged Goods
CPI	Continuous Process Improvement
CPT	Carriage Paid To
CRM	Customer Relationship Management
CRP	Continuous Replenishment Planning
CSCMP	Council of Supply Chain Management Professionals
CSF	Critical Success Factor
CSI	Container Security Initiative
CSL	Container Stuffing List
CSR	Customer Service Representative
CTP	Capable to Promise
C-TPAT	Customs-Trade Partnership against Terrorism
CWT	Hundredweight
CY	Container Yard
CY/CY	CY/CY
DAF	Delivered at Frontier
DBR	Drum-Buffer-Rope
DC	Distribution Center
DDP	Delivered Duty Paid
DDU	Delivered Duty Unpaid
DEQ	Delivered Ex Quay
DES	Delivered Ex Ship

ACRONYMS

DFMA	Design For Manufacture / Assembly
DFZ	Duty Free Zone
DGI	Defective goods inventory
DISA	Data Interchange Standards Association
DOA	Dead on Arrival
DOD	Distribution On Demand
DOE	Design of Experiments
DPC	Dynamic Process Control
DPL	Denied Party List
DPP	Direct Product Profitability
DPS	Dynamic Planning and Scheduling
DRP	Disaster Recovery Planning
DRP	Distribution Requirements Planning
DRP-II	Distribution Resource Planning
DSD	Direct Store Delivery
DSO	Days Sales Outstanding
DSS	Decision Support System
DTD	Door-to-Door
DTF	Demand Time Fence
DTP	Door to Port
EAI	Enterprise Application Integration
EAN	European Article Number
EBIT	Earnings Before Interest and Taxes
EC	E-Commerce
EC	Electronic Commerce
ECO	Engineering Change Order
ECR	Efficient Consumer Response
EDI	Electronic Data Interchange
EFT	Electronic Funds Transfer
EIN	Exporter Identification Number
EIR	Equipment Interchange Receipt
EOQ	Economic Order Quantity
EPC	Electronic Product Code
ERP	Enterprise Resource Planning System
ERS	Evaluated Receipts Settlement
ESI	Early Supplier Involvement
ETA	Estimated Time of Arrival
EVA	Economic Value Added
EXW	Ex Works
FA	Functional Acknowledgment
FAA	Federal Aviation Administration
FAK	Freight-All-Kinds
FAS	Final Assembly Schedule
FAS	Free Alongside Ship
FAST	Fast and Secure Trade
FB	Freight Bill
FCA	Free Carrier
FCL	Full Container Load
FF&E	Furniture, Fixtures and Equipment
FFE	Forty-foot equivalent unit
FFG	Field Finished Goods
FGI	Finished Goods Inventory

GLOSSARY OF TERMS IN LOGISTICS & SHIPPING

FIFO	First In First Out
FIO	FIO
FMC	Federal Maritime Commission
FMEA	Failure Modes Effects Analysis
FOB	Free On Board
FRM	Floor-Ready Merchandise
FTE	Full-time Equivalents
FTL	Full Truckload
FTP	File Transfer Protocol
FTZ	Foreign Trade Zone
GBL	Government Bill of Lading
GIF	Graphics Interchange Format
GMP	Good manufacturing practices
GNP	Gross National Product
GOH	Garment-on-Hanger
GPS	Global Positioning System
GRN	Goods Received Note
GTIN	Global Trade Item Number
HAWB	House Airwaybill
HR	Human Resources
HS-code	Harmonized Commodity Description & Coding System
HTML	HyperText Markup Language
HTS	Harmonize Tariff Schedule of the United States
HTTP	HTTP
ICC	Interstate Commerce Commission
IMC	Intermodal Marketing Company
IP	Intellectual Property
IPI	Inland Point Intermodal
IPO	International Procurement Organization
IS	Information systems
ISDN	Integrated Services Digital Network
ISO	International Standards Organization
ITE	Independent Trading Exchange
ITIGG	International Transport Implementation Guidelines Group
ITU	Intermodal Transport Unit
JIT	Just-in-Time
JIT-II	Just-in-Time II
JOC	Journal of Commerce
JPEG	Joint Photographic Expert Group
JSA	Joint Supplier Agreement
KD	Knocked Down
KPI	Key Performance Indicator
L/H	Line-Haul
LAN	Local Area Network
LC	Letter of Credit
LCL	Less-Than-Carload
LCL	Less-Than-Container Load
LDI	Logistics Data Interchange
LIFO	Last In, First Out
LLP	Lead Logistics Partner
LLP	Lead Logistics Provider
LTL	Less-Than-Truckload

ACRONYMS

M2M	Machine-to-Machine interface
MAWB	Master Air Waybill
MES	Manufacturing Execution Systems
MPS	Master Production Schedule
MRO	Maintenance, Repair, and Operating supplies
MRP	Material Requirements Planning
MRP-II	Manufacturing Resource Planning
MSDS	Material Safety Data Sheet
MTO	Make-to-Order
MTS	Make-to-Stock
NCV	No Customs Value
NMFC	National Motor Freight Classification
NPI	New Product Introduction
NSN	National Stock Number
NVOCC	Non Vessel Operating Common Carrier
OCP	Overland Common Port
OEE	Overall Equipment Effectiveness
OEM	Original Equipment Manufacturer
OLE	Object Linking and Embedding
OS&D	Over, Short, and Damaged
OTIF	On Time In Full
P2P	Path to Profitability
P2P	Peer to Peer
PBIT	Profit Before Interest and Tax
PDA	Personal Digital Assistant
PDCA	Plan-Do-Check-Action
PM	Preventative Maintenance
PO	Purchase Order
POD	Proof of Delivery
POP	Point-of-Purchase
POS	Point Of Sale
PPB	Part Period Balancing
PSP	Procurement Services Provider
PTSC	Port & Terminal Service Charge
QFD	Quality Function Deployment
QR	Quick Response
RF	Radio Frequency
RFI	Request for Information
RFID	Radio Frequency Identificatrion
RFP	Request for Proposal
RFQ	Request for Quote
RM	Raw Materials
RMA	Return Material Authorization
ROA	Return on Assets
ROF	Return on owner's equity
ROI	Return of Investment
RO-RO	Roll on-roll-off
RPA	Return Product Authorization
RTF	Rich Text Format
RTV	Return to Vendor
S&OP	Sales and Operations Planning
SBT	Scan-Based Trading

GLOSSARY OF TERMS IN LOGISTICS & SHIPPING

SCE	Supply Chain Execution
SCEM	Supply Chain Event Management
SCI	Supply Chain Integration
SCM	Supply Chain Management
SCOR	Supply Chain Operations Reference Model
SET	Secure Electronic Transaction
SIC	Standard Industrial Classification
SIT	Storage in Transit
SKU	Stock Keeping Unit
SL&C	Shipper's Load & Count
SMART	Specific, Measurable, Achievable, Realistic, Time-Based
SOA	Service Oriented Architecture
SOP	Standard Operationg Procedure
SOW	Statement of Work
SPC	Statistical Process Control
SS	Safety Stock
SST	Smart and Secure Trade Lanes
SWOT	SWOT Analysis
TCO	Total Cost of Ownership
TEU	Twenty-foot Equivalent Unit
TL	Truckload
TMS	Transportation Management System
TOC	Theory of Constraints
TOFC	Trailer on a Flatcar
TPM	Total Productive Maintenance
TQM	Total quality management
TRP	Transportation requirements planning
T's & C's	Terms and conditions
UCC	Uniform Code Council
UCS	Uniform Communication Standard
ULD	Unit Load Device
UN/SPSC	United Nations Standard Product and Service Code
UOM	Unit of Measure
UPC	Uniform Product Code
URL	Uniform Resource Locator
VAN	Value-Added Network
VAT	Value-Added Tax
VBM	Value-Based Management
VBR	Value Based Return
VMI	Vendor-Managed Inventory
VOI	Vendor Owned Inventory
WAN	Wide Area Network
WIP	Work-in-Process
WMF	Windows Meta File
WMS	Warehouse Management System
WWW	World Wide Web
WYSIWYG	What You See Is What You Get
XML	Extensible Markup Language
YMS	Yard Management System

Definitions

14 Points - W. Edwards Deming's 14 management practices to help companies increase their quality and productivity: 1. create constancy of purpose for improving products and services, 2. adopt the new philosophy, 3. cease dependence on inspection to achieve quality, 4. end the practice of awarding business on price alone; instead, minimize total cost by working with a single supplier, 5. improve constantly and forever every process for planning, production and service, 6. institute training on the job, 7. adopt and institute leadership, 8. drive out fear, 9. break down barriers between staff areas, 10. eliminate slogans, exhortations and targets for the workforce, 11. eliminate numerical quotas for the workforce and numerical goals for management, 12. remove barriers that rob people of pride of workmanship, and eliminate the annual rating or merit system, 13. institute a vigorous program of education and self-improvement for everyone and 14. put everybody in the company to work to accomplish the transformation. SUPPLY CHAIN and LOGISTICS

24/7 - Referring to operations that are conducted 24 hours a day, 7 days a week

24/7/365 - Referring to operations that are conducted 24 hours a day, 7 days a week, 365 days per year, with no breaks for holidays, etc

24-hour Manifest Rule (24-hour Rule) - U.S. Customs rule requiring carriers to submit a cargo declaration 24 hours before cargo is laden aboard a vessel at a foreign port.

3D Loading - 3D loading is a method of space optimizing designed to help quickly and easily plan the best compact arrangement of any 3D rectangular object set (boxes) within one or more larger rectangular enclosures (containers). It's based on threedimensional, most-dense packing algorithms

3PL - see Third party logistics providers.

4PL - see Fourth party logistics providers.

5-Point Annual Average - Method frequently used in PMG studies to establish a representative average for a one year period. Calculation: [12/31/05 + 3/31/06 + 6/30/06 + 9/30/06 + 12/31/06] / 5

5-S Program - A program for organizing work areas. Sometimes referred to as elements, each of the five components of the program begins with the letter "S." They include sort, systemize, shine or sweep, standardize, and sustain. In the UK, the concept is converted to the 5-C program comprising five comparable components: clear out, configure, clean and check, conformity, and custom and practice.

80-20 Rule - A term referring to the Pareto principle. The principle suggests that most effects come from relatively few causes; that is, 80% of the effects (or sales or costs) come from 20% of the possible causes (or items). Also see: ABC Classification, Pareto

———————— A ————————

A/P - see Accounts Payable

A/R - see Accredited Standards Committee

Abandonment - The decision of a carrier to give up or to discontinue service over a route. Railroads must seek ICC permission to abandon routes.

ABB - see Activity Based Budgeting

ABC - see Activity Based Costing

ABC Classification - Classification of a group of items in decreasing order of annual dollar volume or other criteria. This array is then split into three classes called A, B, and C. The A group represents 10 to 20% by number of items, and 50 to 70% by projected dollar volume. The next grouping, B, represents about 20% of the items and about 20% of the dollar volume. The C class contains 60 to 70% of the items, and represents about 10 to 30% of the dollar volume.

ABC Costing - See Activity Based Costing

ABC Inventory Control - An inventory control approach based on the ABC volume or sales revenue classification of products (A items are highest volume or revenue, C--or perhaps D--are lowest-volume SKUs).

ABC Model - In cost management, a representation of resource costs during a time period that are consumed through activities and traced to products, services, and customers or to any other object that creates a demand for the activity to be performed.

ABC System - In cost management, a system that maintains financial and operating data on an organization's resources, activities, drivers, objects and measures. ABC models are created and maintained within this system.

ABM - see Activity Based Management

Abnormal Demand - Demand in any period that is outside the limits established by management policy. This demand may come from a new customer or from existing customers whose own demand is increasing or decreasing. Care must be taken in evaluating the nature of the demand, is it a volume change, is it a change in product mix, or is it related to the timing of the order? Also see: Outlier.

ABP - see Activity Based Planning

Absorption - The assumption that the carrier will cover extraordinary or other special charges without increasing the price to the shipper.

Absorption Costing - In cost management, an approach to inventory valuation in which variable costs and a portion of fixed costs are assigned to each unit of production. The fixed costs are usually allocated to units of output on the basis of direct labor hours, machine hours, or material costs. Synonym: Allocation Costing.

Acceptable Quality Level (AQL) - In quality management, when a continuing series of lots is considered, AQL represents a quality level that, for the purposes of sampling inspection, is the limit of a satisfactory process average. Also see: Acceptance Sampling.

Acceptable Sampling Plan - In quality management, a specific plan that indicates the sampling sizes and the associated acceptance or non-acceptance criteria to be used. Also see: Acceptance Sampling.

Acceptance Number - In quality management, (1) A number used in

DEFINITIONS

acceptance sampling as a cutoff at which the lot will be accepted or rejected. For example, if x or more units are bad within the sample, the lot will be rejected. (2) The value of the test statistic that divides all possible values into acceptance and rejection regions. Also see: Acceptance Sampling.

Acceptance Sampling - (1) The process of sampling a portion of goods for inspection rather than examining the entire lot. The entire lot may be accepted or rejected based on the sample even though the specific units in the lot are better or worse than the sample. There are two types: attributes sampling and variables sampling. In attributes sampling, the presence or absence of a characteristic is noted in each of the units inspected. In variables sampling, the numerical magnitude of a characteristic is measured and recorded for each inspected unit; this type of sampling involves reference to a continuous scale of some kind.(2) A method of measuring random samples of lots or batches of products against predetermined standards.

Accessibility - The ability of a carrier to provide service between an origin and a destination.

Accessorial - (1) Accessorial Charges - Charges made for additional, special or supplemental services, normally over and above the line haul services. (2) Accessorial Service - Service rendered by a carrier in addition to transportation services. (e.g. sorting, packing, precooling, heating and storage.)

Accessorial charges - A carrier's charge for accessorial services such as loading, unloading, pickup, and delivery. See also: Upcharges.

Accessory - A choice or feature added to the good or service offered to the customer for customizing the end product. An accessory enhances the capabilities of the product but is not necessary for the basic function of the product. In many companies, an accessory means that the choice does not have to be specified before shipment but can

be added at a later date. In other companies, this choice must be made before shipment.

Accountability - Being answerable for, but not necessarily personally charged with, doing specific work. Accountability cannot be delegated, but it can be shared. For example, managers and executives are accountable for business performance even though they may not actually perform the work.

Accounts Payable (A/P) - The value of goods and services acquired for which payment has not yet been made.

Accounts receivable (A/R) - The value of goods shipped or services rendered to a customer on whom payment has not yet been received. Usually includes an allowance for bad debts.

Accreditation - Certification by a recognized body of the facilities, capability, objectivity, competence, and integrity of an agency, service, operational group, or individual to provide the specific service or operation needed. For example, the Registrar Accreditation Board accredits those organizations that register companies to the ISO 9000 Series Standards.

Accredited Standards Committee (ASC) - A committee of the ANSI chartered in 1979 to develop uniform standards for the electronic interchange of business documents. The committee develops and maintains U.S. generic standards for Electronic Data Interchange.

Accumulation bin - A place, usually a physical location, used to accumulate all components that go into an assembly before the assembly is sent out to the assembly floor. Synonym: assembly bin.

Accuracy - In quality management, the degree of freedom from error or the degree of conformity to a standard. Accuracy is different from precision. For example, four-significant-digit numbers are less precise than six-significant-digit numbers; however, a

17

properly computed four-significant-digit number might be more accurate than an improperly computed sixsignificant- digit number.

ACD - see Automated Call Distribution

ACE - see Automated Commercial Environment

ACH - see Automated Clearinghouse

Acknowledgment - A communication by a supplier to advise a purchaser that a purchase order has been received. It usually implies acceptance of the order by the supplier.

Acquisition Cost - In cost accounting, the cost required to obtain one or more units of an item. It is order quantity times unit cost.

ACSI - see American Customer Satisfaction Index

Act of God - An extraordinary force of nature (such as a severe flood or earthquake) that experience, prescience or care cannot reasonably foresee or prevent.

Action Message - An output of a system that identifies the need for and the type of action to be taken to correct a current or potential problem. Examples of action messages in an MRP system include release order, reschedule in, reschedule out, and cancel. Synonym: exception message, action report.

Action plan - A specific method or process to achieve the results called for by one or more objectives. An action plan may be a simpler version of a project plan.

Action Report - See Action Message

Activation - In constraint management, the use of non-constraint resources to make parts or products above the level needed to support the system constraint(s). The result is excessive work-in-process inventories or finished goods inventories, or both. In contrast, the term utilization is used to describe the situation in which non-constraint resource(s) usage is synchronized to support the needs of the constraint.

Active Inventory - The raw materials, work in process, and finished goods that will be used or sold within a given period.

Active Stock - Goods in active pick locations and ready for order filling.

Activity - Work performed by people, equipment, technologies or facilities. Activities are usually described by the "action-verbadjective- noun" grammar convention. Activities may occur in a linked sequence and activity-to-activity assignments may exist.(1) In activity-based cost accounting, a task or activity, performed by or at a resource, required in producing the organization's output of goods and services. A resource may be a person, machine, or facility. Activities are grouped into pools by type of activity and allocated to products.(2) In project management, an element of work on a project. It usually has an anticipated duration, anticipated cost, and expected resource requirements. Sometimes "major activity" is used for larger bodies of work.

Activity Analysis - The process of identifying and cataloging activities for detailed understanding and documentation of their characteristics. An activity analysis is accomplished by means of interviews, group sessions, questionnaires, observations, and reviews of physical records of work.

Activity Based Budgeting (ABB) - An approach to budgeting where a company uses an understanding of its activities and driver relationships to quantitatively estimate workload and resource requirements as part of an ongoing business plan. Budgets show the types, number of and cost of resources that activities are expected to consume based on forecasted workloads. The budget is part of an organization's activity-based planning process and can be used in evaluating its success in setting and pursuing strategic goals.

DEFINITIONS

Activity Based Costing (ABC) - A methodology that measures the cost and performance of cost objects, activities and resources. Cost objects consume activities and activities consume resources. Resource costs are assigned to activities based on their use of those resources, and activity costs are reassigned to cost objects (outputs) based on the cost objects proportional use of those activities. Activity-based costing incorporates causal relationships between cost objects and activities and between activities and resources. ABC links activities to a particular product so that the cost impact of that product is more readily visible. ABC combines financial data with nonfinancial data (activity costs) to report the actual per-unit cost of outputs. ABC is a refined form of absorption accounting that replaces misleading overhead cost allocations with cause-and-effect driver relationships that do a better job of segmenting and tracing the diversity and variation of the outputs of the processes. For example, an ABC approach might measure the cost incurred by the accounts receivable department in handling calls for billing errors, whereas the traditional accounting approach ignores the activity and measures the cost of the accounts receivable department as a percentage of revenue.

Activity Based Costing Model - In activity-based cost accounting, a model, by time period, of resource costs created because of activities related to products or services or other items causing the activity to be carried out.

Activity Based Costing System - A set of activity-based cost accounting models that collectively define data on an organization's resources, activities, drivers, objects, and measurements.

Activity Based Management (ABM) - A discipline focusing on the management of activities within business processes as the route to continuously improve both the value received by customers and the profit earned in providing that value. ABM uses activity-based cost information and performance measurements to influence management action. See Activity-Based Costing

Activity Based Planning (ABP) - Activity-based planning (ABP) is an ongoing process to determine activity and resource requirements (both financial and operational) based on the ongoing demand of products or services by specific customer needs. Resource requirements are compared to resources available and capacity issues are identified and managed. Activity-based budgeting (ABB) is based on the outputs of activity-based planning.

Activity Dictionary - A listing and description of activities that provides a common/standard definition of activities across the organization. An activity dictionary can include information about an activity and/or its relationships, such as activity description, business process, function source, whether value-added, inputs, outputs, supplier, customer, output measures, cost drivers, attributes, tasks, and other information as desired to describe the activity.

Activity Driver - The best single quantitative measure of the frequency and intensity of the demands placed on an activity by cost objects or other activities. It is used to assign activity costs to cost objects or to other activities.

Activity Level - A description of types of activities dependent on the functional area. Product-related activity levels may include unit, batch, and product levels. Customer-related activity levels may include customer, market, channel, and project levels.

Activity network diagram - An arrow diagram used in planning and managing processes and projects.

Activity Ratio - A financial ratio used to determine how an organization's resources perform relative to the revenue the resources produce. Activity ratios include inventory turnover, receivables conversion period, fixed-asset turnover, and return on assets.

Actual Cost System - A cost system that collects costs historically as they are applied to production and allocates indirect costs to products based on the specific costs and achieved volume of the products.

Actual Costs - The labor, material, and associated overhead costs that are charged against a job as it moves through the production process.

Actual Demand - Actual demand is composed of customer orders (and often allocations of items, ingredients, or raw materials to production or distribution). Actual demand nets against or "consumes" the forecast, depending upon the rules chosen over a time horizon. For example, actual demand will totally replace forecast inside the sold-out customer order backlog horizon (often called the demand time fence), but will net against the forecast outside this horizon based on the chosen forecast consumption rule.

Actual to Theoretical Cycle Time - The ratio of the measured time required to produce a given output divided by the sum of the time required to produce a given output based on the rated efficiency of the machinery and labor operations.

Ad Valorem (Latin) - According to Value (English); For example, if a bill of lading shows a value for the cargo being carried, an Ad Valorem charge will be levied. This charge is required because the insurance liability of the carrier increases. This charge may be a levied as a percentage of the value that has been shown.

Adaptive Control - (1) The ability of a control system to change its own parameters in response to a measured change in operating conditions.(2) Machine control units in which feeds and/or speeds are not fixed. The control unit, working from feedback sensors, is able to optimize favorable situations by automatically increasing or decreasing the machining parameters. This process ensures optimum tool life or surface finish and/or machining costs or production rates.

Adaptive Smoothing - In forecasting, a form of exponential smoothing in which the smoothing constant is automatically adjusted as a function of one or many items, for example, forecast error measurement, calendar characteristics (launch, replenishment, end of life), or demand volume.

Addendum - Authorized supplement or addition to a shipping or other transportation document that identifies additional services, changes in services and accompanying charges.

Add-Ons - Additional charges above ocean freight.

Advance Material Request - Ordering materials before the release of the formal product design. This early release is required because of long lead times.

Advanced Planning and Scheduling (APS) - Techniques that deal with analysis and planning of logistics and manufacturing over the short, intermediate, and long-term time periods. APS describes any computer program that uses advanced mathematical algorithms or logic to perform optimization or simulation on finite capacity scheduling, sourcing, capital planning, resource planning, forecasting, demand management, and others. These techniques simultaneously consider a range of constraints and business rules to provide real-time planning and scheduling, decision support, available-to-promise, and capable-to-promise capabilities. APS often generates and evaluates multiple scenarios. Management then selects one scenario to use as the "official plan." The five main components of APS systems are demand planning, production planning, production scheduling, distribution planning, and transportation planning.

DEFINITIONS

Advanced Planning Systems (APS) - An analytic decision support tool for production scheduling. The APS applications consist of an intelligent engine that assists planners and schedulers in developing schedules. APS applications take into consideration production constraints, with the assumption that capacities are finite.

Advanced Shipping Notice (ASN) - Detailed shipment information transmitted to a customer or consignee in advance of delivery, designating the contents (individual products and quantities of each) and nature of the shipment. May also include carrier and shipment specifics including time of shipment and expected time of arrival. See also: Assumed Receipt

Advising Bank - Bank where a shipper negotiates documents or where documents are first presented, usually at country of origin. Also, often referred to as the negotiating bank.

Aftermarket - An aftermarket is a customer segmentation that has demand for accessory, replacement, or refurbished parts. For example, a market for new cars. There is a different market (aftermarket) for floor mats (accessory), tires and batteries (replacement), and rebuilt starter motors (refurbish). An aftermarket continues well beyond the purchase of the new car

After-Sale Service - Services provided to the customer after products have been delivered. This can include repairs, maintenance and/or telephone support. Synonym: Field Service.

Agency tariff - A publication of a rate bureau that contains rates for many carriers.

Agent - (1) Abbreviation for 'Freight Agent'. (2) A person, association or corporation authorised to publish and file rates and provisions for a carrier's account in tariffs published in the agent's name. (3) One that acts for, or in the place of, another by authority from him, e.g. a (business)

representative, emissary, or official of a government. (4) A person, association or corporation authorised to publish and file rates and provisions for a carrier's account in tariffs published in the agent's name. (5) An enterprise authorized to transact business for, or in the name of, another enterprise. (6) Warehouse that provides storage, local pickup, local delivery, installation or other services.

Agglomeration - A net advantage gained by a common location with other companies.

Aggregate Forecast - An estimate of sales, often time phased, for a grouping of products or product families produced by a facility or firm. Stated in terms of units, dollars, or both, the aggregate forecast is used for sales and production planning (or for sales and operations planning) purposes.

Aggregate Inventory - The inventory for any grouping of items or products involving multiple stock-keeping units. Also see: Base Inventory Level.

Aggregate Inventory Management - Establishing the overall level (dollar value) of inventory desired and implementing controls to achieve this goal.

Aggregate Plan - A plan that includes budgeted levels of finished goods, inventory, production backlogs, and changes in the workforce to support the production strategy. Aggregated information (e.g., product line, family) rather than product information is used, hence the name aggregate plan.

Aggregate Planning - A process to develop tactical plans to support the organization's business plan. Aggregate planning usually includes the development, analysis, and maintenance of plans for total sales, total production, targeted inventory, and targeted customer backlog for families of products. The production plan is the result of the aggregate planning process. Two approaches to aggregate planning exist-- production planning and sales and operations planning.

21

Glossary of Terms in Logistics & Shipping

Aggregate tender rate - A reduced rate offered to a shipper who tenders two or more class-rated shipments at one time and one place.

Aggregated Shipments - Numerous shipments from different shippers delivered to one consignee, that are consolidated and treated as a single consignment.

Agile manufacturing - Tools, techniques, and initiatives that enable a plant or company to thrive under conditions of unpredictable change. Agile manufacturing not only enables a plant to achieve rapid response to customer needs, but also includes the ability to quickly reconfigure operations--and strategic alliances--to respond rapidly to unforeseen shifts in the marketplace. In some instances, it also incorporates "mass customization" concepts to satisfy unique customer requirements. In broad terms, it includes the ability to react quickly to technical or environmental surprises.

Agility - The ability to successfully manufacture and market a broad range of low-cost, high-quality products and services with short lead times and varying volumes that provides enhanced value to customers through customization. Agility merges the four distinctive competencies of cost, quality, dependability, and flexibility.

AGVS - see Automated Guided Vehicle System

AI - All Inclusive.

Air cargo - Freight that is moved by air transportation.

Air Cargo Containers - Containers designed to conform to the inside of an aircraft. There are many shapes and sizes of containers. Air cargo containers fall into three categories: (1) air cargo pallets (2) lower deck containers (3) box type containers.

Air Freight - A service providing the air transportation of goods. This mode of transportation allows for decreased shipping time, low damage ratios and for certain commodities, lower shipping costs.

Air Freight Forwarder - A non-asset based firm that negotiates low shipping rates with airlines, then takes orders at a higher rate in order to make a profit using the airline's assets to move the product.

Air taxi - An exempt for-hire air carrier that will fly anywhere on demand: air taxis are restricted to a maximum payload and passenger capacity per plane.

Air Transport Association of America - A U.S. airline industry association.

Air Waybill (AWB) - A document issued by a carrier to a shipper that supplies written evidence regarding the receipt of goods, the mode of transportation and the arrangement to deliver goods at the requested destination to the lawful holder of the bill of lading. A standard air waybill accommodates both domestic and international traffic.

Airport and Airway Trust Fund - A federal fund that collects passenger ticket taxes and disburses those funds for airport facilities.

Alaskan carrier - A for-hire air carrier that operates within the state of Alaska.

Alert - See Action Message.

Algorithm - A clearly specified mathematical process for computation; a set of rules, which, if followed, give a prescribed result.

All Water - When a shipment is transported from its origin to its destination solely by water transportation.

All-cargo carrier - An air carrier that transports cargo only.

Alliance - A union of one or more companies having relationship in qualities.

Supply chain alliances consist of trading partners having complimentary goals and objectives that are willing to collaborate in the areas of planning, forecasting and replenishments.

Allocated item - In an MRP system, an item for which a picking order has been released to the stockroom but not yet sent from the stockroom.

Allocation - (1)In cost accounting, a distribution of costs using calculations that may be unrelated to physical observations or direct or repeatable cause-and-effect relationships. Because of the arbitrary nature of allocations, costs based on cost causal assignment are viewed as more relevant for management decision-making.(2) In order management, allocation of available inventory to customer and production orders.

Allocation Costing - See Absorption Costing

Alpha release - A very early release of a product to get preliminary feedback about the feature set and usability.

Alternate Routing - A routing, usually less preferred than the primary routing, but resulting in an identical item. Alternate routings may be maintained in the computer or off-line via manual methods, but the computer software must be able to accept alternate routings for specific jobs.

American Customer Satisfaction Index (ACSI) - Released for the first time in October 1994, an economic indicator and cross industry measure of the satisfaction of U.S. household customers with the quality of the goods and services available to them-- both those goods and services produced within the United States and those provided as imports from foreign firms that have substantial market shares or dollar sales. The ACSI is co-sponsored by the University of Michigan Business School, ASQ and the CFI Group.

American National Standards Institute (ANSI) - A non-profit organization chartered to develop, maintain, and promulgate voluntary U.S. national standards in a number of areas, especially with regards to setting EDI standards. ANSI is the U.S. representative to the International Standards Organization (ISO).

American Society for Quality (ASQ) - Founded in 1946, a not-for-profit educational organization consisting of 144,000 members who are interested in quality improvement.

American Society for Testing and Materials (ASTM) - Not-for-profit organization that provides a forum for the development and publication of voluntary consensus standards for materials, products, systems and services.

American Society for Training and Development (ASTD) - A membership organization providing materials, education and support related to workplace learning and performance.

American Society of Transportation & Logistics - A professional organization founded in 1946 with goals of establishing; promoting and maintaining high standards of knowledge and professional training; serving as a source of information and guidance for the fields of logistics.

American Standard Code for Information Interchange (ASCII) - ASCII format - simple text based data with no formatting. The standard code for information exchange among data processing systems. Uses a coded character set consisting of 7-bit coded characters (8 bits including parity check).

American Trucking Association, Inc. - A motor carrier industry association that is made up of subconferences representing various sectors of the motor carrier industry.

Glossary of terms in Logistics & Shipping

American Waterway Operators - A domestic water carrier industry association representing barge operators on the inland waterways.

Amtrak - The National Railroad Passenger Corporation, a federally created corporation that operates most of the United States' intercity passenger rail service.

Animated GIF - A file containing a series of GIF (Graphics Interchange Format) images that are displayed in rapid sequence by some Web browsers, giving an animated effect. Also see: GIF.

ANSI - see American National Standards Institute

ANSI ASC X12 - American National Standards Institute Accredited Standards Committee X1(2) The committee of ANSI that is charted with setting EDI standards.

ANSI Standard - A published transaction set approved by ANSI. The standards are reviewed every six months.

Anticipated Delay Report - A report, normally issued by both manufacturing and purchasing to the material planning function, regarding jobs or purchase orders that will not be completed on time and explaining why the jobs or purchases are delayed and when they will be completed. This report is an essential ingredient of the closed-loop MRP system. It is normally a handwritten report. Synonym: delay report.

Anticipation Inventories - Additional inventory above basic pipeline stock to cover projected trends of increasing sales, planned sales promotion programs, seasonal fluctuations, plant shutdowns, and vacations.

Any Quantity [AQ] - A rating that applies to an item regardless of weight.

Any-quantity rate (AQ) - The same rate applies to any size shipment tendered to a carrier; no discount rate is available for large shipments.

Applicability Statement 2 (AS2) - A specification for Electronic Data Interchange between businesses using the Internet's Web page protocol, the Hypertext Transfer Protocol (HTTP). The specification is an extension of the earlier version, Applicability Statement 1 (AS1). Both specifications were created by EDI over the Internet (EDIINT), a working group of the Internet Engineering Task Force (IETF) that develops secure and reliable business communications standards.

Application Service Provider (ASP) - A company that offers access over the Internet to application (examples of applications include word processors, database programs, Web browsers, development tools, communication programs) and related services that would otherwise have to be located in their own computers. Sometimes referred to as "apps-on-tap", ASP services are expected to become an important alternative, especially for smaller companies with low budgets for information technology. The purpose is to try to reduce a company's burden by installing, managing, and maintaining software.

Application-to-Application - The direct interchange of data between computers, without re-keying.

Appraisal Costs - Those costs associated with the formal evaluation and audit of quality in the firm. Typical costs include inspection, quality audits, testing, calibration, and checking time.

Approved Vendor List (AVL) - List of the suppliers approved for doing business. The AVL is usually created by procurement or sourcing and engineering personnel using a variety of criteria such as technology, functional fit of the product, financial stability, and past performance of the supplier.

DEFINITIONS

APS - see Advanced Planning and Scheduling

APS - see Advanced Planning Systems

AQ - see Any-quantity rate

AQI - Agriculture Quarantine Inspection.

AQL - see Acceptable Quality Level

Arbitrary - (1) A fixed amount which a transportation line agrees to accept in a dividing joint rate. (2) A fixed amount added to or deducted from one station to make a rate from another station. (3) A fixed amount added to or deducted from a rate to one station to make a rate to another station. (4) An allowance added to an employee's rate of pay in addition to regular wages, based on provisions included in the union contract.

Army Corps of Engineers - A federal agency responsible for the construction and maintenance or waterways.

Arrival Notice - Documentation that notifies the consignee of arrival information for the goods and the freight charges due to be paid in exchange for the goods.

Arrow diagram - A planning tool to diagram a sequence of events or activities (nodes) and the interconnectivity of such nodes. It is used for scheduling and especially for determining the critical path through nodes.

Artificial Intelligence - Understanding and computerizing the human thought process.

Artificial Tween Decks (ATD) - Forty feet long, eight feet wide, one foot thick steel platform with hardwood flooring. Equipped with ten bulrings for securing oversized, heavy lift or wheeled cargo.

AS/RS - see Automated Storage/Retrieval System

AS2 - see Applicability Statement 2

ASC - See Accredited Standards Committee of ANSI.

ASC X12 - Accredited Standards Committee X1(2) A committee of ANSI chartered in 1979 to develop uniform standards for the electronic interchange of business documents.

ASCII - see American Standard Code for Information Interchange

ASN - see Advanced Shipping Notice

ASP - see Application Service Provider

ASQ - see American Society for Quality

Assemble to Order - A production environment performed in a warehouse, where product is assembled after receipt of a customer's order. The key components used in the assembly process are scheduled and usually stocked in expectation of a customer order. The receipt of an order initiates the assembly of the customized product.

Assemble-to-order - A production environment where a good or service can be assembled after receipt of a customer's order. The key components (bulk, semi-finished, intermediate, subassembly, fabricated, purchased, packing, and so on) used in the assembly or finishing process are planned and usually stocked in anticipation of a customer order. Receipt of an order initiates assembly of the customized product. This strategy is useful where a large number of end products (based on the selection of options and accessories) can be assembled from common components. Synonym: Finish to Order. Also see: Make to Order, Make to Stock.

Assembly - A group of subassemblies and/or parts that are put together and that constitute a major subdivision for the final product. An assembly may be an end item or a component of a higher level assembly.

Assembly Line - An assembly process in which equipment and work centers are laid

GLOSSARY OF TERMS IN LOGISTICS & SHIPPING

out to follow the sequence in which raw materials and parts are assembled.

Asset - Any inventory or item owned by a corporation or association of value.

Asset Management - Identifying the assets of a project and creating solutions that help identify, track and manage.

Asset Swap - An asset swap allows the pre-placement of assets at a new business location, supporting a quick and efficient turnover during the actual relocation to minimize downtime. See Equipment Relocation.

Asset-Based, Third Party Provider - A third party provider that owns transportation and/or warehouse assets.

Assignment - (1) The transfer to another of one's own legal interests or rights. (2) Especially the transfer of property to be held in trust or to be used for the benefit of creditors. (3) The document by which such an interest or right is transferred. (4) A distribution of costs using causal relationships. Because cost causal relationships are viewed as more relevant for management decision-making, assignment of costs is generally preferable to allocation techniques. (Synonymous with Tracing. Contrast with Allocation.)

Association of American railroads: A railroad industry association that represents the larger U.S. railroads. -

Assumed Receipt - The principle of assuming that the contents of a shipment are the same as those presented on a shipping or delivery note. Shipping and receiving personnel do not check the delivery quantity. This practice is used in conjunction with bar codes and an EDI-delivered ASN to eliminate invoices and facilitate rapid receiving.

ASTD - see American Society for Training and Development

ASTM - see American Society for Testing and Materials

ATD - see Artificial Tween Decks

ATP - see Available-to-Promise

ATS - see Available to Sell

Attachment - An accessory that has to be physically attached to the product.

Attributes - A label used to provide additional classification or information about a resource, activity, or cost object. Used for focusing attention and may be subjective. Examples are a characteristic, a score or grade of product or activity, or groupings of these items, and performance measures.

Audit - (1) The inspection and examination of a process or quality system to ensure compliance to requirements. An audit can apply to an entire organization or may be specific to a function, process or production step. (2) In reference to freight bills, the term audit is used to verify the accuracy of freight bills.

Audit Trail - Manual or computerized tracing of the transactions affecting the contents or origin of a record.

Auditability - A characteristic of modern information systems, gauged by the ease with which data can be substantiated by trading it to source documents and the extent to which auditors can rely on pre-verified and monitored control processes.

Auditing - Determining the correct transportation charges due the carrier

Authentication - (1) The process of verifying the eligibility of a device, originator, or individual to access specific categories of information or to enter specific areas of a facility. This process involves matching machine-readable code with a predetermined list of authorized end users.(2) A practice of establishing the validity of a transmission, message, device, or originator, which was designed to provide protection against fraudulent transmissions.

Authentication Key - A short string of characters used to authenticate transactions between trading partners.

Autodiscrimination - The functionality of a bar code reader to recognize the bar code symbology being scanned thus allowing a reader to read several different symbologies consecutively

AutoID - Referring to an automated identification system. This includes technology such as bar coding and radio frequency tagging (RFID).

Automated Call Distribution (ACD) - A feature of large call center or "Customer Interaction Center" telephone switches that routes calls by rules such as next available employee, skill-set etc.

Automated Clearinghouse (ACH) - Automated Clearinghouse. A nationwide electronic payments system, which more than 15,000 financial institutions use, on behalf of 100,000 corporations and millions of consumer in the U.S. The funds transfer system of choice among businesses that make electronic payments to vendors, it is economical and can carry remittance information in standardized, computer processable data formats.

Automated Commercial Environment (ACE) - Update of outmoded Automated Commercial System (ACS). It is intended to provide automated information system to enable the collection, processing and analysis of commercial import and export data, allowing for moving goods through the ports faster and at lower cost, as well as detection of terrorist threats.

Automated Guided Vehicle System (AGVS) - A transportation network that automatically routes one or more material handling devices, such as carts or pallet trucks, and positions them at predetermined destinations without operator intervention.

Automated Storage/Retrieval System (AS/RS) - A high-density rack inventory storage system with un-manned vehicles automatically loading and unloading products to/from the racks.

Automatic Relief - A set of inventory bookkeeping methods that automatically adjusts computerized inventory records based on a production transaction. Examples of automatic relief methods are backflushing, direct-deduct, pre-deduct, and post-deduct processing.

Automatic Rescheduling - Rescheduling done by the computer to automatically change due dates on scheduled receipts when it detects that due dates and need dates are out of phase. Antonym: manual rescheduling.

Availability - A term used to describe the access a customer has to equipment, data or assets during a relocation or migration event.

Available Inventory - The on-hand inventory balance minus allocations, reservations, backorders, and (usually) quantities held for quality problems. Often called "beginning available balance". Synonyms: Beginning Available Balance, Net Inventory. Available to Promise (ATP): The uncommitted portion of a company's inventory and planned production maintained in the master schedule to support customer-order promising. The ATP quantity is the uncommitted inventory balance in the first period and is normally calculated for each period in which an MPS receipt is scheduled. In the first period, ATP includes on-hand inventory less customer orders that are due and overdue. Three methods of calculation are used: discrete ATP, cumulative ATP with lookahead, and cumulative ATP without lookahead.

Available to Sell (ATS) - Total quantity of goods committed to the pipeline for a ship to or selling location. This includes the current inventory at a location and any open purchase orders.

Available-to-Promise (ATP) - The uncommitted portion of a company's inventory and planned production, maintained in the master schedule to support customer order promising. The ATP quantity is the uncommitted inventory balance in the first period and is normally calculated for each period in which an MPS receipt is scheduled. In the first period, ATP includes on-hand inventory less customer orders that are due and overdue.

Average Annual Production Materials Related A/P (Accounts Payable) - The value of direct materials acquired in that year for which payment has not yet been made. Production-related materials are those items classified as material purchases and included in the Cost of Goods Sold (COGS) as raw material purchases. Calculate using the 5-Point Annual Average.

Average Cost per Unit - The estimated total cost, including allocated overhead, to produce a batch of goods divided by the total number of units produced.

Average Inventory - The average inventory level over a period of time. Implicit in this definition is a "sampling period" which is the amount of time between inventory measurements. For example, daily inventory levels over a two-week period of time, hourly inventory levels over one day, etc. The average inventory for the same total period of time can fluctuate widely depending upon the sampling period used.

Average Payment Period (for materials) - The average time from receipt of production-related materials and payment for those materials. Production-related materials are those items classified as material purchases and included in the Cost of Goods Sold (COGS) as raw material purchases. (An element of Cash-to-Cash Cycle Time) Calculation: [Five point annual average production-related material accounts payable]

/ [Annual production-related material receipts/365]

AVL - see Approved Vendor List

Avoidable Cost - A cost associated with an activity that would not be incurred if the activity was not performed (e.g., telephone cost associated with vendor support).

AWB - see Air Waybill

B2C - see Business-to-Consumer

Back Haul - To obtain transport on the home run from B to A after having performed a full transport from A to B.

Back Order - Product ordered but out of stock and promised to ship when the product becomes available.

Back Scheduling - A technique for calculating operation start dates and due dates. The schedule is computed starting with the due date for the order and working backward to determine the required start date and/or due dates for each operation.

Backflush - A method of inventory bookkeeping where the book (computer) inventory of components is automatically reduced by the computer after completion of activity on the component's upper-level parent item based on what should have been used as specified on the bill of material and allocation records. This approach has the disadvantage of a built-in differential between the book record and what is physically in stock. Synonym: explode-to-deduct. Also see: Pre-deduct Inventory Transaction Processing

Backhaul - The process of a transportation vehicle returning from the original destination point to the point of origin. The 1980 Motor Carrier Act deregulated interstate commercial trucking and thereby allowed carriers to contract for the return trip. The backhaul can be with a full, partial, or empty load. An empty backhaul is called deadheading. Also see: Deadhead

Backlog Customer - Customer orders received but not yet shipped; also includes backorders and future orders.

Backorder - (1) The act of retaining a quantity to ship against an order when other order lines have already been shipped. Backorders are usually caused by stock shortages.(2) The quantity remaining to be shipped if an initial shipment(s) has been processed. Note: In some cases backorders are not allowed, this results in a lost sale when sufficient quantities are not available to completely ship and order or order line. Also see: Balance to Ship

Backsourcing - Pulling a function back in-house as an outsourcing contract expires

BAF - see Bunker Adjustment Factor

Balance sheet - A financial statement showing the resources owned, the debts owed, and the owner's share of a company at a given point in time.

Balance to Ship (BTS) - Balance or remaining quantity of a promotion or order that has yet to ship. Also see: Backorder

Balanced Scorecard - A structured measurement system developed by David Norton and Robert Kaplan of the Harvard Business School. It is based on a mix of financial and non financial measures of business performance. A list of financial and operational measurements used to evaluate organizational or supply chain performance. The dimensions of the balanced scorecard might include customer perspective, business process perspective, financial perspective, and innovation and learning perspectives. It formally connects overall objectives, strategies, and measurements. Each dimension has goals and measurements. Also see: Scorecard

Balance-of-Stores Record - A double-entry record system that shows the balance of inventory items on hand and the balances of items on order and available for future orders. Where a reserve system of materials control is used, the balance of material on reserve is also shown.

BAM - see Business Activity Monitoring

Bank Guarantee - (1) Under certain circumstances, accepted in lieu of original bill of lading to release cargo. (2) A statement issued by an importer's bank guaranteeing the payment of (L/C) drafts to the exporter or to the carrier. (3) Other forms of guarantees by banks in favour of a beneficiary.

Banker's Acceptance - A form of financing used in import/export transactions.

Bar Code - A symbol consisting of a series of printed bars representing values. A system of optical character reading, scanning, and tracking of units by reading a series of printed bars for translation into a numeric or alphanumeric identification code. A popular example is the UPC code used on retail packaging.

Bar Code Scanner - An electrical device to read bar codes and communicate accurate data to computer programs.

Barcode - A series of bars and spaces read by a scanning device for translation into a numeric or alphanumeric identification code that represents data in machine-readable or computerised form.

Barcode, 2-D - The PDF 1000 style barcode is used to store up to 1800 characters of text. Designed to allow more information to be stored and retrieved electronically; it has not achieved wide use.

Barge - (1) Conveyance used to carry loose cargo or containers in small volumes. (2) The cargo-carrying vehicle used primarily by inland water carriers. The basic barges have open tops, but there are covered barges for both dry and liquid cargoes.

Barrier to Entry - Factors that prevent companies from entering into a particular market, such as high initial investment in equipment.

Base Demand - The percentage of a company's demand that is derived from continuing contracts and/or existing customers. Because this demand is well known and recurring, it becomes the basis of management's plans. Synonym: Baseload Demand.

Base Index - See Base Series

Base Inventory Level - The inventory level made up of aggregate lot-size inventory plus the aggregate safety stock inventory. It does not take into account the anticipation inventory that will result from the production plan. The base inventory level should be known before the production plan is made. Also see: Aggregate Inventory.

Base Port - Ports from which standard tariff rates apply to those normally serviced directly by members.

Base Rate - Rate used only for construction of other rates.

Base Series - A standard succession of values of demand-over-time data used in forecasting seasonal items. This series of factors is usually based on the relative level of demand during the corresponding period of previous years. The average value of the base series over a seasonal cycle will be 1.0. A figure higher than 1.0 indicates that the demand for that period is more than the average; a figure less than 1.0 indicates less than the average. For forecasting purposes, the base series is superimposed upon the average demand and trend in demand for the item in question. Synonym: Base Index. Also see: Seasonality

Base Stock System - A method of inventory control that includes as special cases most of the systems in practice. In this system, when an order is received for any item, it is used as a picking ticket, and duplicate copies, called replenishment orders, are sent back to all stages of production to initiate replenishment of stocks. Positive or negative orders (called base stock orders) are also used from time to time to adjust the level of the base stock of each item. In actual practice, replenishment orders are usually accumulated when they are issued and are released at regular intervals.

Baseload Demand - See Base Demand

Basic Producer - A manufacturer that uses natural resources to produce materials for other manufacturing. A typical example is a steel company that processes iron ore and produces steel ingots; others are those making wood pulp, glass, and rubber.

Basing Points - A point (location) used in construction of through rates between other points.

Batch Control Totals - The result of grouping transactions at the input stage and establishing control totals over them to ensure proper processing. These control totals can be based on document counts, record counts, quantity totals, dollar totals, or hash (mixed data, such as customer AR numbers) totals.

Batch Number - A sequence number associated with a specific batch or production run of products and used for tracking purposes. Synonym: Lot Number.

Batch Picking - A method of picking orders specific to the order requirements that reduces movement to and from product locations. The aggregated quantities of each product are then relocated to a common area where individual orders are constructed.

Batch Processing - A computer term which refers to the processing of computer information after it has been accumulated in one group, or batch. This is the opposite of "real-time" processing where transactions are processed in their entirety as they occur.

Baud - A computer term describing the rate of transmission over a channel or circuit. The baud rate is equal to the number of pulses that can be transmitted in one second, often the same as the number of bits per second. Common rates are now 1200, 2400, 4800, 9600 bits and 19.2 and 56 kilobytes (Kbs) for "dial-up" circuits, and may be much higher for broadband circuits.

Bay - Section of vessel in which containers are held.

BCP - see Business Continuity Plan

Beginning Available Balance - See Available Inventory

Benchmarking - The process of comparing a firm's performance against the practices of other leading companies - in or outside of an industry - for the purpose of improving performance. Companies also benchmark internally by tracking and comparing past performance.

Benefit-cost ratio - An analytical tool used in public planning; a ratio of total measurable benefits divided by the initial capital cost.

Berth - Vessel docking area.

Best Practice - A specific process or group of processes which have been recognized as the best method for conducting an action. Best Practices may vary by industry or geography depending on the environment being used. Best practices methodology may be applied with respect to resources, activities, cost object, or processes. Also known as competitive benchmarking, the methodology that determines state-of-industry performance or application.

Best-in-Class - An organization, usually within a specific industry, recognized for excellence in a specific process area.

Beta release - A pre-released version of a product that is sent to customers for evaluation and feedback.

Bilateral Contract - An agreement wherein each party makes a promise to the other party.

Bill of Activities - A listing of activities required by a product, service, process output or other cost object. Bill of activity attributes could include volume and or cost of each activity in the listing.

Bill of Exchange - (1) A signed, written order by one company that instructs another company to pay a third party a specific amount. (2) An unconditional written order addressed by one person to another and signed by the person placing it. It requires the person, to whom it is addressed, to pay on demand or at a fixed or determinable future time, a certain sum of money to the order of a specified person or to bearer. The drawee is not liable on it until he has accepted it.(3) Usually used in foreign transactions.

Bill of Lading (BOL) - A transportation document that is the contract of carriage containing the terms and conditions between the shipper and carrier. The document is issued by a carrier to a shipper, signed by the captain, agent, or owner of a vessel, furnishing written evidence regarding receipt of freight, the conditions on which transportation is made and the date to deliver goods at the prescribed port of destination to the lawful holder of the bill of lading.

Bill of Material (BOM) - A structured list of all the materials or parts and quantities needed to produce a particular finished product, assembly, subassembly, or manufactured part, whether purchased or not.

Bill of Material Accuracy - Conformity of a list of specified items to administrative specifications, with all quantities correct

Bill of Resources - A listing of resources required by an activity. Resource attributes could include cost and volumes.

Billed Weight - Weight stated in a waybill and/or (freight) bill of lading.

Bin - (1) A storage device designed to hold small discrete parts. (2) A shelving unit with physical dividers separating the storage locations.

Binary - A computer term referring to a system of numerical notation that assumes only two possible states or values, zero (0) and one (1). Computer systems use a binary technique where an individual bit or "Binary Digit" of data can be "on" or "off" (1 or 0). Multiple bits are combined into a "Byte" which represents a character or number.

Bisynchronous - A computer term referring to a communication protocol whereby messages are sent as blocks of characters. The blocks of data are checked for completeness and accuracy by the receiving computer.

Bitmap Image (BMP) - The standard image format on Windows-compatible computers. Bitmap images can be saved for Windows or OS/2 systems and support 24-bit color.

Blanket Order - See Blanket Purchase Order

Blanket Purchase Order - A long-term commitment to a supplier for material against which short-term releases will be generated to satisfy requirements. Often blanket orders cover only one item with predetermined delivery dates. Synonym: Blanket Order, Standing Order.

Blanket Rate - A rate will not increase according to the distance a commodity is shipped.

Blanket Release - The authorization to ship and/or produce against a blanket agreement or contract.

Blanket Wrap - A service provided by moving companies and specific carriers that eliminate packaging material by wrapping product in padded "blankets". This will protect the goods during transit, usually on "air ride" vans. See Pad Wrap.

Bleeding Edge - An unproven process or technology so far ahead of its time that it may create a competitive disadvantage.

Blind Counts - Describes a method used in cycle counting and physical inventories providing inventory counters with the item number and location but no quantity information.

Block diagram - A diagram that shows the operation, interrelationships and interdependencies of components in a system. Boxes, or blocks (hence the name), represent the components; connecting lines between the blocks represent interfaces. There are two types of block diagrams: a functional block diagram, which shows a system's subsystems and lower level products and their interrelationships and which interfaces with other systems; and a reliability block diagram, which is similar to the functional block diagram except that it is modified to emphasize those aspects influencing reliability.

Blocking bug - A defect that prevents further or more detailed analysis or verification of a functional area or feature, or any issue that would prevent the product from shipping.

Blow Through - An MRP process which uses a "phantom bill of material" and permits MRP logic to drive requirements straight through the phantom item to its components. The MRP system usually retains its ability to net against any occasional inventories of the item. Also see: Phantom Bill of Material

BMP - see Bitmap Image

Body of knowledge (BOK) - The prescribed aggregation of knowledge in a particular area an individual is expected to have mastered to be considered or certified as a practitioner.

BOK - see Body of knowledge

BOL - see Bill of Lading

Bolero - Bolero is a neutral, open platform, intended to be a cross-industry community moving world trade onto the Internet. The focus is to process trade documents fully electronically via a secure communication platform (CMP). The initial focus has been on the carrier's bill of lading through the Title Registry replicating the paper bill of lading functionality and bill of lading parties' roles. Lately, Bolero's focus has changed towards the trade settlement engine, 'SURF', Settlement Utility for Risk and Finance, which Bolero has developed together with some major banks.

BOM - see Bill of Material

Bonded Goods - A dutiable goods upon excise duty has not been paid, i.e., good in transit or warehouse pending usage. The bond is the agreement entered into by the owner of the dutiable goods with Customs and the excise authority that the owner agrees to pay the duty when goods are released for final distribution or usage.

Bonded Warehouse - Warehouse owned by persons approved by the relevant customs and excise authorities (for example in the USA it is the Treasury Department), and under bond (or guarantee) for the strict observance of the revenue laws. Utilised for storing goods until duties are paid or goods are otherwise properly released.

Bonded Warehouse - Export - A secure building or area, approved by customs, where cargo, for which export clearance has been performed, is stored. Goods are considered foreign and must go out for export. In some countries, a bonded warehouse is defined as a warehouse with customs officials onsite. In others, it is a warehouse in which customs inspect cargo prior to authorising export clearance. Ensure the local definition is established. In some countries, some manufacturers are also granted a licence to operate a bonded warehouse in which they can store manufactured products in anticipation of export and hence suspend payment of local taxes (e.g. on cigarettes).

Bonded Warehouse - Import - A secure building or area, approved by customs, where cargo, for which export clearance has been performed, is stored.

Book Inventory - An accounting definition of inventory units or value obtained from perpetual inventory records rather than by actual count.

Booking - (1) Act of recording arrangements for the movement/transportation of goods by vessel or other conveyance. (2) To express in advance a desire for something in order to reserve it e.g. transportation of goods. (3) Also known as a booking request.

Booking Number - The unique number assigned to a certain space reservation by the carrier or the carrier's agent.

Bookings - The sum of the value of all orders received (but not necessarily shipped), net of all discounts, coupons, allowances, and rebates.

Bottleneck - A constraint, obstacle or planned control that limits throughput or the utilization of capacity.

Bottom-up Replanning - In MRP, the process of using pegging data to solve material availability or other problems. This process is accomplished by the planner (not the computer system), who evaluates the effects of possible solutions. Potential solutions include compressing lead time, cutting order quantity, substituting material, and changing the master schedule.

Box Rate - A lump sum charged to move cargo in various size containers from origin to destination.

Boxcar - An enclosed rail car typically 40 to 50 feet long; used for packaged freight and some bulk commodities.

Box-Jenkins Model - A forecasting method based on regression and moving average models. The model is based not on regression of independent variables, but on past observations of the item to be forecast at varying time lags and on previous error values from forecasting. See: Forecast.

BPM - see Business Performance Measurement

BPO - see Business Process Outsourcing

BPR - see Business Process Reengineering

Bracing - Securing a shipment inside a carrier's vehicle to prevent damage.

Bracketed Recall - Recall from customers of suspect lot numbers plus a specified number of lots produced before and after the suspect ones.

Branding - The use of a name, term, symbol, or design, or a combination of these, to identify a product.

Breadman - A specific application of Kanban, used in coordinating vendor replenishment activities. In making bread or other route type deliveries, the deliveryman typically arrives at the customer's location and fills a designated container or storage location with product. The size of the order is not specified on an ongoing basis, nor does the customer even specify requirements for each individual delivery. Instead, the supplier assumes the responsibility for quantifying the need against a prearranged set of rules and delivers the requisite quantity.

Break-Bulk - (1) The separation of a single consolidated bulk load into smaller individual shipments for delivery to the ultimate consignees. This is preceded by a consolidation of orders at the time of shipment, where many individual orders which are destined for a specific geographic area are grouped into one shipment in order to reduce cost. (2) Cargo which is not containerised due to its weight and/or size e.g. steel pipes, boats etc.

Break-Even Chart - A graphical tool showing the total variable cost and fixed cost curve along with the total revenue curve. The point of intersection is defined as the break-even point, i.e., the point at which total revenues exactly equal total costs. Also see: Total Cost Curve

Break-Even Point - The level of production or the volume of sales at which operations are neither profitable nor unprofitable. The break-even point is the intersection of the total revenue and total cost curves. Also see: Total Cost Curve

Bricks and Mortar - The act of selling through a physical location. The flip side of clicks and mortar, where selling is conducted via the Internet. An informal term for representing the old economy versus new economy or the Industrial economy versus information economy.

Broadband - A high-speed, high-capacity transmission channel. Broadband channels are carried on radio wave, coaxial or fiberoptic cables that have a wider bandwidth than conventional telephone lines, giving them the ability to carry video, voice, and data simultaneously.

Broken case - An open case. The term is often used interchangeably with "repack" or "less-than-full-case" to name the area in which materials are picked in that form.

Broker - A person or firm, other than a motor carrier or agent of a motor carrier that as a principal or agent sells, offers for sale, or holds itself out by solicitation, advertisement or otherwise as selling, providing or arranging for transportation by motor carrier for competition. A broker is a middleman that brings together the shipper and carrier; a broker does not take responsibility for the transportation. An agent/middleman who for a fee or commission negotiates contract e.g.

Definitions

purchase and sale (such as real estate, commodities or securities) between buyers and sellers without himself taking title to that which is the subject of negotiation and usually without having physical possession of it.

Brokerage Licence - Authority granted by the Interstate Commerce Commission (ICC) to persons to engage in the business of arranging for the transportation of persons or property in interstate commerce.

Brokered Systems - Independent computer systems, owned by independent organizations or entities, linked in a manner to allow one system to retrieve information from another. For example, a customer's computer system is able to retrieve order status from a supplier's computer.

Browser - A utility that allows an internet user to look through collections of things. For example, Netscape Navigator and Microsoft Explorer allow you to view contents on the World Wide Web.

BTS - see Balance to Ship

Bucketed System - An MRP, DRP, or other time-phased system in which all time-phased data are accumulated into time periods, or buckets. If the period of accumulation is one week, then the system is said to have weekly buckets.

Bucketless system - An MRP, DRP, or other time-phased system in which all time-phased data are processed, stored, and usually displayed using dated records rather than defined time periods, or buckets.

Buffer - (1) A quantity of materials awaiting further processing. It can refer to raw materials, semifinished stores or hold points, or a work backlog that is purposely maintained behind a work center.(2) In the theory of constraints, buffers can be time or material and support throughput and/or due date performance. Buffers can be maintained at the constraint, convergent points (with a constraint part), divergent points, and shipping points.

Buffer Management - In the theory of constraints, a process in which all expediting in a shop is driven by what is scheduled to be in the buffers (constraint, shipping, and assembly buffers). By expediting this material into the buffers, the system helps avoid idleness at the constraint and missed customer due dates. In addition, the causes of items missing from the buffer are identified, and the frequency of occurrence is used to prioritize improvement activities.

Buffer Stock - See Safety Stock.

Bulk area - A storage area for large items which at a minimum are most efficiently handled by the pallet load.

Bulk packing - The process or act of placing numbers of small cartons or boxes into a larger single box to aid in the movement of product and to prevent damage or pilferage to the smaller cartons or boxes.

Bulk storage - The process of housing or storing materials and packages in larger quantities, generally using the original packaging or shipping containers or boxes.

Bulletin Board - An electronic forum that hosts posted messages and articles related to a common subject.

Bullwhip Effect - An extreme change in the supply position upstream in a supply chain generated by a small change in demand downstream in the supply chain. Inventory can quickly move from being backordered to being excess. This is caused by the serial nature of communicating orders up the chain with the inherent transportation delays of moving product down the chain. The bullwhip effect can be eliminated by synchronizing the supply chain.

Bundle - A group of products that are shipped together as an unassembled unit.

Glossary of terms in Logistics & Shipping

Bunker Adjustment Factor (BAF) - Surcharge assessed by carrier which is applied to freight rates to supplement an unexpected rise in fuel costs.

Bunker Surcharge - Surcharge assessed by carrier which is applied to freight rates to supplement an unexpected rise in fuel costs.

Burn Rate - The rate of consumption of cash in a business. Burn rate is used to determine cash requirements on an on-going basis. A burn-rate of $50,000 would mean the company spends $50,000 a month above any incoming cash flow to sustain its business. Entrepreneurial companies will calculate their burn-rate in order to understand how much time they have before they need to raise more money, or show a positive cash flow.

Business Activity Monitoring (BAM) - A term which refers to capturing operational data in real-time or close to it, making it possible for an enterprise to react more quickly to events. This is typically done through software and includes features to provide alerts / notifications when specific events occur. See also: Supply Chain Event Management

Business Application - Any computer program, set of programs, or package of programs created to solve a particular business problem or function.

Business Continuity - Any process, item or asset that is needed for a customer to maintain operations during a disaster or contingency.

Business Continuity Plan (BCP) - A contingency plan for sustained operations during periods of high risk, such as during labor unrest or natural disaster. CSCMP provides suggestions for helping companies do continuity planning in their Securing the Supply Chain Research. A copy of the research is available on the CSCMP website.

Business Logistics - The process of planning, implementing, and controlling the efficient, effective flow and storage of product from the point of origin to the point of destination for the purpose of conforming to customer requirements. The systematic and coordinated set of activities required to provide the physical movement and storage of goods (raw materials, parts, finished goods) from vendor/supply services through company facilities to the customer (market) and the associated activities--packaging, order processing, etc.--in an efficient manner necessary to enable the organization to contribute to the explicit goals of the company.

Business Performance Measurement (BPM) - A technique which uses a system of goals and metrics to monitor performance. Analysis of these measurements can help businesses in periodically setting business goals, and then providing feedback to managers on progress towards those goals. A specific measure can be compared to itself over time, compared with a preset target or evaluated along with other measures.

Business Plan - (1) A statement of long-range strategy and revenue, cost, and profit objectives usually accompanied by budgets, a projected balance sheet, and a cash flow (source and application of funds) statement. A business plan is usually stated in terms of dollars and grouped by product family. The business plan is then translated into synchronized tactical functional plans through the production planning process (or the sales and operations planning process). Although frequently stated in different terms (dollars versus units), these tactical plans should agree with each other and with the business plan. See: long-term planning, strategic plan.(2) A document consisting of the business details (organization, strategy, and financing tactics) prepared by an entrepreneur to plan for a new business.

Business Process Outsourcing (BPO) - The practice of outsourcing non-core internal functions to third parties. Functions typically outsourced include logistics, accounts payable, accounts receivable, payroll and human resources. Other areas can include IT development or complete management of the IT functions of the enterprise.

Business Process Reengineering (BPR) - The fundamental rethinking and oftentimes, radical redesign of business processes to achieve dramatic organizational improvements.

Business Unit - A division or segment of an organization generally treated as a separate profit-and-loss center.

Business-to-Business (B2B) - As opposed to business-to-consumer (B2C). Many companies are now focusing on this strategy, and their sites are aimed at businesses (think wholesale) and only other businesses can access or buy products on the site. Internet analysts predict this will be the biggest sector on the Web.

Business-to-Consumer (B2C) - The hundreds of e-commerce Web sites that sell goods directly to consumers are considered B2C. This distinction is important when comparing Websites that are B2B as the entire business model, strategy, execution, and fulfillment is different.

Buyer Behavior - The way individuals or organizations behave in a purchasing situation. The customer-oriented concept finds out the wants, needs, and desires of customers and adapts resources of the organization to deliver need-satisfying goods and services.

Byte - A computer term used to define a string of 7 or 8 bits, or binary digits. The length of the string determines the amount of data that can be represented. The 8-bit byte can represent numerous special characters, 26 uppercase and lowercase alphabetic characters, and 10 numeric digits, totaling 256 possible combinations.

──────── **C** ────────

Caboose - A caboose (US railway terminology) or brake van or guard's van (British terminology) is a manned rail transport vehicle coupled at the end of a freight train. Although cabooses were once used on nearly every freight train in North America, their use has declined and they are seldom seen on trains, except on locals and smaller railroads.

Cabotage - (1) Trade or transport in coastal waters or between two ports/points within a country especially by parties other than domestic carriers. Many countries, such as the USA, have laws requiring domestic-owned vessels to perform domestic interport water transportation services. (2) A federal law that requires coastal and inter-coastal traffic to be carried in U.S.-built and registered ships.

CAD - see Computer Aided Design

CAE - see Computer Aided Engineering

CAF - see Currency Adjustment Factor

Cage - (1) A secure enclosed area for storing highly valuable items, (2) a pallet-sized platform with sides that can be secured to the tines of a forklift and in which a person may ride to inventory items stored will above the warehouse floor.

Caged - Referring to the practice of placing high-value or sensitive products in a fenced off area within a warehouse.

Calculation - To convert from working days to calendar days: if work week = 4 days, multiply by 1.75 = 5 days, multiply by 1.4 = 6 days, multiply by 1.17

Call Center - A facility housing personnel who respond to customer phone queries. These personnel may provide customer service or technical support. Call center services may be in-house or outsourced. Synonym: Customer Interaction Center.

CAM - see Computer Aided Manufacturing

Canadian Customs Invoice - A document required by Canadian Customs identifying shipper, seller, consignee, terms, date of shipment, material being sold/shipped, classification code, quantity, unit and total prices. Additional information may be required pertaining to the shipper and consignee arrangements.

Can-order Point - An ordering system used when multiple items are ordered from one vendor. The can-order point is a point higher than the original order point. When any one of the items triggers an order by reaching the must-order point, all items below their can-order point are also ordered. The can-order point is set by considering the additional holding cost that would be incurred should the item be ordered early.

Capability maturity model (CMM) - A framework that describes the key elements of an effective software process. It's an evolutionary improvement path from an immature process to a mature, disciplined process. The CMM covers practices for planning, engineering and managing software development and maintenance. When followed, these key practices improve the ability of organizations to meet goals for cost, schedule, functionality and product quality.

Capable to Promise (CTP) - A technique used to determine if product can be assembled and shipped by a specific date. Component availability throughout the supply chain, as well as available materials, is checked to determine if delivery of a particular product can be made. The process of committing orders against available capacity as well as inventory. This process may involve multiple manufacturing or distribution sites. Capable-to-promise is used to determine when a new or unscheduled customer order can be delivered. Capable-to-promise employs a finite-scheduling model of the manufacturing system to determine when an item can be delivered. It includes any constraints that might restrict the production, such as availability of resources, lead times for raw materials or purchased parts, and requirements for lower-level components or subassemblies. The resulting delivery date takes into consideration production capacity, the current manufacturing environment, and future order commitments. The objective is to reduce the time spent by production planners in expediting orders and adjusting plans because of inaccurate delivery-date promises.

Capacity - The physical facilities, personnel and process available to meet the product or service needs of customers. Capacity generally refers to the maximum output or producing ability of a machine, a person, a process, a factory, a product, or a service. Also see: Capacity Management

Capacity Management - The concept that capacity should be understood, defined, and measured for each level in the organization to include market segments, products, processes, activities, and resources. In each of these applications, capacity is defined in a hierarchy of idle, non-productive, and productive views.

Capacity Planning - Assuring that needed resources (e.g., manufacturing capacity, distribution center capacity, transportation vehicles, etc.) will be available at the right time and place to meet logistics and supply chain needs.

CAPEX - A term used to describe the monetary requirements (CAPital EXPenditure) of an initial investment in new machines or equipment.

Capital - The resources, or money, available for investing in assets that produce output.

CAPP - see Computer Aided Process Planning

Definitions

Car supply charge - A railroad charge for a shipper's exclusive use of special equipment.

Cargo - The goods or merchandise transported by airplane, ship or vehicle.

Cargo Bays - Doors in a warehouse where vehicles back up to load/unload cargo.

Cargo Manifest - An invoice of all cargo loaded on board a vessel. Listing of all cargo on board a vessel is required by the relevant local authorities. Also Manifest

Carload Lot - A shipment that qualifies for a reduced freight rate because it is greater than a specified minimum weight. Since carload rates usually include minimum rates per unit of volume, the higher LCL (less than carload) rate may be less expensive for a heavy but relatively small shipment.

Carmack Amendment - An Interstate Commerce Act amendment that delineates the liability of common carriers and the bill of lading provision.

Carnet - Known as a "Merchandise Passport", this Customs document permits the holder to carry or send special categories of goods temporarily into certain foreign countries without paying duties or posting bonds.

Carousel - Carousels are a technology used to store items for eventual picking or retrieval. There are two primary types of carousels and one related technology, all of which operate under some form of computer control. Since the late 1990s, carousels have been placed under the more general category of AS/RS.

Carriage and Insurance Paid To (CIP) - Incoterm. Title and risk pass to buyer when delivered to carrier by seller who pays transportation and insurance cost to destination. Used for any mode of transportation.

Carriage Paid To (CPT) - Incoterm. Title, risk and insurance cost pass to buyer when delivered to carrier by seller who pays transportation cost to destination. Used for any mode of transportation.

Carrier - Entity that is a motor carrier, water carrier or freight forwarder engaged in the business of transporting goods or people who, through a contract of carriage, procure the performance of carriage by rail, road, sea, air, inland waterway, or by a combination of modes.

Carrier Certificate and Release Order - Used to advise Customs of the shipment's detailed information. Having this document, the carrier certifies that the firm or individual named in the certificate is the owner or consignee of the cargo.

Carrier Liability - A carrier is liable for all shipment loss, damage, and delay with exception's of acts of God, act of a public enemy, act of a public authority, act of the shipper, and the goods' inherent nature. Carriers may limit their liability based on the commodity code of the item.

Carrier's Certificate - A release order used to advise customs of the details of the shipment, its ownership, port of lading, etc. By means of this document the carrier certifies that the firm or individual named in the certificate is the owner or consignee of the cargo. A U.S. Customs form used in lieu of a bill of lading.

Cartage - The motor freight connection on each end of an air freight link in a supply chain. See also drayage.

Cartage Agent - A ground transportation service company who provides pickup and delivery of freight in locations that cannot be served directly by an air or ocean carrier.

Cartel - A group of companies that agree to cooperate, rather than compete, in producing a product or service, thus limiting or regulating competition.

Glossary of terms in Logistics & Shipping

Case Code - The UPC number for a case of product. The UPC case code is different from the UPC item code. This is sometimes referred to as the "Shipping Container Symbol" or ITF-14 code.

Cash Conversion Cycle - (1) In retailing, the length of time between the sale of products and the cash payments for a company's resources.(2) In manufacturing, the length of time from the purchase of raw materials to the collection of accounts receivable from customers for the sale of products or services. Also see: Cash-to-Cash Cycle Time

Cash flow statement - See funds flow statement.

Cash-to-Cash Cycle Time - The time it takes for cash to flow back into a company after it has been spent for raw materials. Synonym: Cash Conversion Cycle. Calculation: Total Inventory Days of Supply + Days of Sales Outstanding - Average Payment Period for Material in days

Catalog Channel - A call center or order processing facility that receives orders directly from the customer based on defined catalog offerings and ships directly to the customer.

Categorical Plan - A method of selecting and evaluating suppliers that considers input from many departments and functions within the buyer's organization and systematically categorizes that input. Engineering, production, quality assurance, and other functional areas evaluate all suppliers for critical factors within their scope of responsibility. For example, engineering would develop a category evaluating suppliers' design flexibility. Rankings are developed across categories, and performance ratings are obtained and supplier selections are made. Also see: Weighted-Point Plan

Category management - Process of managing one category of a multi-category specified product as strategic business units. The practice empowers a category manager with full responsibility for the assortment decisions, inventory levels, shelf-space allocation, promotions and buying. With this authority and responsibility, the category manager is able to judge more accurately the consumer buying patterns, product sales and market trends of that category.

Causal Forecast - In forecasting, a type of forecasting that uses cause-and-effect associations to predict and explain relationships between the independent and dependent variables. An example of a causal model is an econometric model used to explain the demand for housing starts based on consumer base, interest rates, personal incomes, and land availability.

Cause and Effect Diagram - In quality management, a structured process used to organize ideas into logical groupings. Used in brainstorming and problem solving exercises. Also known as Ishikawa or fish bone diagram.

CBM - Cubic Metre. 1 cubic metre = 35,314 cubic feet.

CBT - see Computer Based Training

Cell - (1) A manufacturing or service unit consisting of a number of workstations, and the materials transport mechanisms and storage buffers that interconnect them. (2) Container slot where container fits into place on vessel.

Cellular manufacturing - A manufacturing approach in which equipment and workstations are arranged to facilitate small-lot, continuous-flow production. In a manufacturing "cell," all operations necessary to produce a component or subassembly are performed in close proximity, thus allowing for quick feedback between operators when quality problems and other issues arise. Workers in a manufacturing cell typically are cross-trained and, therefore, able to perform multiple tasks as needed.

Center-of-Gravity Approach - A supply chain planning methodology for locating distribution centers at approximately the location representing the minimum transportation costs between the plants, the distribution centers, and the markets.

Centralized authority - Management authority to make decisions is restricted to few managers.

Centralized Dispatching - The organization of the dispatching function into one central location. This structure often involves the use of data collection devices for communication between the centralized dispatching function, which usually reports to the production control department, and the shop manufacturing departments.

Centralized Inventory Control - Inventory decision making (for all SKUs) exercised from one office or department for an entire company.

Certificate of Analysis (COA) - A certification of conformance to quality standards or specifications for products or materials. It may include a list or reference of analysis results and process information. It is often required for transfer of the custody/ownership/title of materials.

Certificate of Compliance - A supplier's certification that the supplies or services in question meet specified-requirements.

Certificate of Insurance - Insurance statement evidencing that a policy has been written and stating the coverage's in general terms.

Certificate of origin - Document used to assure the buying country precisely which country produced the goods being shipped. Usually completed by a recognised chamber of commerce.

Certificate of public convenience and necessity - The grant of operating authority that is given to common carriers. A carrier must prove that a public need exists and that the carrier is fit, willing, and able to provide the needed service. The certificate may specify the commodities to be hauled, the area to be served, and the routes to be used.

Certificated carrier - A for-hire air carrier that is subject to economic regulation and requires an operating certification to provide service.

Certified Supplier - A status awarded to a supplier who consistently meets predetermined quality, cost, delivery, financial, and count objectives. Incoming inspection may not be required.

CFD - see Continuous Flow Distribution

CFR - see Cost and Freight

CFS - see Container Freight Station

CGMP - see Current good manufacturing practices

Chain of Customers - The sequence of customers who in turn consume the output of each other, forming a chain. For example, individuals are customers of a department store, which in turn is the customer of a producer, who is the customer of a material supplier.

Chain reaction - A chain of events described by W. Edwards Deming: improve quality, decrease costs, improve productivity, increase market with better quality and lower price, stay in business, provide jobs and provide more jobs.

Challenge and Response - A method of user authentication. The user enters an ID and password and, in return, is issued a challenge by the system. The system compares the user's response to the challenge to a computed response. If the responses match, the user is allowed access to the system. The system issues a different challenge each time. In effect, it requires a new password for each logon.

Champion - A business leader or senior manager who ensures that resources are available for training and projects, and who is

GLOSSARY OF TERMS IN LOGISTICS & SHIPPING

involved in project tollgate reviews; also an executive who supports and addresses Six Sigma organizational issues.

Change agent - An individual from within or outside an organization who facilitates change within the organization. May or may not be the initiator of the change effort.

Change Management - The business process that coordinates and monitors all changes to the business processes and applications operated by the business as well as to their internal equipment, resources, operating systems, and procedures. The change management discipline is carried out in a way that minimizes the risk of problems that will affect the operating environment and service delivery to the users.

Change Order - A formal notification that a purchase order must be modified resulting in a change of quantity, date, or specification by the customer; change in inventory requirement data; etc.

Changeover - Process of making necessary adjustments to change or switchover the type of products produced on a manufacturing line. Changeovers usually lead to downtime and for the most part companies try to minimize changeover time to help reduce costs.

Channel - (1) A method whereby a business dispenses its product, such as a retail or distribution channel, call center or web based electronic storefront.(2) A push technology that allows users to subscribe to a website to browse offline, automatically display updated pages on their screen savers, and download or receive notifications when pages in the website are modified. Channels are available only in browsers that support channel definitions, such as Microsoft Internet Explorer version 4.0 and above.

Channel Charging area - A warehouse area where a company maintains battery chargers and extra batteries to support a fleet of electrically powered materials handling equipment. The company must maintain this area in accordance with government safety regulations.

Channel Conflict - This occurs when various sales channels within a company's supply chain compete with each other for the same business. An example is where a retail channel is in competition with a web based channel set up by the company.

Channel Partners - Members of a supply chain (i.e. suppliers, manufacturers, distributors, retailers, etc.) who work in conjunction with one another to manufacture, distribute, and sell a specific product.

Channels of Distribution - Any series of firms or individuals that participates in the flow of goods and services from the raw material supplier and producer to the final user or consumer. Also see: Distribution

Chargeable Weight - The weight or volume of a shipment used in determining charges. The chargeable weight could be the dimensional weight or on container shipments, the gross weight of the shipment minus the containers tare weight.

Chassis - Trailer or wheeled unit on which a container is placed in order to move container over the road.

Chock - (1) Material, such as a piece of wood, that is placed at the side of cargo to prevent rolling or sideways movement. (2) A wedge, usually made of hard rubber or steel, that is firmly placed under the wheel of a trailer, truck, or boxcar to stop it from rolling.

CI - see Continuous Improvement

CIF - see Cost, Insurance and Freight

CIM - see Computer Integrated Manufacturing

CIP - see Carriage and Insurance Paid To

City driver - A motor carrier driver who drives a local route as opposed to a long-distance, intercity route.

Civil Aeronautics Board - A federal regulatory agency that implemented economic regulatory controls over air carriers.

CL - Carload rail service requiring shipper to meet minimum weight.

Claim - A charge made against a carrier for loss, damage, delay, or overcharge.

Claim Tracer - Request for advice concerning the status of a claim.

Claims - Shipper's statement of shipment loss or damage and a demand for compensation.

Class I carrier - A classification of regulated carriers based upon annual operating revenues--motor carriers of property: > or = $5 million; railroads: > or =$50 million; motor carriers of passengers: > or =$3 million.

Class II carrier - A classification of regulated carriers based upon annual operating revenues--motor carriers of property: $1-$5 million; railroads: $10-$50 million; motor carriers of passengers: < or = $3 million.

Class III carrier - A classification of regulated carriers based upon annual operating revenues--motor carriers of property: < or = $1 million; railroads: < or = $10 million.

Class rate - A rate constructed from a classification and a uniform distance system. A class rate is available for any product between any two points.

Class Rates - Numeral assigned by the American Trucking Associations to an item or group of items to determine the applicable rate. All the items in the group make up a class. The freight rates that apply to all items in the class are known as "class rates."

Classification - An alphabetical listing of commodities, the class or rating into which the commodity is placed, and the minimum weight necessary for the rate discount; used in the class rate structure. This systematic categorization of cargo is done for the purpose of applying class rates, combined with governing rules and regulations for transportation. In Customs, the classification determines the duty status of imported merchandise within the Harmonized Tariff Schedule of the United States (HSUS). The classification is the responsibility of an importer Customs broker or designated individual preparing the entry papers.

Classification yard - A railroad terminal area where rail cars are grouped together to form train units.

CLCA - see Closed-loop corrective action

Clean On Board - A clause inserted in the bill of lading by some shipping/transportation companies, stating that they have not noted or are not familiar with any irregularities or discrepancies in the packing or in the general condition of any part of the goods or its description.

Clearance - The completion of Customs entry requirements resulting in the release of goods from Customs authority to the importer.

Clearinghouse - A conventional or limited purpose entity generally restricted to providing specialized services, such as clearing funds or settling accounts.

Cleat - A strip of wood or metal that is used for additional strength and support, to prevent warping and allowing for support.

Click-and-Mortar - With reference to a traditional brick-and-mortar company that has expanded its presence online. Many brickand- mortar stores are now trying to establish an online presence but often have a difficult time doing so for many reasons. Clickand-mortar is "the successful combination of online and real world experience."

Clip Art - A collection of icons, buttons, and other useful image files, along with sound and video files that can be inserted into documents/web pages.

Clipboard - A temporary storage area on a computer for cut or copied items.

CLM - see Council of Logistics Management

Closed-loop corrective action (CLCA) - A sophisticated engineering system designed to document, verify and diagnose failures, recommend and initiate corrective action, provide follow-up and maintain comprehensive statistical records.

Closed-loop MRP - A system built around material requirements planning that includes the additional planning processes of production planning (sales and operations planning), master production scheduling, and capacity requirements planning. Once this planning phase is complete and the plans have been accepted as realistic and attainable, the execution processes come into play. These processes include the manufacturing control processes of input-output (capacity) measurement, detailed scheduling and dispatching, as well as anticipated delay reports from both the plant and suppliers, supplier scheduling, and so on. The term closed loop implies not only that each of these processes is included in the overall system, but also that feedback is provided by the execution processes so that the planning can be kept valid at all times.

CMI - see Co-Managed Inventory

CMM - see Capability maturity model

CMMS - see Computerized Maintenance Management Systems

COA - see Certificate of Analysis

Coastal carriers - Water carriers that provide service along coasts serving ports on the Atlantic or Pacific oceans or on the Gulf of Mexico

Codabar - Codabar is a variable length barcode that can encode 16 data characters including 0-9, plus the symbols - $; / . +. Codabar is used primarily for numeric data.

Code - A numeric, or alphanumeric, representation of text for exchanging commonly used information. For example: commodity codes, carrier codes,

Code 128 Auto - Code 128 is a variable length barcode capable of encoding the entire 128 character ASCII character set. Code 128 allows three subsets, A, B and C. This version, "Code 128 Auto", automatically selects the subset that will produce the smallest barcode.

Code 128A - Code 128 is a variable length barcode capable of encoding the entire 128 character ASCII character set. Code 128 allows three subsets, A, B and C. This subset (A) allows all standard upper case alphanumeric keyboard characters plus control characters.

Code 128B - Code 128 is a variable length barcode capable of encoding the entire 128 character ASCII character set. Code 128 allows three subsets, A, B and C. This subset (B) allows all standard upper case alphanumeric keyboard characters and lower case alpha characters.

Code 128C - Code 128 is a variable length barcode capable of encoding the entire 128 character ASCII character set. Code 128 allows three subsets, A, B and C. This subset (C) includes a set of 100 digit pairs from 00 to 99 inclusive. This allows double density numeric digits, two digits per barcoded character.

Code 3 of 9 - This barcode is an alphanumeric barcode allowing upper case letters and numbers. Each character consists of nine elements. 3 of the nine elements are wide, hence the name "3 of 9".

Code 93 - Code 93 is an alpha-numeric barcode allowing upper case letters and numbers. BarCode/VBX will convert lower case letters to upper case before encoding them.

Co-destiny - The evolution of a supply chain from intra-organizational management to inter-organizational management.

Codifying - The process of detailing a new standard.

COFC - Container on Flat Car. Rail service whereby a container is loaded onto a flat car without chassis, bogies or wheels.

COGS - see Cost of Goods Sold

Collaboration - Joint work and communication among people and systems including business partners, suppliers, and customers to achieve a common business goal.

Collaborative planning, forecasting, and replenishment (CPFR) - (1) A collaboration process whereby supply chain trading partners can jointly plan key supply chain activities from production and delivery of raw materials to production and delivery of final products to end customers. Collaboration encompasses business planning, sales forecasting, and all operations required to replenish raw materials and finished goods. (2) CPFR: A process philosophy for facilitating collaborative communications. CPFR is considered a standard, endorsed by the Voluntary Interindustry Commerce Standards.

Collaborative Product Commerce (CPC) - A set of activities and functions that enable collaboration between business partners in the supply chain.

Co-Managed Inventory (CMI) - A form of continuous replenishment in which the manufacturer is responsible for replenishment of standard merchandise, while the retailer manages the replenishment of promotional merchandise.

Combined Lead Time - See Cumulative Lead Time

Combined Transport Bill of Lading - Provides a combined transport by at least two different modes of transportation from a place from which the goods are taken to a place designated for delivery.

Commercial Invoice - A document produced by the shipper/seller of goods which contains an accurate description of the merchandise and the country of origin. All items are itemised and with actual price. required document identifying the transaction between a seller and buyer. The form should have the invoice number, date, shipping date, the mode of transport, delivery and payment terms, description of goods and the quantity. Custom's requires a commercial invoice that includes the following information. (1) The port of entry. (2) Name of shipper and receiver. (3) Description of items. (4) Quantity in weight and measures. (5) Country of origin. The invoice and any attachments must be in the English language.

Commercial zone - The area surrounding a city or town to which rates quoted for the city or town also apply; the area is defined by the ICC.

Committed Capability - The portion of the production capability that is currently in use, or is scheduled for use.

Committee of American Steamship Lines - An industry association representing subsidized U.S. Flag steamship firms.

Commodities - Any article of goods shipped.

Glossary of terms in Logistics & Shipping

Commodities clause - A clause that prohibits railroads from hauling commodities that they produced, mined, owned, or had an interest in.

Commodity - An item that is traded in commerce. The term usually implies an undifferentiated product competing primarily on price and availability. A specification of goods/product types, e.g. toys, electronics or welding machinery.

Commodity Buying - Grouping like parts or materials under one buyer's control for the procurement of all requirements to support production.

Commodity Code - A code describing a commodity or a group of commodities pertaining to the goods classification.

Commodity Procurement Strategy - The purchasing plan for a family of items. This would include the plan to manage the supplier base and solve problems.

Commodity Rate - A rate that will be used for a specific commodity and its origin-destination locations.

Common Carrier - Transportation available to the public that does not provide special treatment to any one party and is regulated as to the rates charged, the liability assumed, and the service provided. A common carrier must obtain a certificate of public convenience and necessity from the Federal Trade Commission for interstate traffic. See also dedicated carrier.

Common carrier duties - Common carriers are required to serve, deliver, charge reasonable rates, and not discriminate.

Common cost - A cost that cannot be directly assignable to particular segments of the business but that is incurred for the business as a whole.

Common Point - Point reached by two or more transportation lines.

Common Tariff - Tariff published by or for the account of two or more transportation lines as issuing carriers.

Communication Protocol - The method by which two computers coordinate their communications. BISYNC and MNP are two examples.

Commuter - An exempt for-hire air carrier that publishes a time schedule on specific routes; a special type of air taxi.

Company Culture - A system of values, beliefs, and behaviors inherent in a company. To optimize business performance, top management must define and create the necessary culture.

Company Guarantee - A letter of guarantee from a company indemnifying the carrier of responsibility associated with the release of goods in lieu of a bill of lading.

Comparative advantage - A principle based on the assumption that an area will specialize in the production of goods for which it has the greatest advantage or least comparative disadvantage.

Competitive Advantage - Value created by a company for its customers that clearly distinguishes it from the competition, and provides its customers a reason to remain loyal.

Competitive Benchmarking - Benchmarking a product or service against competitors. Also see: Benchmarking

Competitive Bid - A price/service offering by a supplier that must compete with offerings from other suppliers.

Complete & On-Time Delivery (COTD) - A measure of customer service. All items on any given order must be delivered on time for the order to be considered as complete and on time

DEFINITIONS

Complete Manufacture to Ship Time - Average time from when a unit is declared shippable by manufacturing until the unit actually ships to a customer.

Compliance - Meaning that products, services, processes and/or documents comply with requirements.

Compliance Checking - The function of EDI processing software that ensures that all transmissions contain the mandatory information demanded by the EDI standard. Compares information sent by an EDI user against EDI standards and reports exceptions. Does not ensure that documents are complete and fully accurate, but does reject transmissions with missing data elements or syntax errors.

Compliance Monitoring - A check done by the VAN/third party network or the translation software to ensure the data being exchanged is in the correct format for the standard being used.

Compliance Program - A method by which two or more EDI trading partners periodically report conformity to agreed upon standards of control and audit. Management produces statements of compliance, which briefly note any exceptions, as well as corrective action planned or taken, in accordance with operating rules. Auditors produce an independent and objective statement of opinion on management statements.

Component - Material that will contribute to a finished product but is not the finished product itself. Examples would include tires for an automobile, power supply for a personal computer, or a zipper for a ski parka. Note that what is a component to the manufacturer may be considered the finished product of their supplier.

Computer Aided Design (CAD) - Computer-based systems for product design that may incorporate analytical and "what if" capabilities to optimize product designs. Many CAD systems capture geometric and other product characteristics for engineeringdata- management systems, producibility and cost analysis, and performance analysis. In many cases, CAD-generated data

Computer Aided Engineering (CAE) - The use of computers to model design options to stimulate their performance.

Computer Aided Manufacturing (CAM) - Computerized systems in which manufacturing instructions are downloaded to automated equipment or to operator workstations.

Computer Aided Process Planning (CAPP) - Software-based systems that aid manufacturing engineers in creating a process plan to manufacture a product who's geometric, electronic, and other characteristics have been captured in a CAD database. CAPP systems address such manufacturing criteria as target costs, target lead times, anticipated production volumes, availability of

Computer Based Training (CBT) - Training that is delivered via computer workstation and includes all training and testing materials.

Computer Integrated Manufacturing (CIM) - A variety of approaches in which computer systems communicate or interoperate over a local-area network. Typically, CIM systems link management functions with engineering, manufacturing, and support operations. In the factory, CIM systems may control the sequencing of production operations, control operation of automated equipment and conveyor systems, transmit manufacturing instructions, capture data at various stages of the manufacturing or assembly process, facilitate tracking and analysis of test results and operating parameters, or a combination of these.

Computerized Maintenance Management Systems (CMMS) - Software-based systems that analyze operating conditions of production equipment : vibration, oil analysis, heat, etc. : and equipment-failure data, and apply that data to the scheduling of maintenance and repair inventory orders and routine maintenance functions. A CMMS prevents unscheduled machine downtime and optimizes a plant's ability to process product at optimum volumes and quality levels.

Computerized process simulation - Use of computer simulation to facilitate sequencing of production operations, analysis of production flows, and layout of manufacturing facilities.

Computerized SPC - See Statistical process control

Concealed Damage - Damage to the contents of a package that is in good condition externally.

Concurrent engineering - A cross-functional, team-based approach in which the product and the manufacturing process are designed and configured within the same time frame, rather than sequentially. Ease and cost of manufacturability, as well as customer needs, quality issues, and product-life-cycle costs are taken into account earlier in the development cycle. Fully configured concurrent engineering teams include representation from marketing, design engineering, manufacturing engineering, and purchasing, as well as supplierand even customercompanies.

Conference - Defined in the 1984 Shipping Act as: ... an association of ocean common carriers permitted, pursuant to an approved or effective agreement, to engage in concerted activity and to utilise a common tariff; but the term does not include a joint service, consortium, pooling, sailing or transshipment arrangement. It is basically a group of steamship companies offering equitable freight rates, standardised shipping practices and regularly scheduled services between designated ports. These arrangements are given anti-trust immunity as authorised by the 1984 Shipping Act.

Configuration - The arrangement of components as specified to produce an assembly of product.

Configure/Package-to-Order - A process where the trigger to begin manufacture, final assembly or packaging of a product is an actual customer order or release, rather than a market forecast. In order to be considered a Configure-to-Order environment, less than 20% of the value-added takes place after the receipt of the order or release, and virtually all necessary design and process documentation is available at time of order receipt.

Confirmation - With regards to EDI, a formal notice (by message or code) from a electronic mailbox system or EDI server indicating that a message sent to a trading partner has reached its intended mailbox or been retrieved by the addressee.

Confirming Order - A purchase order issued to a supplier, listing the goods or services and terms of an order placed orally or otherwise before the usual purchase document.

Conformance - An affirmative indication or judgment that a product or service has met the requirements of a relevant specification, contract, or regulation. Synonym: Compliance.

Conrail - The Consolidated Rail Corporation established by the Regional Reorganization Act of 1973 to operate the bankrupt Penn Central Railroad and other bankrupt railroads in the Northeast; funding was provided by the 4-R Act of 1976.

Consensus - A state in which all the members of a group support an action or decision, even if some of them don't fully agree with it.

DEFINITIONS

Consignee - The party to whom goods are shipped and delivered. The receiver of a freight shipment.

Consignment - (1) A shipment that is handled by a common carrier. (2) The process of a supplier placing goods at a customer location without receiving payment until after the goods are used or sold. (3) Agreement by which one signs over the delivery of a quantity of goods to another. See: Consignment Inventory

Consignment Inventory - (1) Goods or product that are paid for when they are sold by the reseller, not at the time they are shipped to the reseller. (2) Goods or products which are owned by the vendor until they are sold to the consumer.

Consignor - Person normally shown on shipping documents as authorized at origin to release goods to a transportation company. The party who originates a shipment of goods (shipper). The sender of a freight shipment, usually the seller.

Consolidation - (1) A number of separate shipments that are assembled into one shipment for movement on one waybill from one location to another. Consolidation of freight can result in reduced shipping rates. (2) The placing of LCL/LTL cargo from several sources into a container in order to fill the container and obtain a better per-unit cost for shipping.

Consortium - A group of companies that work together to jointly produce a product, service, or project.

Constraint - A bottleneck, obstacle or planned control that limits throughput or the utilization of capacity.

Constraint-based planning and scheduling - Planning and scheduling following the Theory of Constraints rules

Consul - A government official residing in a foreign country representing the interests of her or his country and its nationals.

Consular Declaration - A formal statement describing goods to be shipped; filed with and approved by the consul of the country of destination prior to shipment.

Consular Invoice - A document, certified by a consular official, may be required in some countries to describe a shipment. Used by Customs of the foreign country, to verify the value, quantity and nature of the cargo.

Consular Visa - An official signature or seal affixed to certain documents by the consul of the country of destination.

Consumer Packaged Goods (CPG) - Consumable goods such as food and beverages, footwear and apparel, tobacco, and cleaning products. In general, CPGs are things that get used up and have to be replaced frequently, in contrast to items that people usually keep for a long time, such as cars and furniture.

Consumer-Centric Database - Database with information about a retailer's individual consumers, used primarily for marketing and promotion.

Consuming the Forecast - The process of reducing the forecast by customer orders or other types of actual demands as they are received. The adjustments yield the value of the remaining forecast for each period.

Container - (1) A reusable, rigid exterior shipping box, typically 10 to 40 feet long that is used to ship goods by ship, truck or rail. It is a weatherproof box designed for the shipment of freight, generally used for overseas shipments. The container is separable from the chassis when loaded onto vessels or rail cars. (2) The packaging type including a carton, case, box, that an item is packed and transported in.

Container Depot - Location, other than a container yard, maintained by or on behalf of an ocean carrier at which shippers or consignees may pick up or drop off empty equipment. No loaded containers may be received at CDs and such locations may not be owned or controlled by a shipper or his agent.

Container Freight Station (CFS) - The physical facility where goods are received by carrier for loading into containers or unloading from containers and where carrier may assemble, hold, or store its containers or trailers.

Container Security Initiative (CSI) - U.S. Customs program to prevent global containerized cargo from being exploited by terrorists. Designed to enhance security of sea cargo container.

Container Service Charge - The charge assessed by the terminal for the positioning of containers within the terminal/yard.

Container Stuffing List (CSL) - List showing how cargo is stowed in each container.

Container Yard (CY) - Area adjacent to the vessel berth where containers are delivered to and received from the vessel or inland carrier. The facility for holding Full Container Load (FCL) and empty containers that are received from or delivered to consignors or consignees by or on behalf of a carrier. It also provides a location to receive merchandise from consignors for packing into containers.

Containerization - A shipment method in which commodities are placed in containers, and after initial loading, the commodities per se are not re-handled in shipment until they are unloaded at the destination.

Contingency planning - Preparing to deal with calamities (e.g., floods) and non-calamitous situations (e.g., strikes) before they occur

Continuous Flow Distribution (CFD) - The streamlined pull of products in response to customer requirements while minimizing the total costs of distribution.

Continuous Improvement (CI) - A structured measurement driven process that continually reviews and improves performance.

Continuous Process Improvement (CPI) - A never-ending effort to expose and eliminate root causes of problems; small-step improvement as opposed to big-step improvement. Synonym: Continuous Improvement. Also see: Kaizen

Continuous Replenishment - Continuous Replenishment is the practice of partnering between distribution channel members that changes the traditional replenishment process from distributor-generated purchase orders, based on economic order quantities, to the replenishment of products based on actual and forecasted product demand.

Continuous Replenishment Planning (CRP) - A program that triggers the manufacturing and movement of product through the supply chain when the identical product is purchased by an end user.

Continuous-flow, fixed-path equipment - Materials handling devices that include conveyors and drag lines.

Contract - An agreement between two or more competent persons or companies to perform or not to perform specific acts or services or to deliver merchandise. A contract may be oral or written. A purchase order, when accepted by a supplier, becomes a contract. Acceptance may be in writing or by performance, unless the purchase order requires acceptance in writing.

Contract Administration - Managing all aspects of a contract to guarantee that the contractor fulfills his obligations.

Contract Carrier - A carrier that does not serve the general public, but provides

Definitions

transportation for hire for one or a limited number of shippers under a specific contract.

Contribution - The difference between sales price and variable costs. Contribution is used to cover fixed costs and profits.

Contribution Margin - An amount equal to the difference between sales revenue and variable costs.

Controlled Access - Referring to an area within a warehouse or yard that is fenced and gated. These areas are typically used to store high-value items and may be monitored by security cameras

Conveyor - A materials handling device that moves freight from one area to another in a warehouse. Roller conveyors make sue of gravity, whereas belt conveyors use motors.

Cookie - A computer term. A piece of information from your computer that references what the user has clicked on, or references information that is stored in a text file on the user's hard drive (such as a username). Another way to describe cookies is to say they are tiny files containing information about individual computers that can be used by advertisers to track online interests and tastes. Cookies are also used in the process of purchasing items on the Web. It is because of the cookie that the "shopping cart" technology works. By saving in a text file, the name, and other important information about an item a user "clicks" on as they move through a shopping Website, a user can later go to an order form, and see all the items they selected, ready for quick and easy processing.

Cooperative associations - Groups of firms or individuals having common interests: agricultural cooperative associations may haul up to 25% of their total interstate tonnage in nonfarm, nonmenber goods in movements incidental and necessary to their primary business.

Co-opetition - A combination of cooperation and competition that offers the counter intuitive possibility for rivals to benefit from each other's seemingly competitive activities. In short, there are circumstances where having more players to cut the pie means bigger pieces of pie for everyone. An example would be found in the group buying setting where its use refers to the activity of multiple, normally competitive buying group members leveraging each other's buying power to gain reduced pricing.

Coordinated transportation - Two or more carriers of different modes transporting a shipment.

Co-Packer - A contract co-packer produces goods and/or services for other companies, usually under the other company's label or name. Co-Packers are more frequently seen in CPG and Foods.

Co-product - The term co-product is used to describe multiple items that are produced simultaneously during a production run. Co-products are often used to increase yields in cutting operations such as die cutting or sawing when it is found that scrap can be reduced by combining multiple-sized products in a single production run. Co-products are also used to reduce the frequency of machine setups required in these same types of operations. Co-products, also known as byproducts, are also common in process manufacturing such as in chemical plants. Although the concept of co-products is fairly simple, the programming logic required to provide for planning and processing of co-products is very complicated.

Core Competency - A company's primary function considered essential to its success. Bundles of skills or knowledge sets that enable a firm to provide the greatest level of value to its customers in a way that is difficult for competitors to emulate and that provides for future growth. Core competencies are embodied in the skills of the workers and in the organization. They are developed through -collective -learning, communication, and commitment to work across levels and functions in the organization and with the customers and suppliers. For example, a core competency could be the capability of a firm to coordinate and harmonize diverse production skills and multiple technologies. To illustrate, advanced casting processes for making steel require the integration of machine design with sophisticated sensors to track temperature and speed, and the sensors require mathematical modeling of heat transfer. For rapid and effective development of such a process, materials scientists must work closely with machine designers, software engineers, process specialists, and operating personnel. Core competencies are not directly related to the product or market.

Core Process - That unique capability that is central to a company's competitive strategy.

Cost Accounting - The branch of accounting that is concerned with recording and reporting business operating costs. It includes the reporting of costs by departments, activities, and products.

Cost Allocation - In accounting, the assignment of costs that cannot be directly related to production activities via more measurable means, e.g., assigning corporate expenses to different products via direct labor costs or hours.

Cost and Freight (CFR) - Incoterm. Title, risk and insurance cost pass to buyer when delivered on board the ship by seller who pays the transportation cost to the destination port. Used for sea or inland waterway transportation.

Cost Center - In accounting, a sub-unit in an organization that is responsible for costs.

Cost Driver - In accounting, any situation or event that causes a change in the consumption of a resource, or influences quality or cycle time. An activity may have multiple cost drivers. Cost drivers do not necessarily need to be quantified; however, they strongly influence the selection and magnitude of resource drivers and activity drivers.

Cost Driver Analysis - In cost accounting, the examination, quantification, and explanation of the effects of cost drivers. The results are often used for continuous improvement programs to reduce throughput times, improve quality, and reduce cost.

Cost Element - In cost accounting, the lowest level component of a resource, activity, or cost object.

Cost Management - The management and control of activities and drivers to calculate accurate product and service costs, improve business processes, eliminate waste, influence cost drivers, and plan operations. The resulting information will have utility in setting and evaluating an organization's strategies.

Cost of Capital - The cost to borrow or invest capital.

Cost of Goods Sold (COGS) - The amount of direct materials, direct labor, and allocated overhead associated with products sold during a given period of time, determined in accordance with Generally Accepted Accounting Principles (GAAP)

Cost of lost sales - The forgone profit associated with a stockout.

Cost trade-off - The interrelationship among system variables indicates that a change in one variable has cost impact upon other variables. A cost reduction in one variable may be at the expense of increased cost for other variables, and vice versa.

Cost Variance - In cost accounting, the difference between what has been budgeted for an activity and what it actually costs.

Cost, Insurance and Freight (CIF) - Incoterm. Title and risk pass to buyer when delivered on board the ship by seller who pays transportation and insurance cost to destination port. Used for sea or inland waterway transportation.

DEFINITIONS

Cost-optimized - A product or service in which the trade-off between cost and performance has been analyzed and optimized from a cost point of view.

COTD - see Complete & On-Time Delivery

Council of Logistics Management (CLM) - See Council of Supply Chain Management Professionals.

Council of Supply Chain Management Professionals (CSCMP) - The CSCMP is a not-for-profit professional business organization consisting of individuals throughout the world who have interests and/or responsibilities in logistics and supply chain management, and the related functions that make up these professions. Its purpose is to enhance the development of the logistics and supply chain management professions by providing these individuals with educational opportunities and relevant information through a variety of programs, services, and activities.

Country of Destination - The country that will be the final destination for goods.

Country of Origin - The country where the goods have been manufactured.

Courier service - A fast, door-to-door service for high-valued goods and documents; firms usually limit service to shipments of 50 pounds or less.

CPC - see Collaborative Product Commerce

CPFR - see Collaborative planning, forecasting, and replenishment

CPG - see Consumer Packaged Goods

CPI - see Continuous Process Improvement

CPT - see Carriage Paid To

Crane - A handling device that lifts heavy items, usually serviced by a third party company.

Credit Level - The amount of purchasing credit a customer has available. Usually defined by the internal credit department and reduced by any existing unpaid bills or open orders.

Credit Terms - An agreement between two or more enterprises concerning the amount and timing of payment for goods or services.

Critical Data - A term that defines electronic data that is irreplaceable to a customer. This data is needed to support/maintain business operations.

Critical Differentiators - This is what makes an idea, product, service or business model unique.

Critical Success Factor (CSF) - Those activities and/or processes that must be completed and/or controlled to enable a company to reach its goals.

Critical value analysis - A modified ABC analysis in which a subjective value of criticalness is assigned to each item in the inventory.

CRM - see Customer Relationship Management

Cross Docking - A distribution system in which merchandise received at the warehouse or distribution center is not put away, but instead is readied for shipment to retail stores. Cross docking requires close synchronization of all inbound and outbound shipment movements. By eliminating the put-away, storage and selection operations, it can significantly reduce distribution costs.

Cross functional - A term used to describe a process or an activity that crosses the boundary between functions. A cross functional team consists of individuals from

Glossary of Terms in Logistics & Shipping

more than one organizational unit or function.

Cross Sell - The practice of attempting to sell additional products to a customer during a sales call. For example, when the CSR presents a camera case and accessories to a customer that is ordering a camera

Cross-Docking - The process of moving merchandise directly from the receiving dock to the shipping dock, eliminating the need to place the merchandise in storage.

Cross-Shipment - Material flow activity where materials are shipped to customers from a secondary shipping point rather than from a preferred shipping point.

Cross-Subsidy - In cost accounting, the inequitable assignment of costs to cost objects, which leads to over costing or under costing them relative to the amount of activities and resources actually consumed. This may result in poor management decisions that are inconsistent with the economic goals of the organization.

CRP - see Continuous Replenishment Planning

CSCMP - see Council of Supply Chain Management Professionals

CSF - see Critical Success Factor

CSI - see Container Security Initiative

CSL - see Container Stuffing List

CSR - see Customer Service Representative

CTP - see Capable to Promise

C-TPAT - see Customs-Trade Partnership against Terrorism

Cubage - Cubic volume of space being used or available for shipping or storage.

Cube - The volume of the shipment or package (the product of the length x width x depth).

Cube Utilization - In warehousing, a measurement of the utilization of the total storage capacity of a vehicle or warehouse.

Cubed out - A completely filled trailer or container but could still be below the weight capacity.

Cubic Foot - The unit of volume measurement that is equaled to 1,728 cubic inches.

Cubic Space - In warehousing, a measurement of space available or required in transportation and warehousing.

Cumulative Available-to-Promise - A calculation based on the available-to-promise (ATP) figure in the master schedule. Two methods of computing the cumulative available-to-promise are used, with and without lookahead calculation. The cumulative with lookahead ATP equals the ATP from the previous period plus the MPS of the period minus the backlog of the period minus the sum of the differences between the backlogs and MPSs of all future periods until, but not to include, the period where point production exceeds the backlogs. The cumulative without lookahead procedure equals the ATP in the previous period plus the MPS, minus the backlog in the period being considered. Also see: Available-to-Promise

Cumulative Lead Time - The total time required to source components, build and ship a product.

Cumulative Source/Make Cycle Time - The cumulative internal and external lead time to manufacture shippable product, assuming that there is no inventory on-hand, no materials or parts on order, and no prior forecasts existing with suppliers. (An element of Total Supply Chain Response Time)Calculation: The critical path along the following elements: Total Sourcing Lead

Time, Manufacturing Order Release to Start Manufacturing, Total Manufacture Cycle Time (Make-to-Order, Engineer-to-Order, Configure/Package-to-Order) or Manufacture Cycle Time (Make-to-Stock), Complete Manufacture to Ship Time Note: Determined separately for Make-to-Order, Configure/Package-to-Order, Engineer-to-Order, and Make-to-Stock products

Currency Adjustment Factor (CAF) - Used to adjust ocean freight due to currency fluctuations.

Current good manufacturing practices (CGMP) - Regulations enforced by the U.S. Food and Drug Administration for food and chemical manufacturers and packagers.

Customer - (1) In distribution, the Trading Partner or reseller, i.e. Wal-Mart, Safeway, or CVS. (2) In Direct-to-Consumer, the end customer or user.

Customer Acquisition or Retention - The rate by which new customers are acquired, or existing customers are retained. A key selling point to potential marquis partners. Also see: Marquis Partner

Customer Driven - The end user, or customer, motivates what is produced or how it is delivered.

Customer Facing - Those personnel whose jobs entail actual contact with the customer.

Customer Interaction Center - See Call Center

Customer Order - An order from a customer for a particular product or a number of products. It is often referred to as an actual demand to distinguish it from a forecasted demand.

Customer Profitability - The practice of placing a value on the profit generated by business done with a particular customer.

Customer Receipt of Order to Installation Complete - Average lead-time from receipt of goods at the customer to the time when installation (if applicable) is complete, including the following sub-elements: time to get product up and running, and product acceptance by customer. (An element of Order Fulfillment Lead Time) Note: Determined separately for Make-to-Order, Configure/Package-to-Order, Engineer-to-Order, and Make-to-Stock products.

Customer Relationship Management (CRM) - This refers to information systems that help sales and marketing functions, as opposed to the ERP (Enterprise Resource Planning), which is for back-end integration.

Customer satisfaction - The results of delivering a good or service that meets customer requirements.

Customer Segmentation - Dividing customers into groups based on specific criteria, such as products purchased, customer geographic location, etc.

Customer service - Activities between the buyer and seller that enhance or facilitate the sale or use of the seller's products or services.

Customer Service Ratio - See Percent of Fill

Customer Service Representative (CSR) - The individual who provides customer support via telephone in a call center environment.

Customer Signature/Authorization to Order Receipt - Average lead-time from when a customer authorizes an order to the time that that order is received and order entry can commence. (An element of Order Fulfillment Lead Time) Note: Determined separately for Make-to-Order, Configure/Package-to-Order, Engineer-to-Order, and Make-to-Stock products.

Glossary of Terms in Logistics & Shipping

Customer/Order Fulfillment Process - A series of customers' interactions with an organization through the order filling process, including product/service design, production and delivery, and order status reporting.

Customer-Supplier Partnership - A long-term relationship between a buyer and a supplier characterized by teamwork and mutual confidence. The supplier is considered an extension of the buyer's organization. The partnership is based on several commitments. The buyer provides long-term contracts and uses fewer suppliers. The supplier implements quality assurance processes so that incoming inspection can be minimized. The supplier also helps the buyer reduce costs and improve product and process designs.

Customization - Creating a product from existing components into an individual order. Synonym: Build to Order.

Customs - The designated government authority that regulates the flow of goods to/from a country and collects duties levied by a country on imports and exports.

Customs Bounded Warehouse - A federal warehouse where goods remain until duty has been collected from the importer. Goods that are held under bond are also kept here.

Customs Broker - A firm that represents importers/exporters in dealings with Customs. They are responsible for obtaining and submitting all documents for clearing items through Customs, arranging inland transport, and paying all charges related to these functions.

Customs Clearance - The process of declaring and clearing cargoes by Customs through designated formalities such as presenting import license/permit, payment of import duties and other required documentations by the nature of the cargo such as FCC or FDA approval.

Customs Declaration - An oral or written statement attesting to the accuracy of description, quantity, value, etc. of merchandise offered for importation into the United States.

Customs Duties - A tax levied and government collection by custom officials of duties that is imposed by law on imports.

Customs Entries - Consumption Entry Form required by U.S. Customs for importing goods into the United States. The form contains information as to the origin of the cargo, a description of the merchandise and estimated duties applicable to the particular commodity. Estimated duties must be paid at the time the entry is filled. - Immediate Delivery Entry is used to expedite clearance of cargo. It allows up to ten days for the payment of estimated duty and processing of the consumption entry. In addition, it permits the delivery of the cargo prior to payment of the estimated duty and then allows for the subsequent filing of the consumption entry and duty. Also known as an ID entry. - Immediate Transportation Entry allows the cargo to be moved from the pier to an inland destination via a bonded carrier without the payment of duties or finalisation of the entry at the port of arrival. Known as an IT entry. - Transportation and Exportation Entry allows goods coming from or going to a third country, such as Canada or Mexico, to enter the United States for the purpose of transshipment. Known as a T&E entry. - Vessel Repair Entry is the law known as the "Foreign Vessel Repair Statute". It provides that when any repairs in a foreign country are made on a vessel documented under the laws of the United States, an ad valorem duty of 50% is imposed on the cost of repair, including labour and labour costs, when the vessel arrives in the United States. All equipment, parts or materials purchased, and repairs made outside the United States must be declared on Customs Form 226 (CF-226) and filed at the port of first arrival within 5 working days.

Customs House Broker - A business firm that oversees the progress of international shipments through Customs, and ensures that the documentation accompanying a shipment is complete and accurate.

Customs Invoice - A document that contains a statement by the seller, the shipper, or the agent as to the value of the shipment.

Customs Value - The assessed value of the imported goods on which duties will apply.

Customs-Trade Partnership against Terrorism (C-TPAT) - A joint government/business initiative to build cooperative relationships that strengthen overall supply chain and border security. The voluntary program is designed to share information that will protect against terrorists' compromising the supply chain.

Cut-Off Time - Last possible time when containers/cargoes may be delivered to a ship or designated point.

CWT - see Hundredweight

CY - see Container Yard

CY/CY (CY/CY) - Full container load with cargo to be packed therein and unpacked there from at the shipper's elected point or place and at shipper's expense.

Cycle Count - Counting inventory by checking a particular location or set of locations and comparing the physical counts with the system-maintained inventory levels.

Cycle Counting - An inventory accuracy audit technique where inventory is counted on a cyclic schedule rather than once a year. A cycle inventory count is usually taken on a regular, defined basis (often more frequently for high-value or fast-moving items and less frequently for low-value or slow-moving items). Most effective cycle counting systems require the counting of a certain number of items every workday with each item counted at a prescribed frequency. The key purpose of cycle counting is to identify items in error, thus triggering research, identification, and elimination of the cause of the errors.

Cycle inventory - An inventory system where counts are performed continuously, often eliminating the need for an annual overall inventory. It is usually set up so that A items are counted regularly (i.e., every month), B items are counted semiregularly (every quarter or six months), and C items are counted perhaps only once a year.

Cycle Time - The amount of time it takes to complete a business process.

Cycle Time Reduction - The process of reducing cycle time, cutting costs and improving customer service.

Cycle Time to Process Excess Product Returns for Resale - The total time to process goods returned as Excess by customer or distribution centers, in preparation for resale. This cycle time includes the time a Return Product Authorization (RPA) is created to the time the RPA is approved, from Product Available for Pick-up to Product Received and from Product Receipt to Product Available for use.

Cycle Time to Process Obsolete and End-of-Life Product Returns for Disposal - The total time to process goods returned as Obsolete & End of Life to actual Disposal. This cycle time includes the time a Return Product Authorization (RPA) is created to the time the RPA is approved, from Product Available for Pick-up to Product Received and from Product Receipt to Product Disposal/Recycle.

Cycle Time to Repair or Refurbish Returns for Use - The total time to process goods returned for repair or refurbishing. This cycle time includes the time a Return Product Authorization (RPA) is created to the time the RPA is approved, from Product Available for Pick-up to Product Received, from Product Receipt to Product Repair/Refurbish begin, and from Product

Repair/Refurbish begin to Product Available for use.

Cyclical Demand - A situation where demand patterns for a product run in cycles driven by seasonality or other predictable factors.

DAF - see Delivered at Frontier

Dangerous Goods - Articles or substances capable of posing a significant risk to health, safety, or property when transported by air and that require special attention when being transported. Also called Hazardous Goods.

Dashboard - A performance measurement tool used to capture a summary of the Key Performance Indicators (KPIs)/metrics of a company. Metrics dashboards/scorecards should be easy to read and usually have "red, yellow, green" indicators to flag when the company is not meeting its metrics targets. Ideally, a dashboard/scorecard should be cross-functional in nature and include both financial and non-financial measures. In addition, scorecards should be reviewed regularly at least on a monthly basis and weekly in key functions such as manufacturing and distribution where activities are critical to the success of a company. The dashboard/scorecards philosophy can also be applied to external supply chain partners such as suppliers to ensure that supplier's objectives and practices align. Synonym: Scorecard.

Data Communications - The electronic transmission of data, usually in computer readable form, using a variety of transmission vehicles and paths.

Data Dictionary - Lists the data elements for which standards exist. The Joint Electronic Document Interchange (JEDI) committee developed a data dictionary that is employed by many EDI users.

Data Interchange Standards Association (DISA) - The secretariat, which provides clerical and administrative support to the ASC X12 Committee.

Data Migration/Relocation - A migration or relocation event involves either the physical or electronic relocation of data or electronic media from one location to another.

Data Mining - The process of studying data to search for previously unknown relationships. This knowledge is then applied to achieving specific business goals.

Data Warehouse - A repository of data that has been specially prepared to support decision-making applications. Synonym: Decision-Support Data.

Database - Data stored in computer-readable format, usually indexed or sorted in a logical order by which users can find a particular item of data they need.

Date Code - A label on products with the date of production. In food industries, it is often an integral part of the lot number.

Days of Supply - Measure of quantity of inventory-on-hand, in relation to number of days for which usage which will be covered. For example, if a component is consumed in manufacturing at the rate of 100 per day, and there are 1,585 units available onhand, this represents 15.85 days supply.

Days Sales Outstanding (DSO) - Measurement of the average collection period (time from invoicing to cash receipt). Calculation: [5 Point Annual Gross Accounts Receivables] / [Total Annual Sales / 365]

DBR - see Drum-Buffer-Rope

DC - see Distribution Center

DDP - see Delivered Duty Paid

DDU - see Delivered Duty Unpaid

DEFINITIONS

Dead on Arrival (DOA) - A term used to describe products which are not functional when delivered. Synonym: Defective.

Deadhead - Equipment running completely empty (with no shipment aboard) to transport a container to its point of origin. See: backhauling.

Deadweight - The maximum carrying capacity of a ship, expressed in tons of cargo, including provisions and fuel. The vessel's capacity for cargo is less than its total deadweight tonnage.

Decentralized authority - A situation in which management decision-making authority is given to managers at many levels in the organizational hierarchy.

Decision Support System (DSS) - Software that speeds access and simplifies data analysis, queries, etc. within a database management system.

Decking - Second level that can be used inside of a trailer, allowing for additional tonnage onto the trailer.

Declared Value - Tariff provisions providing for the assumed value of a shipment (unless the shipper declares a higher value). An additional fee will apply if declared at a higher value.

Decomposition - A method of forecasting where time series data are separated into up to three components: trend, seasonal, and cyclical; where trend includes the general horizontal upward or downward movement over time; seasonal includes a recurring demand pattern such as day of the week, weekly, monthly, or quarterly; and cyclical includes any repeating, non-seasonal pattern. A fourth component is random, that is, data with no pattern. The new forecast is made by projecting the patterns individually determined and then combining them.

Dedicated carrier - A carrier that is hired on a contractual basis.

Dedicated Contract Carriage - A third-party service that dedicates equipment (vehicles) and drivers to a single customer for its exclusive use on a contractual basis.

Defective goods inventory (DGI) - Those items that have been returned, have been delivered damaged and have a freight claim outstanding, or have been damaged in some way during warehouse handling.

De-Installation - Providing a service by professional management teams to pickup, pack, inspect, repair, redeployment, sales and disposal.

Delimiters - (1) ASCII, characters which are used to separate data elements within a data stream. (2) EDI, two levels of separators and a terminator that are integrals part of a transferred data stream. Delimiters are specified in the interchange header. From highest to lowest level, the separators and terminator are segment terminator, data element separator, and component element separator (used only in EDIFACT).

Delivered at Frontier (DAF) - Incoterm. Title, risk and responsibility for import clearance pass to buyer when delivered to named border point by seller. Used for any mode of transportation.

Delivered Duty Paid (DDP) - Incoterm. Title and risk pass to buyer when seller delivers goods to named destination point cleared for import. Used for any mode of transportation.

Delivered Duty Unpaid (DDU) - Incoterm. Title, risk and responsibility of import clearance pass to buyer when seller delivers goods to named destination point. Used for any mode of transportation. Buyer is obligated for import clearance.

Delivered Ex Quay (DEQ) - Incoterm. Title and risk pass to buyer when delivered on board the ship at the destination point by the seller who delivers goods on dock at

Glossary of Terms in Logistics & Shipping

destination point cleared for import. Used for sea or inland waterway transportation.

Delivered Ex Ship (DES) - Incoterm. Title, risk, responsibility for vessel discharge and import clearance pass to buyer when seller delivers goods on board the ship to destination port. Used for sea or inland waterway transportation.

Delivery - (1) The physical and legal transfer of a shipment from consignor to carrier and from carrier/ transport agent to consignee. (2) The act of putting property into the legal possession of another, whether involving the actual transfer of the physical control of the object from one to the other or being constructively effected in various other ways.

Delivery Appointment - The time agreed upon by two companies for goods or merchandise to arrive at a predetermined location.

Delivery Date Spread - Range of agreed-upon delivery dates. Shipment can arrive on any of these dates and meet the contractual agreement between a shipper and a carrier.

Delivery Instructions - A document provided to a carrier to pick up goods at a location and deliver them to another location. Specific instructions are included indicating exactly where the goods are to be delivered, the deadline, and the name, address, and telephone number of the person to contact if delivery problems are encountered.

Delivery Order - An order from the consignee, shipper or owner of freight to a terminal operator, carrier or warehouse to deliver freight to another party. On imports, it may also be known as a pier release. A document which is neither a bill of lading or a waybill but contains an undertaking which (1) is given under or for the purposes of a contract for the carriage by sea of goods to which the document relates, or of goods which include those goods; and (2) is an undertaking by the carrier to a person identified in the document to deliver those goods to that person which the document relates. Delivery orders are capable of transferring contractual rights by way of endorsements, but they are not necessarily documents of title in the sense of being able to pass constructive possession.

Delivery Performance to Commit Date - The percentage of orders that are fulfilled on or before the internal Commit date, used as a measure of internal scheduling systems effectiveness. Delivery measurements are based on the date a complete order is shipped or the ship-to date of a complete order. A complete order has all items on the order delivered in the quantities requested. An order must be complete to be considered fulfilled. Multiple line items on a single order with different planned delivery dates constitute multiple orders, and multiple planned delivery dates on a single line item also constitute multiple orders. Calculation: [Total number of orders delivered in full and on time to the scheduled commit date] / [Total number of orders delivered]

Delivery Performance to Request Date - The percentage of orders that are fulfilled on or before the customer's requested date used as a measure of responsiveness to market demand. Delivery measurements are based on the date a complete order is shipped or the ship-to date of a complete order. A complete order has all items on the order delivered in the quantities requested. An order must be complete to be considered fulfilled. Multiple line items on a single order with different planned delivery dates constitute multiple orders, and multiple planned delivery dates on a single line item also constitute multiple orders. Calculation: [Total number of orders delivered in full and on time to the customer's request date] / [Total number of orders delivered]

Delivery Ticket - Documentation signed at the job site confirming receipt of product or service.

Delivery-Duty-Paid - Supplier/manufacturer arrangement in which

DEFINITIONS

suppliers are responsible for the transport of the goods they have produced, which is being sent to a manufacturer. This responsibility includes tasks such as ensuring products get through Customs.

Delphi Method - A qualitative forecasting technique where the opinions of experts are combined in a series of iterations. The results of each iteration are used to develop the next, so that convergence of the experts' opinions is obtained.

Delta Nu Alpha - A professional association of transportation and traffic practitioners.

Demand Chain - Another name for the supply chain, with emphasis on customer or end-user demand pulling materials and product through the chain.

Demand Chain Management - Same as supply chain management, but with emphasis on consumer pull versus supplier push.

Demand creation - The process of creating demand for a company's products or services by utilizing various marketing and selling channels and approaches, including the Internet.

Demand management - The function of recognizing all demands for goods and services to support the marketplace. It involves doing what is required to help make the demand happen and prioritizing demand when supply is lacking. Proper demand management facilitates the planning and use of resources for profitable business results. It encompasses the activities of forecasting, order entry, order promising, and determining branch warehouse requirements, interplant orders, and service parts requirements.

Demand Planning - The process of identifying, aggregating, and prioritizing, all sources of demand for the integrated supply chain of a product or service at the appropriate level, horizon and interval. The sales forecast is comprised of the following concepts: (1) The sales forecasting level is the focal point in the corporate hierarchy where the forecast is needed at the most generic level, i.e. Corporate forecast, Divisional forecast, Product Line forecast, SKU, SKU by Location. (2) The sales forecasting time horizon generally coincides with the time frame of the plan for which it was developed, i.e. Annual, 1-5 years, 1- 6 months, Daily, Weekly, Monthly. (3) The sales forecasting time interval generally coincides with how often the plan is updated, i.e. Daily, Weekly, Monthly, and Quarterly.

Demand Planning Systems - The systems that assist in the process of identifying, aggregating, and prioritizing, all sources of demand for the integrated supply chain of a product or service at the appropriate level, horizon and interval.

Demand Pull - The triggering of material movement to a work center only when that work center is ready to begin the next job. It in effect eliminates the queue from in front of a work center, but it can cause a queue at the end of a previous work center.

Demand Supply Balancing - The process of identifying and measuring the gaps and imbalances between demand and resources in order to determine how to best resolve the variances through marketing, pricing, packaging, warehousing, outsource plans or some other action that will optimize service, flexibility, costs, assets (or other supply chain inconsistencies) in an iterative and collaborative environment.

Demand Time Fence (DTF) - (1) That point in time inside of which the forecast is no longer included in total demand and projected available inventory calculations; inside this point, only customer orders are considered. Beyond this point, total demand is a combination of actual orders and forecasts, depending on the forecast consumption technique chosen.(2) In some contexts, the demand time fence may correspond to that point in the future inside which changes to the master schedule must be approved by an authority higher than the master scheduler. Note, however, that customer orders may still be promised inside the demand time fence without higher authority approval if there are quantities available-to-promise (ATP). Beyond the demand time fence, the master scheduler may change the MPS within the limits of established rescheduling rules, without the approval of higher authority. See: planning time fence, time fence.

Demand-Side Analysis - Techniques such as market research, surveys, focus groups, and performance/cost modeling used to identify emerging technologies.

Deming Circle - The concept of a continuously rotating wheel of plan-do-check-action (PDCA) used to show the need for interaction among market research, design, production, and sales to improve quality. Also see: Plan-Do-Check-Action

Demographic Segmentation - In marketing, dividing potential markets by characteristics of potential customers, such as age, sex, income, and education.

Demurrage - (1) Compensation (as liquidated damages) for delay in removing cargo from terminal facilities. (2) A charge assessed for detaining a container, freight car, truck or other vehicle beyond the freetime stipulated for loading or unloading.

Denied Party List (DPL) - A list of organizations that are unauthorized to submit a bid for an activity or to receive a specific product. For example, some countries have bans for certain products such as weapons or sensitive technology.

Density - (1) A physical characteristic of a commodity measuring its mass per unit volume or pounds per cubic foot; an important factor in rate making, since density affects the utilization of a carrier's vehicle. (2) The weight per cubic foot that is determined by multiplying the Length, Width and Height of a container and dividing the total by 1728.

Density Rate - A rate based upon the density and shipment weight.

DEQ - see Delivered Ex Quay

Deregulation - The revisions or complete elimination of economic regulations controlling the various transportation services. The Motor Carrier Act of 1980 and the Staggers Act of 1980 revised the economic controls over motor carriers and railroads, and the Airline Deregulation Act of 1978 eliminated economic controls over air carriers.

Derived Demand - Demand for component products that arises from the demand for final design products. For example, the demand for steel is derived from the demand for automobiles.

DES - see Delivered Ex Ship

Design For Manufacture / Assembly (DFMA) - A product design methodology that provides a quantitative evaluation of product designs.

Design of Experiments (DOE) - A branch of applied statistics dealing with planning, conducting, analyzing, and interpreting controlled tests to evaluate the factors that control the value of a parameter or group of parameters

Destination - The location designated as the receipt point for goods/shipment.

Destination-Enhanced Consolidation - Ganging of smaller shipments to cut cost, often as directed by a system or via pooling with a third party.

Detention - Costs incurred when a shipper/consignee or his/her agent removes a container from the carrier's origin/destination CY to the shipper/consignee's place of business, and does not return the loaded/empty container to the CY or to another location designated

DEFINITIONS

by the carrier within the permitted freetime as stipulated in the applicable tariff.

Deterministic Models - Models where no uncertainty is included, e.g., inventory models without safety stock considerations.

DFMA - see Design For Manufacture / Assembly

DFZ - see Duty Free Zone

DGI - see Defective goods inventory

Dial Up - Access a network by dialing a phone number or initiating a computer to dial the number. The dial-up line connects to the network access point via a node or a PAD.

Differential - (1) A discount offered by a carrier that faces a service time disadvantage over a route. (2) Amount added or deducted from base rate to create a rate to or from some other point or via another route.

Digital Signature - Electronically generated, digitized (as opposed to graphically created) authorization that is uniquely linkable and traceable to an empowered officer.

Dimensional Weight - A calculated weight based on a minimum density requirement. Length x width x height divided by 194 for domestic shipment, or divided by 166 for international shipments.

Direct Channel - Your own sales force sells to the customer. Your entity may ship to the customer, or a third party may handle shipment, but in either case your entity owns the sales contract and retains rights to the receivable from the customer. Your end customer may be a retail outlet. The movement to the customer may be direct from the factory, or the product may move through a distribution network owned by your company. Order information in this channel may be transmitted by electronic means.

Direct Cost - A cost that can be directly traced to a cost object since a direct or repeatable cause-and-effect relationship exists. A direct cost uses a direct assignment or cost causal relationship to transfer costs. Also see: Indirect Cost, Tracing

Direct Product Profitability (DPP) - Calculation of the net profit contribution attributable to a specific product or product line.

Direct Production Material - Material that is used in the manufacturing/content of a product (example: Purchased parts, solder, SMT glues, adhesives, mechanical parts etc. Bill-of-Materials parts, etc.)

Direct Retail Locations - A retail location that purchases products directly from your organization or responding entity.

Direct Store Delivery (DSD) - Process of shipping direct from a manufacturer's plant or distribution center to the customer's retail store, thus bypassing the customer's distribution center. Also called Direct-to-Store Delivery

Direct Transmission - A transmission whereby data is exchanged directly between sender and receiver computers, without an intervening third-party service. Also called a point-to-point transmission.

Directed tasks - Tasks that can be completed based upon detailed information provided by the computer system. An order picking task where the computer details the specific item, location, and quantity to pick is an example of a directed task. If the computer could not specify the location and quantity forcing the worker to choose locations or change quantities, it would not be a directed task. Directed tasks set up the opportunity for confirmation transactions.

Direct-to-Store (DTS) Delivery - Same as Direct Store Delivery.

DISA - see Data Interchange Standards Association

Disaster Recovery Planning (DRP) - Contingency planning specifically related to recovering hardware and software (e.g. data centers, application software, operations, personnel, telecommunications) in information system outages.

Discontinuous Demand - A demand pattern that is characterized by large demands interrupted by periods with no demand, as opposed to a continuous or steady (e.g., daily) demand. Synonym: Lumpy Demand.

Discrete Available-to-Promise - A calculation based on the available-to-promise figure in the master schedule. For the first period, the ATP is the sum of the beginning inventory plus the MPS quantity minus backlog for all periods until the item is master scheduled again. For all other periods, if a quantity has been scheduled for that time period then the ATP is this quantity minus all customer commitments for this and other periods, until another quantity is scheduled in the MPS. For those periods where the quantity scheduled is zero, the ATP is zero (even if deliveries have been promised). The promised customer commitments are accumulated and shown in the period where the item was most recently scheduled. Also see: Available-to- Promise

Discrete Manufacturing - Discrete manufacturing processes create products by assembling unconnected distinct parts as in the production of distinct items such as automobiles, appliances, or computers.

Discrete Order Picking - A method of picking orders in which the items on one order are picked before the next order is picked. Also see: Batch Picking, Order Picking, Zone Picking

Discrete Order Quantity - An order quantity that represents an integer number of periods of demand. Most MRP systems employ discrete order quantities. Also see: Fixed-period Requirements, Least Total Cost, Least Unit Cost, Lot-for-Lot, Part Period Balancing, Period Order Quantity, Wagner-Whitin Algorithm

Disintermediation - The process of eliminating an intermediate stage or echelon in a supply chain. Total supply chain operating expense is reduced, total supply chain inventory is reduced, total cycle time is reduced, and profits increase among the remaining echelons. See also echelon.

Dispatching - The carrier activities involved with controlling equipment; involves arranging for fuel, drivers, crews, equipment, and terminal space.

Distributed Inventory - Inventory that is geographically dispersed. For example, where a company maintains inventory in multiple distribution centers to provide a higher level of customer service.

Distribution - (1) The full range of activities and planning required to move a product from the production line to the end-user. (2) Outbound logistics, from the end of the production line to the end user. (3) The activities associated with the movement of material, usually finished goods or service parts, from the manufacturer to the customer. These activities encompass the functions of transportation, warehousing, inventory control, material handling, order administration, site and location analysis, industrial packaging, data processing, and the communications network necessary for effective management. It includes all activities related to physical distribution, as well as the return of goods to the manufacturer. In many cases, this movement is made through one or more levels of field warehouses. Synonym: Physical Distribution. (4). The systematic division of a whole into discrete parts having distinctive characteristics.

Distribution Center (DC) - The warehouse facility which holds inventory from manufacturing pending distribution to the appropriate stores.

Definitions

Distribution Channel - One or more companies or individuals who participate in the flow of goods and services from the manufacturer to the final user or consumer.

Distribution On Demand (DOD) - The order fulfillment state a distribution operation achieves when it can respond, closest to real time, to changes in demand while shipping 100 percent customer compliant orders at the least cost.

Distribution Planning - The planning activities associated with transportation, warehousing, inventory levels, materials handling, order administration, site and location planning, industrial packaging, data processing, and communications networks to support distribution.

Distribution Requirements Planning (DRP) - A system of determining demands for inventory at distribution centers and consolidating demand information in reverse as input to the production and materials system.

Distribution Resource Planning (DRP-II) - The extension of distribution requirements planning into the planning of the key resources contained in a distribution system: warehouse space, workforce, money, trucks, freight cars, etc.

Distribution Warehouse - A finished goods warehouse that allows space, tools, and personal the ability to assemble customer orders.

Distributor - A business that does not manufacture its own products, but purchases and resells these products. Such a business usually maintains a finished goods inventory. Synonym: Wholesaler.

DIT - Destination Interchange Terminal. Facility operated by the ocean carrier or his agent at which containers are interchanged with the delivering motor carrier.

Diversion - (1) Authorized change in the route or destination of a shipment in transit. (2) The practice of selling goods to a competitor that the vendor assumes would be used to service that Customer's store. Example; Grocery Store Chain A buys orange juice from Minute Maid. Grocery Store Chain A, because of their sales volume or because of promotion, can buy product for $12.50 per case. Grocery Store Chain B, because of a lower sales volume, buys the same orange juice for $14.50 per case. Grocery Store Chain A and Grocery Store Chain B get together and make a deal. Grocery Store Chain A resells that product to Grocery Store Chain B for $13.50 per case. Grocery Store Chain A makes $1.00 per case and Grocery Store Chain B gets product for $1.00 less per case than it can buy from Minute Maid.

Diversion Charge - Fee for diverting cargo from original intended destination port to a new location.

DOA - see Dead on Arrival

Dock - The loading or unloading platform at an industrial location or carrier terminal.

Dock Receipt - Receipt given for a shipment received or delivered at a pier or dock. When delivery of a foreign shipment is completed, the dock receipt is exchanged for a bill of lading with the transportation line.

Dock-to-Stock - A program by which specific quality and packaging requirements are met before the product is released. Prequalified product is shipped directly into the customer's inventory. Dock-to-stock eliminates the costly handling of components, specifically in receiving and inspection and enables product to move directly into production.

Document - (1) Papers customarily attached to foreign forms, consisting of bills of lading, insurance certificates and commercial invoice where required, including certificates of origin and consular invoices. (2) In EDI, a form can act as an invoice or purchase order, that trading partners have agreed to exchange and that the EDI software handles within its compliance-checking logic.

Documentation - Paperwork that is attached or pertaining to goods requiring transportation and/or transfer of ownership.

DOD - see Distribution On Demand

DOE - see Design of Experiments

Dolly - A piece of equipment with two or four wheels that can be used to move heavy containers, pallets or freight.

Domain - A computer term for the following:(1) Highest subdivision of the Internet, for the most part by country (except in the U.S., where it's by type of organization, such as educational, commercial, and government). Usually the last part of a host name; for example, the domain part of ibm.com is .com, which represents the domain of commercial sites in the U.S.(2) In corporate data networks, a group of client computers controlled by a server system.

Domestic trunk line carrier - An air carrier classification for carriers that operate between major population centers. These carriers are now classified as major carriers.

Door to Port (DTP) - Shipment placed in a container at origin residence and delivered in the same container to the port of entry in the destinations country.

Door-to-Door (DTD) - Shipment placed in a container at origin residence and delivered in the same container to a destinations residence.

Dormant route - A route over which a carrier failed to provide service 5 days a week for 13 weeks out of a 26-week period.

Double bottoms - A motor carrier operation involving two trailers being pulled by one tractor.

Double Order Point System - A distribution inventory management system that has two order points. The smallest equals the original order point, which covers demand during replenishment lead time. The second order point is the sum of the first order point plus normal usage during manufacturing lead time. It enables warehouses to forewarn manufacturing of future replenishment orders.

Double stack - Two containers, one on top of the other, loaded on a railroad flatcar; an intermodal service.

Double Stack Car - Rail car capable of carrying two containers stacked on top of each other.

Double-pallet jack - A mechanized device for transporting two standard pallets simultaneously.

Download - To merge temporary files containing a specific date containing information with the main database in order to update it.

Downstream - Referring to the demand side of the supply chain. One or more companies or individuals who participate in the flow of goods and services moving from the manufacturer to the final user or consumer. Opposite of Upstream.

Downtime - Is a period of time when a customer does not have access to equipment, data or assets during a relocation event.

DPC - see Dynamic Process Control

DPL - see Denied Party List

DPP - see Direct Product Profitability

DPS - see Dynamic Planning and Scheduling

Draft - Marine: The depth to which a vessel's deepest point is under water. Rail: A cut of coupled cars. Financial: A signed, written order by one party that instructs

DEFINITIONS

another party to pay a third party a specific amount. It can also be called a bill of exchange.

Drawback - 99% refund of imported or duty paid materials which are to be re-exported.

Drayage - The service offered by a motor carrier for loading and delivery of ocean containers or rail containers. Drayage providers usually handle full-load containers for ocean and rail carriers.

Driving time regulations - Rules that limit the maximum time a driver may drive in interstate commerce; both daily and weekly maximums are prescribed.

Drop - A trailer or boxcar is left at a facility at which it is to be loaded or unloaded. The van operator that dropped the trailer or boxcar may change after the freight has been loaded. See Trailer Drops.

Drop Ship - To take the title of the product but not actually handle, stock, or deliver it, e.g., to have one supplier ship directly to another or to have a supplier ship directly to the buyer's customer.

DRP - (1) See Distribution Requirements Planning (2) See Disaster Recovery Planning

DRP-II - see Distribution Resource Planning

Drum-Buffer-Rope (DBR) - In the theory of constraints, the generalized process used to manage resources to maximize throughput. The drum is the rate or pace of production set by the system's constraint. The buffers establish the protection against uncertainty so that the system can maximize throughput. The rope is a communication process from the constraint to the gating operation that checks or limits material released into the system to support the constraint. Also see: Finite Scheduling,

Dry Dock) - Used to lay up vessels for repair.

DSD - see Direct Store Delivery

DSO - see Days Sales Outstanding

DSS - see Decision Support System

DTD - see Door-to-Door

DTF - see Demand Time Fence

DTP - see Door to Port

Dual operation - A motor carrier that has both common and contract carrier operating authority.

Dual rate system - An international water carrier pricing system where a shipper signing an exclusive use agreement with the conference pays a lower rate (10% to %15) than non-signing shippers for an identical shipment.

Dumping - Selling goods below costs in selected markets.

Dunnage - Material used around cargo to prevent breakage or shifting, normally provided by shipper. Its weight is included in the rating.

DUNS - Data Universal Numbering System.

DUNS Number - A unique nine-digit number assigned by Dun and Bradstreet to identify a company. DUNS stands for Data Universal Numbering System.

Durable Goods - Generally, any goods whose continuous serviceability is likely to exceed three years (e.g., trucks, furniture).

Duty - A tax levied by a government on merchandise imported, exported from another country. Duties are based on the value of goods, while other factors include weight on quantity or combination of value and other factors (compound duties).

67

GLOSSARY OF TERMS IN LOGISTICS & SHIPPING

Duty Drawback - (1) Payment returned for cargo re-exported or trade show material. (2) A customs refund on re-exported cargo.

Duty Free Zone (DFZ) - Areas where goods or cargo can be stored without have to pay import customs duties while awaiting manufacturing or future transport.

Duty rate - The incremental cost required to import a part into a country.

Dynamic Lot Sizing - Any lot-sizing technique that creates an order quantity subject to continuous recomputation. See: Least total cost, Least unit cost, Part period balancing, Period order quantity, Wagner-Whitin algorithm.

Dynamic Planning and Scheduling (DPS) - Systems designed to provide rapid planning and scheduling information for manufacturers and distributors of short shelf life and fast turnover products. Manufacturers are typically faced with problems of decreasing lead times, smaller batch sizes, increasing product variety and little opportunity to manufacture to stock. DPS systems handle real world production and supply chain resources.

Dynamic Process Control (DPC) - Continuous monitoring of process performance and adjustment of control parameters to optimize process output

E

EAI - see Enterprise Application Integration

EAN - see European Article Number

EAN 13 - EAN barcodes are used when the country origin needs to be known. There are 13 digits in EAN 13, where the first two characters are used to define the country of origin, the next 10 are data, followed by the checksum. Both 2 and 5 digit supplementals are also supported.

EAN 8 - EAN barcodes are used when the country origin needs to be known. There are 8 digits in EAN 8, where the first two characters are used to define the country of origin, the next 5 are data, followed by the checksum. Both 2 and 5 digit supplementals are also supported.

EAN.UCC - European Article Numbering/ Uniform Code Council. The EAN.UCC System provides identification standards to uniquely identify trade items, logistics units, locations, assets, and service relations worldwide. The identification standards define the construction of globally-unique and unambiguous numbers. For additional reference, please see http://www.uccouncil.org/ean

Early Supplier Involvement (ESI) - The process of involving suppliers early in the product design activity and drawing on their expertise, insights, and knowledge to generate better designs in less time and designs that are easier to manufacture with high quality.

Earnings - Income after a company's taxes and all other expenses have been paid. Also called profit or net income.

Earnings Before Interest and Taxes (EBIT) - A measure of a company's earning power from ongoing operations, equal to earnings (revenues minus cost of sales, operating expenses, and taxes) before deduction of interest payments and income taxes. Also called operating profit.

EBIT - see Earnings Before Interest and Taxes

EC - see E-Commerce

EC - see Electronic Commerce

ECCN - Export control classification number.

Definitions

Echelon - A level of supply chain nodes. For example, a supply chain with two independent factory warehouses and nine wholesale warehouses delivering product to 350 retail stores is a supply chain with three echelons between the factory and the end customer. One echelon consists of the two independent factory warehouses. One echelon consists of the nine wholesale warehouses. One echelon consists of the 350 retail stores. Each echelon adds operating expense, holds inventory, adds to the cycle time, and expects to make a profit.

ECO - see Engineering Change Order

E-Commerce (EC) - Conducting business electronically via EDI technologies, or online via the Internet. Software programs run the main functions of e-commerce support, such as product display, ordering, shipment, billing, and inventory management. Also written as electronic commerce (EC).

Economic Order Quantity (EOQ) - An inventory model that determines how much to order by determining the amount that will meet customer service levels while minimizing total ordering and holding costs.

Economic Value Added (EVA) - A measure of the shareholder value as a company's operating profits after tax, less a charge for the capital used in creating the profits. EVA is a registered trademark of Stern & Co. in the USA.

Economy of Scale - A phenomenon whereby larger volumes of production reduce unit cost by distributing fixed costs over a larger quantity.

ECR - see Efficient Consumer Response

EDI - see Electronic Data Interchange

EDI message - An approved, published and maintained formal description of how to structure the data required to perform a specific business function in such a way as to allow for the transfer and handling of this data by electronic means.

EDI Standards - Criteria that define the data content and format requirements for specific business transactions (e.g. purchase orders). Using standard formats allows companies to exchange transactions with multiple trading partners easily. Also see: American National Standards Institute, Uniform Code Council

EDI Transmission - A functional group of one or more EDI transactions that are sent to the same location, in the same transmission, and are identified by a functional group header and trailer.

EDIFACT - EDIFACT stands for Electronic Data Interchange For Administration, Commerce and Transport. EDIFACT is an international standard provided by ISO 9735 (created in 1986): * Provides a set of syntax rules to structure data.* Provides an interactive exchange protocol (I-EDI)* Provides standard messages (allows multi-country and multi-industry exchange)

Efficient Consumer Response (ECR) - A demand driven replenishment system designed to link all parties in the logistics channel to create a massive flow-through distribution network. Replenishment is based upon consumer demand and point of sale information.

EFT - see Electronic Funds Transfer

EIN - see Exporter Identification Number

EIR - see Equipment Interchange Receipt

Electronic Commerce (EC) - Also written as e-commerce. Conducting business electronically via traditional EDI technologies, or online via the Internet. In the traditional sense of selling goods, it is possible to do this electronically because of certain software programs that run the main functions of an e-commerce website, such as product display, online ordering, and inventory management. The definition of e-commerce includes business activity that is business-to-business (B2B), business-to-consumer (B2C).

Electronic Data Interchange (EDI) - Intercompany, computer-to-computer transmission of business information in a standard format. For EDI purists, "computer-to-computer" means direct transmission from the originating application program to the receiving, or processing, application program. An EDI transmission consists only of business data, not any accompanying verbiage or free-form messages. Purists might also contend that a standard format is one that is approved by a national or international standards organization, as opposed to formats developed by industry groups or companies.

Electronic Data Interchange Association - A national body that propagates and controls the use of EDI in a given country. All EDIAs are nonprofit organizations dedicated to encouraging EDI growth. The EDIA in the United States was formerly TDCC and administered the development of standards in transportation and other industries.

Electronic Funds Transfer (EFT) - Payment for goods or services via exchanges of electronic authorisations against bank accounts. Authorisation is sent to an automated clearing house (usually a bank), which verifies the source of the transaction as having control over the accounts, and performs the fund transfer.

Electronic Mail (E-Mail) - The computer-to-computer exchange of messages. E-mail is usually unstructured (free-form) rather than in a structured format. X.400 has become the standard for e-mail exchange.

Electronic Product Code (EPC) - An electronically coded tag that is intended as an improvement to the UPC bar code system. The EPC is a 96-bit tag which contains a number called the Global Trade Identification Number (GTIN). Unlike a UPC number, which only provides information specific to a group of products, the GTIN gives each product its own specific identifying number, giving greater accuracy in tracking.

Electronic Signature - A form of authentication that provides identification and validation of a transaction by means of an authorization code identifying the individual or organization

Elkins Act - An amendment to the IC Act that prohibits giving rebates.

e-Logistics - The processes necessary to transfer the goods sold over the Internet to the customers (Auramo et al., 2001). Another more sophisticated aspect is that E-logistics are a wide-ranging topic related to supply chain integration that has the effect of eliminating intermediaries (such as wholesalers or retailers) and also fosters the emergence of new players like logisticians, whose role is to adapt traditional logistics chains to take into account the requirements of e-business.

E-mail - See Electronic Mail

Empirical - Pertaining to a statement or formula based upon experience or observation rather than on deduction or theory.

Empowerment - A condition whereby employees have the authority to make decisions and take action in their work areas without prior approval. For example, an operator can stop a production process if he or she detects a problem, or a customer service representative can send out a replacement product if a customer calls with a problem.

Encryption - The transformation of readable text into coded text for security purposes.

DEFINITIONS

End item - A product sold as a completed item or repair part; any item subject to a customer order or sales forecast. Synonym: Finished Goods Inventory.

End-of-Life - Planning and execution at the end of the life of a product. The challenge is making just the right amount to avoid A) ending up with excess, which have to be sold at great discounts or scrapped or B) ending up with shortages before the next generation is available.

End-of-Life Inventory - Inventory on hand that will satisfy future demand for products that are no longer in production at your entity.

Engineered flow of information - The method that prevents supply chain flows from happening by chance through reorganizations, outsourcing, mergers, and acquisitions. Instead, supply chains should be engineered for competitiveness, meaning they should be designed and optimized to match the business strategy and deliver the intended product.

Engineering Change - A revision to a drawing or design released by engineering to modify or correct a part. The request for the change can be from a customer or from production, quality control, another department, or a supplier. Synonym: Engineering Change Order.

Engineering Change Order (ECO) - A documented and approved revision to a product or process specification.

Engineer-to-Order - A process in which the manufacturing organization must first prepare (engineer) significant product or process documentation before manufacture may begin.

En-route - Shipment in a carrier's possession and being transported.

Enterprise Application Integration (EAI) - A computer term for the tools and techniques used in linking ERP and other enterprise systems together. Linking systems is key for e-business. Gartner say 'firms implementing enterprise applications spend at least 30% on point-to-point interfaces'.

Enterprise Resource Planning (ERP) System - A class of software for planning and managing "enterprise-wide" the resources needed to take customer orders, ship them, account for them and replenish all needed goods according to customer orders and forecasts. Often includes electronic commerce with suppliers. Examples of ERP systems are the application suites from SAP, Oracle, PeopleSoft and others.

Enterprise-Wide ABM - A management information system that uses activity-based information to facilitate decision making across an organization.

Enveloping - An EDI management software function that groups all documents of the same type, or functional group, and bound for the same destination into an electronic envelope. Enveloping is useful where there are multiple documents such as orders or invoices issued to a single trading partner that need to be sent as a packet.

Environmentally Sensitive Engineering - Designing features in a product and its packaging that improve recycling, etc. It can include elimination of compounds that are hazardous to the environment.

EOQ - see Economic Order Quantity

EPC - see Electronic Product Code

EPS - A computer term. Encapsulated Postscript. An extension of the PostScript graphics file format developed by Adobe Systems. EPS lets PostScript graphics files be incorporated into other documents.

Equalisation - (1) Monetary allowance to a customer for picking up or delivering cargo to or from a point which is not the origin/destination shown on the B/L. (2) Compensation for additional charges incurred by the shipper for delivering cargo to port designated by the carrier other than the closest port to the supplier.

Equipment Interchange Receipt (EIR) - A document used to receive or deliver a full or empty container/chassis at any terminal or inland container pool/depot.

Equipment Relocation - The relocation of any form of business equipment from one location to another that usually involves special handling, packaging, mode of transportation, and de-install/install. The types of equipment could be office gear, IT assets, hospital assets, plant assets, inventory storage assets or any complex gear. Using an asset swap can reduce the downtime associated with these complex items and support a quick and efficient turnover during the actual relocation to minimize downtime. See Asset Swap.

Ergonomic - The science of creating workspaces and products which are human friendly to use.

Error List - Report showing discrepancies (errors) in data input.

ERS - see Evaluated Receipts Settlement

ESI - see Early Supplier Involvement

Estimated Time of Arrival (ETA) - The expected date, including time of arrival of a shipment, passenger or vessel at a port, airport or terminal.

ETA - see Estimated Time of Arrival

ETD - See Estimated Time of Departure.

Ethernet - A computer term for the most commonly used type of local area network (LAN) communication protocol using coaxial or twisted pair wiring.

Ethical standards - A set of guidelines for proper conduct by business professionals.

European Article Number (EAN) - A defined numbering mechanism used in Europe to uniquely identify every retail product and packaging option. The EAN is similar in concept and design to the UPC code and is usually what the barcode represents on goods. Also see: Uniform Product Code.

EVA - see Economic Value Added

Evaluated Receipts Settlement (ERS) - A process for authorizing payment for goods based on actual receipts with purchase order data, when price has already been negotiated. The basic premise behind ERS is that all of the information in the invoice is already transmitted in the shipping documentation. Therefore, the invoice is eliminated and the shipping documentation is used to pay the vendor.

Ex Works (EXW) - Incoterm. Title and risk pass to buyer including payment of all transportation and insurance cost from the seller's door. Used for any mode of transportation.

Exception - Notations made when the cargo is received at the carrier's terminal or loaded aboard a vessel. Irregularities in packaging or actual or suspected damage to the cargo are notated on the bill of lading.

Exception Inventory - Inventory quantities that are above a specific need.

Exception Message - See Action Message

Exception Rate - A change or exception made to the classification affecting the class rate.

Exception-Based Processing - A computer term for applications that automatically highlight particular events or results which fall outside pre-determined parameters. This saves considerable effort by automatically finding problems and alerting the right persons. An example would be where a shorted item on a purchase order receipt would automatically notify a purchasing agent for follow-up.

Exclusive patronage agreements - A shipper agrees to use only member liner firms of a conference in return for a 10% to 15% rate reduction.

Exclusive Use - Service ordered by the shipper, whereby the shipper obtains exclusive use of a vehicle and agrees to the terms for this service.

Exempt Carrier - A for-hire carrier that is free from economic regulation. Trucks hauling certain commodities are exempt from Interstate Commerce Commission economic regulation. By far the largest portion of exempt carriers transports agricultural commodities or seafood.

Expediting - (1) Moving shipments through regular channels at an accelerated rate. (2) To take extraordinary action because of an increase in relative priority. Synonym: Stockchase.

Expert system - A computer program that mimics a human expert.

Explode-to-Deduct - See Backflush

Exponential Smoothing Forecast - In forecasting, a type of weighted moving average forecasting technique in which past observations are geometrically discounted according to their age. The heaviest weight is assigned to the most recent data. The smoothing is termed exponential because data points are weighted in accordance with an exponential function of their age. The technique makes use of a smoothing constant to apply to the difference between the most recent forecast and the critical sales data, thus avoiding the necessity of carrying historical sales data. The approach can be used for data that exhibit no trend or seasonal patterns. Higher order exponential smoothing models can be used for data with either (or both) trend and seasonality

Export - (1) In logistics, the movement of products from one country to another. For example, significant volumes of cut flowers are exported from The Netherlands to other countries of the world. (2) A computer term referring to the transfer of information from a source (system or database) to a target.

Export Broker - A firm that brings together buyer and seller for a fee, then eventually withdraws from the transaction.

Export Compliance - In compliance with rules for exporting products, including packaging, labeling, and documentation.

Export Declaration - (1) Government document permitting designated goods to leave the country. Issued by the U.S. Dept. of Commerce. Includes complete particulars on the shipment. Although customers can submit their declarations themselves to U.S. Customs, the carrier is still responsible for penalties if the documentation is not available by the time a vessel is "cleared" by customs for sailing. Also known as an ex-dec or SED (Shipper´s Export Declaration). (2) Shippers need to obtain a Bureau of Census document which spells out shipment details for entry into a government statistical system. Documents for export shipping, declaring the value of the cargo to the U.S. Customs.

Export License - A certificate secured from a government granting permission to an exporter to export a specific quantity of a controlled commodity to a certain country. An export license is often required if a government has placed embargoes or other restrictions upon exports.

Export sales contract - The initial document in any international transaction; it details the specifics of the sales agreement between the buyer and seller.

Exporter Identification Number (EIN) - A number required for the exporter on the Shipper's Export Declaration. A corporation may use their Federal Employer Identification Number as provided by the

IRS; individuals can use their Social Security Numbers.

Exports - A term used to describe products produced in one country and sold in another. Also see: Export

Express - (1) Carrier payment to its customers when ships, rail cars, or trailers are unloaded or loaded in less than the time allowed by contract and returned to the carrier for use. Also see: demurrage, detention.(2) The use of priority package delivery to achieve overnight or second-day delivery.

Extended 3 of 9 - Similar to Code 3 of 9 except that it allows the full 128 ASCII character set to be encoded by printing two barcode characters for each text character.

Extended Code 93 - Similar to Code 93 except that it allows the full 128 character ASCII character set to be encoded.

Extended Enterprise - The notion that supply chain partners form a larger entity which works together as though it were a single unit.

Extended supply chain community - Supply chains that take advantage of e-market (electronic market) services.

Extensible Markup Language (XML) - A computer term for a language that facilitates direct communication among computers on the Internet. Unlike the older hypertext markup language (HTML), which provides data tags giving instructions to a web browser about how to display information, XML tags give instructions to a browser or to application software which help to define the specifics about the category of information.

External Factory - A situation where suppliers are viewed as an extension of the firm's manufacturing capabilities and capacities. The same practices and concerns that are commonly applied to the management of the firm's manufacturing system should also be applied to the management of the external factory.

Extra Loader - Additional vessel brought into schedule to cope with exceptionally strong market conditions.

Extranet - A computer term describing a private network (or a secured link on the public internet) that links separate organizations and that uses the same software and protocols as the Internet. Used for improving supply chain management. For example, extranets are used to provide access to a supply chain partner's internal inventory data which is not available to unrelated parties. Antonym: Intranet.

Extrinsic Forecast - In forecasting, a forecast based on a correlated leading indicator, such as estimating furniture sales based on housing starts. Extrinsic forecasts tend to be more useful for large aggregations, such as total company sales, than for individual product sales. Antonym: intrinsic forecast method.

EXW - see Ex Works

FA - see Functional Acknowledgment
FAA - see Federal Aviation Administration

Fabricator - A manufacturer that turns the product of a raw materials supplier into a larger variety of products. A fabricator may turn steel rods into nuts, bolts, and twist drills, or may turn paper into bags and boxes.

Facilities - The physical plant, distribution centers, service centers, and related equipment.

Failure Modes Effects Analysis (FMEA) - A pro-active method of predicting faults and failures so that preventive action can be taken.

Definitions

Fair return - A level of profit that enables a carrier to realize a rate of return on investment or property value that the regulatory agencies deem acceptable for that level of risk.

Fair value - The value of the carrier's property; the basis of calculation has included original cost minus depreciation, replacement cost, and market value.

Fair-share Quantity Logic - In inventory management, the process of equitably allocating available stock among field distribution centers. Fair-share quantity logic is normally used when stock available from a central inventory location is less than the cumulative requirements of the field stocking locations. The use of fair-share quantity logic involves procedures that "push" stock out to the field, instead of allowing the field to "pull" in what is needed. The objective is to maximize customer service from the limited available inventory.

FAK - see Freight-All-Kinds

FAS - (1) See Free Alongside Ship (2) See Final Assembly Schedule

FAST - see Fast and Secure Trade

Fast and Secure Trade (FAST) - U.S. Customs program that allows importers on the U.S./Canada border to obtain expedited release for qualifying commercial shipments.

FB - see Freight Bill

FCA - see Free Carrier

FCL - see Full Container Load

Feature - A distinctive characteristic of a good or service. The characteristic is provided by an option, accessory, or attachment. For example, in ordering a new car, the customer must specify an engine type and size (option), but need not necessarily select an air conditioner (attachment).

Federal Aviation Administration (FAA) - The federal agency charged with administering federal safety regulations governing air transportation.

Federal Maritime Commission (FMC) - A regulatory agency that controls services, practices, and agreements of international water common carriers and noncontiguous domestic water carriers.

Feeder - Transportation conveyance utilised to relay cargo from the mother vessel to ultimate destination or from first receipt port to mother vessel.

Feeder Railroad Development Program - Any financially responsible person (except Class I and Class II carriers) with ICC approval can acquire a rail line having a density of less than 3 million gross ton-miles per year.

FEU - see Forty-foot equivalent unit

FF&E - see Furniture, Fixtures and Equipment

FFE - See Forty-foot Equivalent Unit.

FFG - see Field Finished Goods

FGI - see Finished Goods Inventory

Field Finished Goods (FFG) - Inventory maintained at locations outside of the manufacturing plant (i.e., distribution center (dc) or warehouse).

Field Service - See After-Sale Service

Field Service Parts - Parts inventory kept at locations outside the four walls of the manufacturing plant (i.e., distribution center or warehouse).

Field Warehouse - Warehouse that stores goods on the goods' owner's property while the goods are under a bona fide warehouse manager's custody. The owner uses the warehouse receipts as collateral for a loan.

75

Glossary of terms in Logistics & Shipping

FIFO - see First In First Out

File Transfer Protocol (FTP) - The Internet service that transfers files from one computer to another, over standard phone lines.

Filed rate doctrine - The legal rate the common carrier may charge; is the rate published in the carrier's tariff on file with the ICC.

Fill Rate - The percentage of order items that the picking operation actually fills within a given period of time.

Fill Rates by Order - Whether orders are received and released consistently, or released from a blanket purchase order, this metric measures the percentage of ship-from-stock orders shipped within 24 hours of order "release". Make-to-Stock schedules attempt to time the availability of finished goods to match forecasted customer orders or releases. Orders that were not shipped within 24 hours due to consolidation but were available for shipment within 24 hours are reported separately. In calculating elapsed time for order fill rates, the interval begins at ship release and ends when material is consigned for shipment.Calculation: [Number of orders filled from stock shipped within 24 hours of order release] / [Total number of stock orders] Note: The same concept of fill rates can be applied to order lines and individual products to provide statistics on percentage of lines shipped completely and percentage of products shipped completely.

Final Assembly - The highest level assembled product, as it is shipped to customers. This terminology is typically used when products consist of many possible features and options that may only be combined when an actual order is received. Also see: End Item, Assemble to Order

Final Assembly Schedule (FAS) - A schedule of end items to finish the product for specific customers' orders in a make-to-order or assemble-to-order environment. It is also referred to as the finishing schedule because it may involve operations other than just the final assembly; also, it may not involve assembly, but simply final mixing, cutting, packaging, etc. The FAS is prepared after receipt of a customer order as constrained by the availability of material and capacity, and it schedules the operations required to complete the product from the level where it is stocked (or master scheduled) to the end-item level.

Final Destination - Last stopping location for a shipment.

Finance lease - An equipment-leasing arrangement that provides the lessee with a means of financing for the leased equipment; a common method for leasing motor carrier trailers.

Financial responsibility - Motor carriers are required to have body injury and property damage (not cargo) insurance or not less than $500,000 per incident per vehicle; higher financial responsibility limits apply for motor carriers transporting oil or hazardous materials.

Finished Goods Inventory (FGI) - Products that are completely manufactured, packaged, stored, and ready for distribution.

Finite Forward Scheduling - An equipment scheduling technique that builds a schedule by proceeding sequentially from the initial period to the final period while observing capacity limits. A Gantt chart may be used with this technique. Also see: Finite Scheduling

Finite Scheduling - A scheduling methodology where work is loaded into work centers such that no work center capacity requirement exceeds the capacity available for that work center. See: drum-buffer-rope, finite forward scheduling.

FIO (FIO) - Free In Free Out.

Firewall - A computer term for a method of protecting the files and programs on one network from users on another network. A firewall blocks unwanted access to a protected network while giving the protected network access to networks outside of the firewall. A company will typically install a firewall to give users access to the Internet while protecting their internal information.

Firm Planned Order - A planned order which has been committed to production. Also see: Planned Order

First In First Out (FIFO) - (1) The practice of using stock from inventory on the basis of what was received first and is consumed first. (2) Warehouse term meaning first items stored are the first used. In accounting this tem is associated with the valuing of inventory such that the latest purchases are reflected in book inventory. Also see: Book Inventory

First Mover Advantage - Market innovator, putting the company in the leadership position.

First Pass Yield - The ratio of usable, specification conforming output from a process to its input, achieved without rework or reprocessing.

Fixed Costs - Costs, which do not fluctuate with business volume in the short run. Fixed costs include items such as depreciation on buildings and fixtures.

Fixed interval inventory model - A setup wherein each time an order is placed for an item, the same (fixed) quantity is ordered.

Fixed Interval Order System - See Fixed Reorder Cycle Inventory Model

Fixed Order Quantity - A lot-sizing technique in MRP or inventory management that will always cause planned or actual orders to be generated for a predetermined fixed quantity, or multiples thereof if net requirements for the period exceed the fixed order quantity.

Fixed Order Quantity System - See Fixed Reorder Cycle Inventory Model

Fixed Overhead - Traditionally, all manufacturing costs, other than direct labor and direct materials, that continue even if products are not produced. Although fixed overhead is necessary to produce the product, it cannot be directly traced to the final product. Also see: Indirect Cost

Fixed Reorder Cycle Inventory Model - A form of independent demand management model in which an order is placed every "n" time units. The order quantity is variable and essentially replaces the items consumed during the current time period. Let "M" be the maximum inventory desired at any time, and let x be the quantity on hand at the time the order is placed. Then, in the simplest model, the order quantity will be M x. The quantity M must be large enough to cover the maximum expected demand during the lead time plus a review interval. The order quantity model becomes more complicated whenever the replenishment lead time exceeds the review interval, because outstanding orders then have to be factored into the equation. These reorder systems are sometimes called fixed-interval order systems, order level systems, or periodic review systems. Synonyms: Fixed- Interval Order System, Fixed-Order Quantity System, Order Level System, Periodic Review System, Time-Based Order System. Also see: Fixed Reorder Quantity Inventory Model, Hybrid Inventory System, Independent Demand Item Management Models,

Fixed Reorder Quantity Inventory Model - A form of independent demand item management model in which an order for a fixed quantity is placed whenever stock on hand plus on order reaches a predetermined reorder level. The fixed order quantity may be determined by the economic order quantity, by a fixed order quantity (such as a carton or a truckload), or by another model yielding a fixed result. The reorder point may be deterministic or stochastic, and in either instance is large enough to cover the maximum expected demand during the replenishment lead time. Fixed reorder quantity models assume the existence of some form of a perpetual inventory record or some form of physical tracking, e.g., a two-bin system that is able to determine when the reorder point is reached. Synonym: Fixed Order Quantity System, Lot Size System, Order Point-Order Quantity System, Quantity Based Order System. Also see: Fixed Reorder Cycle Inventory Model, Hybrid Inventory System, Independent Demand Item Management Models, Optional Replenishment Model, Order Point Order Management System

Fixed-Location Storage - A method of storage in which a relatively permanent location is assigned for the storage of each item in a storeroom or warehouse. Although more space is needed to store parts than in a random-location storage system, fixed locations become familiar, and therefore a locator file may not be needed. Also see: Random-Location Storage

Fixed-Period Requirements - A lot-sizing technique that sets the order quantity to the demand for a given number of periods. Also see: Discrete Order Quantity

Flag of convenience - A shipowner registers a ship in a nation that offers conveniences in the areas of taxes, manning, and safety requirements; Liberia and Panama are two nations known for flags of convenience.

Flat - A loadable platform having no superstructure whatever but having the same length and width as the base of a container and equipped with top and bottom corner fittings. This is an alternative term used for certain types of specific purpose containers - namely platform containers and platform-based containers with incomplete structures

Flat Bed - Truck designed to haul heavy or oversized non-containerisable cargo.

Flat File - A computer term which refers to any file having fixed-record length, or in EDI, the file produced by EDI translation software to serve as input to the interface. Usually includes the same fields as the original file, but each field is expanded to its maximum length. Does not have delimiters.

Flatbed - Open truck or trailer without sides or top that generally is used for bulky, oversized items.

Flatcar - A rail car without sides; used for hauling machinery.

Flexibility - Ability to respond quickly and efficiently to changing customer and consumer demands.

Flexible Specialization - a strategy based on multi-use equipment, skilled workers and innovative senior management to accommodate the continuous change that occurs in the marketplace.

Flexible-path equipment - Materials handling devices that include hand trucks and forklifts.

Float - The time required for documents, payments, etc. to get from one trading partner to another.

Floating Cranes - Heavy duty cranes that are able to handle exceptionally heavy cargo if unable to use conventional gantry cranes.

Floor-Ready Merchandise (FRM) - Goods shipped by suppliers to retailers with all necessary tags, prices, security devices, etc. already attached, so goods can be cross docked rapidly through retail DCs, or received directly at stores.

Flow rack - Storage rack that utilizes shelves (metal) that are equipped with rollers or wheels. Such an arrangement allows product and materials to "flow" from the back of the rack to the front and therein making the product more accessible for smallquantity order-picking.

FMC - see Federal Maritime Commission

FMEA - see Failure Modes Effects Analysis

FOB - see Free On Board

Force Majeure - A state of emergency or condition that permits a company to depart from the strict terms of contract because of an event or effect that cannot be reasonably anticipated or controlled, i.e: beyond human control (French superior or irresistible force). Compare: ACT OF GOD, INEVITABLE ACCIDENT, VIS MAJOR.

Forecast - An estimate of future demand. A forecast can be constructed using quantitative methods, qualitative methods, or a combination of methods, and it can be based on extrinsic (external) or intrinsic (internal) factors. Various forecasting techniques attempt to predict one or more of the four components of demand: cyclical, random, seasonal, and trend. Also see: Box-Jenkins Model, Exponential Smoothing Forecast, Extrinsic Forecasting Method, Intrinsic Forecasting Method, Qualitative Forecasting Method, Quantitative Forecasting Method

Forecast Accuracy - Measures how accurate your forecast is as a percent of actual units or dollars shipped, calculated as 1 minus the absolute value of the difference between forecasted demand and actual demand, as a percentage of actual demand.Calculation: [1- (|Sum of Variances|/Sum of Actual)]

Forecast Cycle - Cycle time between forecast regenerations that reflect true changes in marketplace demand for shippable endproducts.

Forecasting - Predictions of how much of a product will be purchased by customers. Relies upon both quantitative and qualitative methods. Also see: Forecast

Foreign Trade Zone (FTZ) - Special restricted-access commercial and industrial areas in or near ports of entry that are designated by the government for duty-free entry of any non-prohibited goods. Foreign and domestic merchandise, including raw materials, components, and finished goods may be stored, displayed, and used for manufacturing within the zone and re-exported without duties being paid. Duties are imposed only when the original goods or items manufactured from those goods pass from the zone into an area of the country subject to Customs authority.

For-hire carrier - A carrier that provides transportation service to the public on a fee basis.

For-Hire Carriers - Persons or firms engaged in the transportation of goods or passengers for compensation. Classified into two general categories, specialised and general freight motor carriers.

Forklift Truck - A machine device used to raise and lower freight and to move freight to different warehouse locations.

Form utility - The value created in a good by changing its form, through the production process.

Forty-foot equivalent unit (FFE) - A standard size intermodal container.

Forwarder's Cargo Receipt - A non-negotiable document issued by a forwarder which will satisfy the legal requirements of a letter of credit. Since a forwarder is not an NVOCC it cannot issue actual bills of lading. The FCR is legally binding upon the forwarder and is an industry standard.

Four Party Logistics Provider (4PL) - Businesses that manage a variety of logistics related services for clients by using Third Party Logistics Providers (3PL). The provider integrates the technology and does not perform any of the services. Differs from third party logistics in the following ways;1. 4PL organization is often a separate entity established as a joint venture or long-term contract between a primary client and one or more partners; 2. 4PL organization acts as a single interface between the client and multiple logistics service providers; 3. All aspects (ideally) of the client's supply chain are managed by the 4PL organization; and, 4. It is possible for a major third-party logistics provider to form a 4PL organization within its existing structure.

Four P's - A set of marketing tools to direct the business offering to the customer. The four P's are product, price, place, and promotion.

Four Wall Inventory - The stock which is contained within a single facility or building.

Fourier Series - In forecasting, a form of analysis useful for forecasting. The model is based on fitting sine waves with increasing frequencies and phase angles to a time series.

Free Alongside Ship (FAS) - Incoterm. Title and risk pass to buyer including payment of all transportation and insurance cost once delivered alongside ship by the seller. Used for sea or inland waterway transportation. the export clearance obligation rests with the seller.

Free Carrier (FCA) - Incoterm. Title and risk pass to buyer including transportation and insurance cost when the seller delivers goods cleared for export to the carrier. Seller is obligated to load the goods on the Buyer's collecting vehicle; it is the Buyer's obligation to recieve the Seller's arriving vehicle unloaded.

Free On Board (FOB) - Incoterm. Title and risk pass to buyer including payment of all transportation and insurance cost once delivered on board the ship by the seller. Used for sea or inland waterway transportation.

Free Time - Time allowed for shippers or consignees/receivers to load or unload cargo before demurrage, detention and other charges accrue.

Freezing inventory balances - In most cycle counting programs the term "freezing" refers to copying the current on-hand inventory balance into the cycle count file. This may also be referred to as taking a snapshot of the inventory balance. It rarely means that the inventory is actually frozen in a way that prevents transactions from occurring.

Freight - Goods that are transported from one place to another.

Freight Bill - (1) The carrier's invoice for transportation charges applicable to a freight shipment. (2) Bill rendered by a transportation line to consignee containing description of freight shipper name, point of origin and weight charges (if not prepaid). (3) Bill rendered by a transportation line to shipper containing description of freight, consignee, destination and weight charges (if prepaid).

Freight Bill (FB) - Document for a shipment noting description of the freight, its weight, and amount of carrier's invoice for payment of transport services rendered.

Freight Carriers - Companies that transport freight by trucking, railroads, airlines, and sea borne shipping.

Freight Cashier - Responsible for collections of freight/charges/release of cargo/release of bills of ladings. (1) Person engaged in assembling, collecting, consolidating shipping and distributing less than trailerload freight. (2) Also, a person acting as an agent in the transshipping of freight to or from foreign countries and clearing freight through federal customs.

Freight Charge - The rate that has been established for transporting freight.

Freight Collect - The freight and charges to be paid by the consignee of the order.

Freight Consolidation - The grouping of shipments to obtain reduced costs or improved utilization of the transportation function. Consolidation can occur by market area grouping, grouping according to scheduled deliveries, or using third-party pooling services such as public warehouses and freight forwarders.

Freight Forwarder - An organization which provides logistics services as an intermediary between the shipper and the carrier, typically on international shipments. Freight forwarders provide the ability to respond quickly and efficiently to changing customer and consumer demands and international shipping (import/export) requirements.

Freight Forwarders Institute - The freight forwarder industry association.

Freight Release - Evidence that the freight charges for the cargo have been paid. If in writing, it may be presented at the pier to obtain release of the cargo. Normally, once the freight is paid, freight releases are arranged without additional documentation. Also known as freight bill receipt.

Freight-All-Kinds (FAK) - Consolidated cargo that is shipped at one rate. FAK cargo is usually shipped in a container filled with a variety of merchandise or commodities.

FRM - see Floor-Ready Merchandise

Frozen Zone - In forecasting, this is the period in which no changes can be made to scheduled work orders based on changes in demand. Use of a frozen zone provides stability in the manufacturing schedule.

FTE - see Full-time Equivalents

FTL - see Full Truckload

FTP - see File Transfer Protocol

FTZ - see Foreign Trade Zone

Fulfillment - The act of fulfilling a customer order. Fulfillment includes order management, picking, packaging, and shipping.

Full Container Load (FCL) - (1) A delivery of cargo that fills a given container either by bulk or maximum weight. (2) Containers are charged a specific rate for ocean transit regardless of their (lack of) contents. A full container will thus offer a better price per unit shipped than will a LCL.

Full Truckload (FTL) - A shipment of cargo that fills a given tractor-trailer either by bulk or maximum weight.

Full Visible Capacity - The trailer is loaded as full as the nature of the freight and other conditions permit, so that no more of the same type of freight can be loaded, consistent with safety and damage precautions.

Full-Service Leasing - An equipment-leasing arrangement that includes a variety of services to support leased equipment (i.e., motor carrier tractors).

Full-time Equivalents (FTE) - Frequently organizations make use of contract and temporary employees; please convert contract, part-time, and temporary employees to full-time equivalents. For example, two contract employees who worked for six months full-time and a half-time regular employee would constitute 1.5 full-time equivalents. 1FTE = 2000 hours per year.

Fully allocated cost - The variable cost associated with a particular unit of output plus an allocation of common cost.

Functional Acknowledgment (FA) - A specific EDI Transaction Set (997) sent by the recipient of an EDI message to confirm the receipt of data but with no indication as to the recipient application's response to the message. The FA will confirm that the message contained the correct number of lines, etc. via control summaries, but does not report on the validity of the data.

Functional Group - Part of the hierarchical structure of EDI transmissions, a Functional Group contains one or more related Transaction Sets preceded by a Functional Group header and followed by a Functional Group trailer

Functional Silo - A view of an organization where each department or functional group is operated independent of other groups within the organization. Each group is referred to as a "Silo". This is the opposite of an integrated structure.

Furniture, Fixtures and Equipment (FF&E) - Types of items that can be arranged for installation or de-installation through a Logistics company. See FF&E.

Future order - An order entered for shipment at some future date. This may be related to new products which are not currently available for shipment, or scheduling of future needs by the customer.

Gain Sharing - A method of incentive compensation where supply chain partners share collectively in savings from productivity improvements. The concept provides an incentive to both the buying and supplier organizations to focus on continually reevaluating, re-energizing, and enhancing their business relationship. All aspects of value delivery are scrutinized, including specification design, order processing, inbound transportation, inventory management, obsolescence programs, material yield, forecasting and inventory planning, product performance and reverse logistics. The focus is on driving out limited value cost while protecting profit margins.

Gantry Crane - Port crane used to load and discharge containers from vessels, can be positioned by moving along rail tracks.

Gap analysis - A comparison of the current performance of a business process with that reported to be the best-in-class. A gap analysis is used to prioritize multiple opportunities for improvement within the same supply chain.

Garment-on-Hanger (GOH) - Method of storing apparel in containers for garments that should not be folded.

Gateway - (1) Shipping: Point at which freight moving from one territory to another is interchanged between transportation lines. (2) Computers: Computers, like bridges and routers, are a method of connecting two local area networks. Gateways translate between two LAN protocols. (3) Gateways: are protocol-specific and can only translate between two types of networks, not directly to PCs.

Gathering lines - Oil pipelines that bring oil from the oil well to storage areas.

GBL - see Government Bill of Lading

General commodities carrier - A common motor carrier that has operating authority to transport general commodities, or all commodities not listed as special commodities.

General Commodity - Any commodity that is not household goods or personal effects.

General-merchandise warehouse - A warehouse that is used to store goods that are readily handled, are packaged, and do not req1ire a controlled environment.

Genset - Generator sets which supply power to refrigerated containers when no external source is available. It is used to regulate the temperature in a reefer container. It can use its own power or plugs provided on the pier/vessel.

GIF - see Graphics Interchange Format

Global Positioning System (GPS) - A system that uses satellites equipment to precisely locate over-the-road equipment.

Global Strategy - A strategy that focuses on improving worldwide performance through the sales and marketing of common goods and services with minimum product variation by country. Its competitive advantage grows through selecting the best locations for operations in other countries.

Global Trade Item Number (GTIN) - A unique number that comprises up to 14 digits and is used to identify an item (product or service) upon which there is a need to retrieve pre-defined information that may be priced, ordered or invoiced at any point in the supply chain. The definition covers raw materials through end user products and includes services, all of which have pre-defined characteristics. GTIN is the globally-unique EAN.UCC System identification number, or key, used for trade items (products and services). It's used for uniquely identifying trade items (products and services) sold, delivered, warehoused, and billed throughout the retail and commercial distribution channels. Unlike a UPC number, which only provides information specific to a group of products, the GTIN gives each product its own specific identifying number, giving greater accuracy in tracking. See EPC

Globalization - The process of making something worldwide in scope or application.

GMP - See Good manufacturing practices.

GNP - see Gross National Product

GOH - see Garment-on-Hanger

Going-concern value - The value that a firm has as an entity, as opposed to the sum of the values of each of its parts taken separately; particularly important in determining what constitutes a reasonable railroad rate.

Gondola - A rail car with a flat platform and sides three to five feet high; used for top loading of items that are long and heavy.

Good manufacturing practices (GMP) - That part of the pharmaceutical quality assurance, which ensures that products are consistently produced and controlled in conformity with quality standards appropriate for their intended use and as required by the product specification.

Goods - Merchandise, supplies, raw materials, commodities and finished product. All things are treated as moveable and indicated as sold to a particular buyer.

Goods Received Note (GRN) - Documentation raised by the recipient of materials or products.

Government Bill of Lading (GBL) - The bill of lading used for shipments completed by U.S. Government agencies.

GPS - see Global Positioning System

Grandfather clause - A provision that enabled motor carriers engaged in lawful trucking operations before the passage of the Motor Carrier Act of 1935 to secure common carrier authority without proving public convenience and necessity; a similar provision exists for other modes.

Grandfathering - Clause creating an exemption based on circumstances previously existing.

Granger laws - State laws passed before 1870 in Midwestern states to control rail transportation.

Graphics Interchange Format (GIF) - A graphical file format commonly used to display indexed-color images on the World Wide Web. GIF is a compressed format, designed to minimize file transfer time over standard phone lines.

GLOSSARY OF TERMS IN LOGISTICS & SHIPPING

Great Lakes carriers - Water carriers that operate on the five Great lakes.

GRI - General Rate Increase

Grid technique - A quantitative technique to determine the least-cost center, given raw materials sources and markets, for locating a plant or warehouse.

GRN - see Goods Received Note

Gross Inventory - Value of inventory at standard cost before any reserves for excess and obsolete items are taken.

Gross Margin - The difference between total revenue and the cost of goods sold. Synonym: gross profit margin.

Gross National Product (GNP) - A measure of a nation's output; the total value of all final goods and services produced during a period of time.

Gross Weight - Weight of a shipment together with the weight of a tractor-trailer and any other shipments on board.

Groupthink - A situation in which critical information is withheld from the team because individual members censor or restrain themselves, either because they believe their concerns are not worth discussing or because they are afraid of confrontation.

GTIN - see Global Trade Item Number

GTM - Global Trade Management.

Guaranteed loans - Loans made to railroads that are cosigned and guaranteed by the federal government.

Handling Costs - The cost included in moving, transferring, preparing, and handling.

Hangertainer - Specialised container equipped with hanger beams for the purpose of stowing garments on hangers.

Hard copy - Computer output printed on paper.

Harmless Chemicals - A cargo description, which is a contradiction of terms. A chemical is a substance and whether it is harmless or not, depends on the context in which the substance appears or is used.

Harmonised Tariff System - An international classification system designed to improve the collection of import and export statistics as well as provide a uniform tariff code structure for incorporation into national tariff systems. Promotes a high degree of international uniformity in the presentation of customs tariffs and foreign trade statistics. Consists of approximately 5,000 item descriptions, grouped into 21 sections and 97 chapters.

Harmonize Tariff Schedule of the United States (HTS) - An organized listing of goods and their duty rates which is used as the basis for classifying imported products and identifying the rates of duty to be charged. The tariff schedule is divided into a variety of sections and chapters dealing independently with merchandise in wide-ranging product categories. The U.S. International Trade Commission is responsible for publishing the information.

Harmonized Commodity Description & Coding System (HS-code) - An international classification system that assigns identification numbers to specific products. The coding system ensures that all parties in international trade use consistent classification for the purposes of documentation, statistical control, and duty assessment.

Hawaiian carrier - A for-hire air carrier that operates within the state of Hawaii

HAWB - see House Airwaybill

DEFINITIONS

Hawthorne Effect - From a study conducted at the Hawthorne Plant of Western Electric Company in 1927-1932 which found that the act of showing people that you are concerned usually results in better job performance. Studying and monitoring of activities are typically seen as being concerned and results in improved productivity.

Hazardous Goods - Articles or substances that could have a significant risk to health, safety, or property, and that ordinarily require special attention when transported. Also called Dangerous Goods.

Hazardous Material - A hazardous material is defined as any substance or material could adversely affect the safety of the public, handlers or carriers during transportation. There are nine classes of hazardous materials:

Heavy Lift Charge - Charge for cargo which is too heavy to be lifted by standard cranes or ship's tackle.

Hedge Inventory - A form of inventory buildup to buffer against some event that may not happen. Hedge inventory planning involves speculation related to potential labor strikes, price increases, unsettled governments, and events that could severely impair a company's strategic initiatives. Risk and consequences are unusually high, and top management approval is often required.

Heijunka - In the Just-in-Time philosophy, an approach to level production throughout the supply chain to match the planned rate of end product sales.

Hierarchy of Cost Assignability - In cost accounting, an approach to group activity costs at the level of an organization where they are incurred, or can be directly related to. Examples are the level where individual units are identified (unit-level), where batches of units are organized or processed (batch-level), where a process is operated or supported (process-level), or where costs cannot be objectively assigned to lower level activities or processes (facility-level). This approach is used to better understand the nature of the costs, including the level in the organization at which they are incurred, the level to which they can be initially assigned (attached) and the degree to which they are assignable to other activity and/or cost object levels, i.e. activity or cost object cost, or sustaining costs.

Highway Trust Fund - Federal highway use tax revenues are paid into this fund, and the federal government's share of highway construction is paid from the fund.

Highway use taxes - Taxes assessed by federal and state governments against users of the highway (the fuel tax is an example). The use tax money is used to pay for the construction, maintenance, and policing of highways.

Hi-low - Usually refers to a forklift truck on which the operator must stand rather than sit.

Hitchment - Marrying 2 or more portions of one shipment that originate at different geographical locations, moving under one bill of lading, from one shipper to one consignee. Authority for this service must be granted by tariff publication.

Holds - Section of vessel in which containers are stored. See Bays

Home Page - The starting point for a website. It is the page that is retrieved and displayed by default when a user visits the website. The default home-page name for a server depends on the server's configuration. On many web servers, it is index.html or default.htm. Some web servers support multiple home pages.

Honeycombing - (1) The practice of removing merchandise in pallet load quantities where the space is not exhausted in an orderly fashion. This results in inefficiencies due to the fact that the received merchandise may not be efficiently stored in the space which is created by the honey-combing. (2) The storing or withdrawal or supplies in a manner that results in vacant space that is not usable for storage of other items. (3) Creation of unoccupied space resulting from withdrawal of unit loads. This is one of the major hidden costs of warehousing.

Hopper cars - Rail cars that permit top loading and bottom unloading of bulk commodities; some hopper cars have permanent tops with hatches to provide protection against the elements.

Horizontal Play/Horizontal Hub - This is a term for a function that cuts across many industries, usually defines a facility or organization that is providing a common service.

Hoshin Planning - Breakthrough planning. A Japanese strategic planning process in which a company develops up to four vision statements that indicate where the company should be in the next five years. Company goals and work plans are developed based on the vision statements. Periodic audits are then conducted to monitor progress.

Hospitality - The division of service that provides receiving, warehousing, inspection, installation of furniture, fixtures and equipment (FF&E) for new or renovated hotels, restaurants or assisted living center.

Hostler - An individual employed to move trucks and trailers within a terminal or warehouse yard area.

House Airwaybill (HAWB) - Document issued by agent. Used for consolidation of cargo. Reference numbers are normally issued by agent for identification of individual shipments within a consolidation.

Household goods warehouse - A warehouse that is used to store household goods.

HR - see Human Resources

HS-code - see Harmonized Commodity Description & Coding System

HTML - see HyperText Markup Language

HTS - see Harmonize Tariff Schedule of the United States

HTTP (HTTP) - See HyperText Transport Protocol

Hub - (1). A large retailer or manufacturer having many trading partners. (2) A reference for a transportation network as in "hub and spoke" which is common in the airline and trucking industry. For example, a hub airport serves as the focal point for the origin and termination of long-distance flights where flights from outlying areas are fed into the hub airport for connecting flights. (3) A common connection point for devices in a network. (4) A Web "hub" is one of the initial names for what is now known as a "portal". It came from the creative idea of producing a website, which would contain many different "portal spots" (small boxes that looked like ads, with links to different yet related content). This content, combined with Internet technology, made this idea a milestone in the development and appearance of websites, primarily due to the ability to display a lot of useful content and store one's preferred information on a secured server. The web term "hub" was replaced with portal.

Hub airport - An airport that serves as the focal point for the origin and termination of long-distance flights; flights from outlying areas are fed into the hub airport for connecting flights.

Human Resources (HR) - The function broadly responsible for personnel policies and practices within an organization.

Human-machine interface - Any point where data is communicated from a worker to a computer or from a computer to a worker. Data entry programs, inquire programs, reports, documents, LED displays,

DEFINITIONS

and voice commands are all examples of human-machine interfaces.

Hundredweight (CWT) - A pricing unit used in transportation.

Hustler - Tractor that pulls containers around the pier for positioning. Also known as a yard hustler.

Hybrid Inventory System - An inventory system combining features of the fixed reorder quantity inventory model and the fixed reorder cycle inventory model. Features of the fixed reorder cycle inventory model and the fixed reorder quantity inventory model can be combined in many different ways. For example, in the order point-periodic review combination system, an order is placed if the inventory level drops below a specified level before the review date; if not, the order quantity is determined at the next review date. Another hybrid inventory system is the optional replenishment model. Also see: Fixed Reorder Cycle Inventory Model, Fixed Reorder Quantity Inventory Model, Optional Replenishment Model

Hyperlink - A computer term. Also referred to as "link". The text you find on a website which can be "clicked on" with a mouse which, in turn, will take you to another web page or a different area of the same web page. Hyperlinks are created or "coded" in HTML.

HyperText Markup Language (HTML) - The standard language for describing the contents and appearance of pages on the

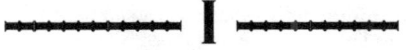

ICC - see Interstate Commerce Commission

Igloos - Pallets and containers used in air transportation; the igloo shape is designed to fit the internal wall contours of a narrowbody airplane.

Image Processing - allows a company to take electronic photographs of documents. The electronic photograph then can be stored in a computer and retrieved from computer storage to replicate the document on a printer. The thousands of bytes of data composing a single document are encoded in an optical disk. Many carriers now use image processing to provide proof-ofdelivery documents to a shipper. The consignee signs an electronic pad that automatically digitizes a consignee's signature for downloading into a computer. A copy of that signature then can be produced to demonstrate that a delivery took place.

IMC - see Intermodal Marketing Company

IMCO - International Maritime Control Organisation. See IMO.

IMCO Classification - International Maritime Control Organisation classification for hazardous cargo.

IMO - International Maritime Organisation. Formally IMCO.

Import - Movement of products from one country into another. The import of automobiles from Germany to the U.S. is an example.

Import/Export License - Official authorization issued by a government allowing the shipping or delivery of a product across national boundaries.

Importation Point - The location where goods are cleared for importation into a country.

Imports - Goods and services which one country's residents purchase and transport from another country into their own country.

Impressions - With regard to online advertising, it is the number of times an ad banner is downloaded and presumably seen by users. Guaranteed impressions refer to the minimum number of times an ad banner will be seen by users.

87

Glossary of terms in Logistics & Shipping

In Bond - A Customs program for inland ports that provides for cargo arriving at a seaport to be shipped under a Customs bond to a more conveniently located inland port where the entry documents have been filed. Customs clears the shipment there and the cargo is trucked to its destination, which normally is close to the inland port.

Inbound - Import Shipment.

Inbound Logistics - The movement of materials from suppliers and vendors into production processes or storage facilities.

Incentive rate - A rate designed to induce the shipper to ship heavier volumes per shipment.

Income statement - A financial statement showing the net income for a business over a given period of time. See also balance sheet, funds flow statement.

INCOTERMS - International terms of sale developed by the International Chamber of Commerce to define sellers' and buyers' responsibilities.

Independent Action - A separate action taken by an individual member of a conference agreement to change rates or terms of carriage as laid out in the conference agreements. A carrier can take an independent action in a conference, resulting in a unique rate for that carrier within a conference; ability to file a rate independently of other carriers' actions.

Independent Carrier - Carrier that is not a member of a shipping conference.

Independent Demand Item Management Models - Models for the management of items whose demand is not strongly influenced by other items managed by the same company. These models can be characterized as follows: (1) stochastic or deterministic, depending on the variability of demand and other factors; (2) fixed quantity, fixed cycle, or hybrid - (optional replenishment). Also see: Fixed Reorder Cycle Inventory Model, Fixed Reorder Quantity Inventory Model, Optional Replenishment Model

Independent Trading Exchange (ITE) - Often used synonymously with B2B, e-marketplace or Virtual Commerce Network. ITE is a more precise term, connoting many-to-many transactions, whereas the others do not specify the transactions.

Indirect Cost - A resource or activity cost that cannot be directly traced to a final cost object since no direct or repeatable cause-and-effect relationship exists. An indirect cost uses an assignment or allocation to transfer cost. Also see: Direct Cost, Support Costs

Indirect Retail Locations - A retail location that ultimately sells your product to consumers, but who purchases your products from an intermediary, like a distributor or wholesaler.

Indirect/Distributor Channel - Your company sells and ships to the distributor. The distributor sells and ships to the end user. This may occur in multiple stages. Ultimately your products may pass through the Indirect/Distributor Channel and arrive at a retail outlet. Order information in this channel may be transmitted by electronic means. These means may include EDI, brokered systems, or linked electronic systems.

Infinite Loading - Calculation of the capacity required at work centers in the time periods required regardless of the capacity available to perform this work.

Information System Agreement (ISA0 - Leading organisation of ocean carriers that develops, promotes and implements electronic commerce solutions for the maritime industry.

Information systems (IS) - Managing the flow of data in an organization in a systematic, structured way to assist in planning, implementing, and controlling.

DEFINITIONS

Information Technology - The branch of engineering that deals with the use of computers and telecommunications to retrieve and store and transmit information. It is a term that encompasses all forms of technology used to create, store, exchange, and use information in its various forms (business data, voice conversations, still images, motion pictures, multimedia presentations, and other forms, including those not yet conceived). It's a convenient term for including both telephony and computer technology in the same word. It is the technology that is driving what has often been called "the information revolution."

Inherent advantage - The cost and service benefits of one mode compared with other modes.

Inland Carrier - Transportation company which hauls imports or exports between ports and inland points.

Inland Point Intermodal (IPI) - Cargo moving via land from/to an inland point. See Micro Bridge.

Insourcing - The opposite of outsourcing, that is, a serve performed in-house.

Installation - Providing a service by professional management teams to knock-down, move, set-up and reconfiguration services.

Insurance Certificate - Document which assures the consignee that insurance is provided to cover loss or damage to the cargo while in transit. A certificate issued by an insurer to a shipper (or other party) as evidence that a shipment of merchandise is covered under a marine policy.

Integrated Carriers - Carriers that have both air and ground fleets or other combinations, such as sea, rail and truck. They usually handle thousands of small parcels an hour.

Integrated Logistics - A comprehensive, system-wide view of the entire supply chain as a single process, from raw materials supply through finished goods distribution. All functions that make up the supply chain are managed as a single entity, rather than managing individual functions separately.

Integrated Services Digital Network (ISDN) - A computer term describing the networks and equipment for integrated broadband transmissions of data, voice, and image, from rates of 144 Kbps to 2 Mbps. ISDN allows integration of data, voice, and video over the same digital links.

Integrated tow barge - A series of barges that are connected together to operate as one unit.

Intellectual Property (IP) - Property of an enterprise or individual which is typically maintained in a digital form. This may

Interchange - (1) In Logistics, the exchange relating to interchanging trailers or rail cars between carriers, usually agreed in writing with an Interchange Agreement. Liability between the carriers exists for the actual equipment (trailer or rail car) while in possession of the other carrier. (2) In EDI, the exchange of electronic information between companies.

Intercoastal carriers - Water carriers that transport freight between East and West Coast ports, usually by way of the Panama Canal.

Intercorporate hauling - A private carrier hauling the goods of a subsidiary and charging the subsidiary a fee: this is legal if the subsidiary is wholly owned (100%) or if the private carrier has common carrier authority.

Interleaved 2 of 5 - This is strictly a numeric barcode. Each encoded character is made up of five elements, two are wide and three are narrow. The number of characters to be printed must be an even number. If the

89

number of characters to be printed is odd, a zero will be appended to the beginning of the code.

Interleaving - The practice of assigning an employee multiple tasks which are performed concurrently.

Interline - The movement of a single shipment via two or more carriers. Carriers may interchange equipment but usually they handle the shipment without transferring the equipment.

Intermediately Positioned Warehouse - A warehouse located between customers and manufacturing plants to provide increased customer service and reduced distribution cost.

Intermittent-flow, fixed-path equipment - Materials handling devices that include cranes, monorails, and stacker cranes.

Intermodal - Coordinated transport of freight, especially in connection with relatively long-haul movements, using any combination of freight forwarders, piggyback, containerisation, air freight, assemblers, rail and road.

Intermodal Marketing Company (IMC) - An intermediary that sells intermodal services to shippers.

Intermodal Transport Unit (ITU) - Container, swap body or semi-trailer/goods road motor vehicle suitable for intermodal transport.

Intermodal Transportation - Transporting freight by using two or more transportation modes such as by truck and rail or truck and oceangoing vessel.

Internal customer - The recipient (person or department) of another person's or department's output (good, service, or information) within an organization. Also see: Customer

Internal Labor and Overhead - The portion of COGS that is typically reported as labor and overhead, less any costs already classified as "outsourced."

Internal water carriers - Water carriers that operate over internal, navigable rivers such as the Mississippi, Ohio, and Missouri.

International Air Transport Association - An international air carrier rate bureau for passenger and freight movements.

International Civil Aeronautics Organization - An international agency that is responsible for air safety and for standardizing air traffic control, airport design, and safety features worldwide.

International Freight Forwarders - Freight forwarders that handle booking, paperwork and consolidation of exports.

International Procurement Organization (IPO) - A combined procurement, materials engineering, and logistics team that is located in the supplier's country of export and hired by the importer.

International Standards Organization (ISO) - An organization within the United Nations to which all national and other standard setting bodies defer. Develops and monitors international standards, including OSI, EDIFACT, and X.400

International Transport Implementation Guidelines Group (ITIGG) - ITIGG is an international group of experts engaged in the development and implementation of UN/EDIFACT-standard messages for electronic trading in the transport industry. ITIGG is a subgroup of D4, the UN/EDIFACT Message Development Group for Transport. ITIGG develops recommendations which provide software developers with a series of simple, straightforward tools to assist in designing applications which can be used for trading electronically throughout the world, and to

DEFINITIONS

clarify the intentions of the designers of key UN/EDIFACT messages.

Internet - A computer term which refers to an interconnected group of computer networks from all parts of the world, i.e. a network of networks. Accessed via a modem and an on-line service provider, it contains many information resources and acts as a giant electronic message routing system.

Interstate commerce - The transportation of persons or property between states; in the course of the movement, the shipment cresses a state boundary line.

Interstate Commerce Commission (ICC) - An independent regulatory agency that implements federal economic regulations controlling railroads, motor carriers, pipelines, domestic water carriers, domestic surface freight forwarders, and brokers.

Interstate System - The National System of Interstate and Defense Highways, 42,000 miles of four-lane, limited-access roads connecting major population centers.

Intra-Manufacturing Re-plan Cycle - Average elapsed time, in calendar days, between the time a regenerated forecast is accepted by the end-product manufacturing/assembly location, and the time that the revised plan is reflected in the Master Production Schedule of all the affected internal sub-assembly/component producing plant(s). (An element of Total Supply Chain Response Time)

Intranet - A private network based on internet protocols such as TCP/IP but designed for information management within a company or organization. Its uses include such services as document distribution, software distribution, access to databases, and training. An intranet is so called becasue it looks like a World Wide Web site and is based on the same technologies, yet is strictly internal to the organization and is not connected to the Internet proper. Some intranets also offer access to the Internet, but such connections are directed through a firewall that protects the internal network from the external Web.

In-transit Inventory - Material moving between two or more locations, usually separated geographically; for example, finished goods being shipped from a plant to a distribution center. In-transit inventory is an easily overlooked component of total supply chain availability.

Intrastate commerce - The transportation of persons or property between points within a state. A shipment between two points within a state may be interstate if the shipment had a prior or subsequent move outside of the state and the intent of the shipper was an interstate shipment at the time of shipment.

Intrinsic Forecast Method - In forecasting, a forecast based on internal factors, such as an average of past sales.

Inventory - (1) Raw materials, work in process, finished goods, and supplies required for creation of a company's goods and services. The number of units and/or value of the stock of goods held by a company. (2) A detailed list of your goods, describing each item and its condition at loading. The inventory is prepared for you as your goods are professionally packed, and is used as a Customs document for clearance of your shipment. Upon delivery, you also can use the inventory to check for any possible loss or damage.

Inventory Accuracy - When the on-hand quantity is equivalent to the perpetual balance (plus or minus the designated count tolerances).

Inventory Balance Location Accuracy - When the on-hand quantity in the specified locations is equivalent to the perpetual balance (plus or minus the designated count tolerances).

Inventory Carrying Cost - One of the elements comprising a company's total

91

GLOSSARY OF TERMS IN LOGISTICS & SHIPPING

supply-chain management costs. These costs consist of the following: 1. Opportunity Cost: The opportunity cost of holding inventory. This should be based on your company's own cost of capital standards using the following formula. Calculation: Cost of Capital x Average Net Value of Inventory 2. Shrinkage: The costs associated with breakage, pilferage, and deterioration of inventories. Usually pertains to the loss of material through handling damage, theft, or neglect. 3. Insurance and Taxes: The cost of insuring inventories and taxes associated with the holding of inventory. 4. Total Obsolescence for Raw Material, WIP, and Finished Goods Inventory: Inventory reserves taken due to obsolescence and scrap and includes products exceeding the shelf life, i.e. spoils and is no good for use in its original purpose (do not include reserves taken for Field Service Parts). 5. Channel Obsolescence: Aging allowances paid to channel partners, provisions for buy-back agreements, etc. Includes all material that goes obsolete while in a distribution channel. Usually, a distributor will demand a refund on material that goes bad (shelf life) or is no longer needed because of changing needs. 6. Field Service Parts Obsolescence: Reserves taken due to obsolescence and scrap. Field Service Parts are those inventory kept at locations outside the four walls of the manufacturing plant i.e., distribution center or warehouse.

Inventory Carrying Costs - Generally, carrying costs or holding costs are financial measurements that calculate all the costs associated with holding goods in storage. It includes inventory-in-storage, warehousing, obsolescence, deterioration, spoilage and labour costs, as well as insurance and taxes.

Inventory Control - Control of current stock (shelf, warehouse, on-order, etc.) so merchandise received conforms to sales demands, therefore out-of-stock or over-stocks are avoided.

Inventory Cost - The cost of keeping goods; includes the cost of capital, warehousing, taxes, insurance, depreciation, and obsolescence.

Inventory Days of Supply - Total gross value of inventory for the category (raw materials, work in process, partially finished goods, or fully-finished goods) at standard cost before reserves for excess and obsolescence. It includes only inventory that is on the books and currently owned by the business entity. Future liabilities such as consignments from suppliers are not included. Calculation: [5 Point Annual Average Gross Inventory] / [Calendar Year Value of Transfers / 365]

Inventory deployment - The process of strategically locating inventory at company and customer locations for the purpose of improving product availability and decreasing replenishment times.

Inventory In Transit - Inventory in a carrier's possession that is in the process of being transported to the buyer.

Inventory Management - The process of ensuring the availability of products through inventory administration.

Inventory Planning Systems - The systems that help in strategically balancing the inventory policy and customer service levels throughout the supply chain. These systems calculate time-phased order quantities and safety stock, using selected inventory strategies. Some inventory planning systems conduct what-if analysis and that compares the current inventory policy with simulated inventory scenarios and improves the inventory ROI.

Inventory Turnover - The cost of goods sold, divided by the average level of inventory on hand. The ratio measures how many times a company's inventory has been sold during the year.

Inventory Turns - The cost of goods sold divided by the average level of inventory on hand. This ratio measures how many times a company's inventory has been sold during a period of time. Operationally, inventory turns are measured as total throughput divided by

DEFINITIONS

average level of inventory for a given period; How many times a year the average inventory for a firm changes over, or is sold.

Inventory Velocity - The speed with which inventory moves through a defined cycle (i.e., from receiving to shipping).

Inventory, Days of - The number of days that goods are on-hand in inventory at any given time.

Invoice - A detailed report showing goods sold or shipped and amounts for each item. The invoice is prepared by the seller and acts as the document that the buyer will use to process payment.

IP - see Intellectual Property

IPI - see Inland Point Intermodal

IPO - see International Procurement Organization

Irregular Route Carrier - (1) A carrier that does not have fixed lanes, patterns or routes. (2) Motor carriers that may provide service utilizing any route.

IS - see Information systems

ISDN - see Integrated Services Digital Network

ISO - see International Standards Organization

ISO 14000 Series Standards - A series of generic environmental management standards under development by the International Organization of Standardization, which provide structure and systems for managing environmental compliance with legislative and regulatory requirements and affect every aspect of a company's environmental operations.

ISO 9000 - A series of quality assurance standards compiled by the Geneva, Switzerland-based International Standards Organization. In the United States, the American National Standards Institute based in Washington, DC represents ISO. UniGroup Worldwide companies are certified ISO.

Issuing Carrier - The carrier whose name is printed on the bill of lading.

IT - (1) Immediate Transportation Entry: refers to an IT entry (U.S. Customs). Allows the cargo to move beyond the vessel entry point in bond for customs clearance at the destination named in the I.T. movement from one customs district to another, e.g. cargo entering the U.S. at Los Angeles destined for Chicago can move to Chicago before having a customs inspection. 2. See Information Technology.

ITE - see Independent Trading Exchange

Item - Any unique manufactured or purchased part, material, intermediate, subassembly, or product.

ITIGG - see International Transport Implementation Guidelines Group

ITL - International Trade Logistics

ITU - see Intermodal Transport Unit

Java - A computer term for a general-purpose programming language created by Sun Microsystems. Java can be used to create

Java Applet - A computer term for a short program written in Java that is attached to a web page and executed by the computer on which the Web browser is installed.

Java applets - A Java program is downloaded from the web server and interpreted by a program running on the computer running the Web browser.

Java Script - A computer term for a cross-platform, World Wide Web scripting language developed by Netscape

Communications. JavaScript code is inserted directly into an HTML page.

Jidoka - The concept of adding an element of human judgment to automated equipment. In doing this, the equipment becomes capable of discriminating against unacceptable quality, and the automated process becomes more reliable. This concept, also known as autonomation, was pioneered by Sakichi Toyoda at the turn of the twentieth century when he invented automatic looms that stopped instantly when any thread broke. This permitted one operator to oversee many machines with no risk of producing large amounts of defective cloth. The term has since been extended beyond its original meaning to include any means of stopping production to prevent scrap (for example the andon cord which allows assembly-plant workers to stop the line), even where this capability is not built-in to the production machine itself

JIT - see Just-in-Time

JIT/QC - Just-In-Time/Quality Control.

JIT-II - see Just-in-Time II

Job costing - A cost accounting system in which costs are assigned to specific jobs. This system can be used with either actual or standard costs in the manufacturing of distinguishable units or lots of production.

JOC - see Journal of Commerce

Joint cost - A type of common cost where products are produced in fixed proportions, and the cost incurred to produce on product necessarily entails the production of another; the backhaul is an example.

Joint Photographic Expert Group (JPEG) - A computer term which is an abbreviation for the Joint Photographic Expert Group. A graphical file format used to display high-resolution color images on the World Wide Web. JPEG images apply a userspecified compression scheme that can significantly reduce the large file size usually associated with photo-realistic color images. A higher level of compression results in lower image quality, whereas a lower level of compression results in higher image quality.

Joint rate - A rate over a route that involves two or more carriers to transport the shipment.

Joint Supplier Agreement (JSA) - Indicative of Stage 3 Sourcing Practices, the JSA includes terms & conditions, objectives, process flows, performance targets, flexibility, balancing and incentives.

Jones Act - Section 27 of the Merchant Marine Act of 1920, requiring that all shipments by water between ports in the United States (including Puerto Rico) be carried by U.S.-flag, be U.S.-built, and U.S.-crewed vessels.

Journal of Commerce (JOC) - A trade publication. Trade transportation journal.

JPEG - see Joint Photographic Expert Group

JSA - see Joint Supplier Agreement

Just-in-Time (JIT) - An inventory control system that controls material flow into assembly and manufacturing plants by coordinating demand and supply to the point where desired materials arrive just in time for use. An inventory reduction strategy that feeds production lines with products delivered "just in time". Developed by the auto industry, it refers to shipping goods in smaller, more frequent lots.

Just-in-Time II (JIT-II) - Vendor-managed operations taking place within a customer's facility. JIT II was popularized by the Bose Corporation. The supplier reps, called "inplants," place orders to their own companies, relieving the customer's buyers from this task. Many also become involved at a deeper level, such as participating in new product development projects, manufacturing planning.

Kaizen - The Japanese term for improvement; continuing improvement involving everyone--managers and workers. In manufacturing, kaizen relates to finding and eliminating waste in machinery, labor, or production methods. Also see: ContinuousProcess Improvement

Kaizen Blitz - A rapid improvement of a limited process area, for example, a production cell. Part of the improvement team consists of workers in that area. The objectives are to use innovative thinking to eliminate non-value-added work and to immediately implement the changes within a week or less. Ownership of the improvement by the area work team and the development of the team's problem-solving skills are additional benefits.

Kanban - Japanese word for "visible record", loosely translated means card, billboard or sign. Popularized by Toyota Corporation, it uses standard containers or lot sizes to deliver needed parts to assembly line "just in time" for use.

KD - see Knocked Down

Keiretsu - A form of cooperative relationship among companies in Japan where the companies largely remain legally and economically independent, even though they work closely in various ways such as sole sourcing and financial backing. A member of a eiretsu generally owns a limited amount of stock in other member companies. A keiretsu generally forms around a bank and a trading company but "distribution" (supply chain) keiretsus exist linking companies from raw material suppliers to retailers.

Key Custodians - The persons, assigned by the security administrators of trading partners, that send or receive a component of either the master key or exchange key used to encrypt data encryption keys. This control technique involves dual control, with split knowledge that requires two key custodians.

Key Performance Indicator (KPI) - A measure which is of strategic importance to a company or department. For example, a supply chain flexibility metric is Supplier On-time Delivery Performance which indicates the percentage of orders that are fulfilled on or before the original requested date. Also see: Scorecard

Kitting - Light assembly of components or parts into defined units. Kitting reduces the need to maintain an inventory of pre-built completed products, but increases the time and labor consumed at shipment. Also see: Postponement

Knocked Down (KD) - Articles that are partially or totally disassembled to reduce the cubic footage or to ensure safer transportation.

Known Damage - Damage discovered before or at the time a shipment is delivered.

Known Loss - Loss discovered before or at the time a shipment is delivered.

KPI - See Key Performance Indicator

L/H - see Line-Haul

Label Cargo - Cargo, including all commodities, requiring a label according to the provisions of the International Maritime Dangerous Goods Code.

Lading - The cargo carried in a transportation vehicle.

Laid-down cost - The sum of the product and transportation costs. The laid-down cost is useful in comparing the total cost of a product shipped from different supply sources to a customer's point of use.

LAN - see Local Area Network

Land bridge - The movement of containers by ship-rail-sip on Japan-to-Europe moves; ships move containers to the U.S. Pacific Coast, rails move containers to an East Coast port, and ships deliver containers to Europe.

Land grants - Grants of land given to railroads during their developmental stage to build tracks.

Landed Cost - Cost of product plus relevant logistics costs such as transportation, warehousing, handling, etc. Also called Total Landed Cost or Net Landed Costs

Lash barges - Covered barges that are loaded on board oceangoing ships for movement to foreign destinations.

Last In, First Out (LIFO) - Accounting method of valuing inventory that assumes latest goods purchased are first goods used during accounting period.

LC - see Letter of Credit

LCL - see Less-Than-Carload

LCL - see Less-Than-Containerload

LDI - see Logistics Data Interchange

Lead Logistics Partner (LLP) - An organization that organizes other 3rd party logistics partners for outsourcing of logistics functions. Also see: Fourth Party Logistics

Lead Logistics Provider (LLP) - The logistics provider is the integrator for multiple carriers and other Third Party Logistics Providers for a customer. The LLP has the technology that brings the parties together for a customer and will also performing part of the service.

Lead Time - The total time that elapses between an order's placement and its receipt. It includes the time required for order transmittal, order processing, order preparation, and transit.

Lead Time from Complete Manufacture to Customer Receipt - Includes time from when an order is ready for shipment to customer receipt of order. Time from complete manufacture to customer receipt including the following elements: pick/pack time, prepare for shipment, total transit time (all components to consolidation point), consolidation, queue time, and additional transit time to customer receipt.

Lead Time from Order Receipt to Complete Manufacture - Includes times from order receipt to order entry complete, from order entry complete to start to build, and from start to build to ready for shipment. Time from order receipt to order entry complete includes the following elements: order revalidation, configuration check, credit check, and scheduling. Time from order entry complete to start to build includes the following elements: customer wait time and engineering and design time. Time from start to build to ready for shipment includes the following elements: release to manufacturing or distribution, order configuration verification, production scheduling, and build or configure time.

Least Total Cost - A dynamic lot-sizing technique that calculates the order quantity by comparing the setup (or ordering) costs and the carrying cost for various lot sizes and selects the lot size where these costs are most nearly equal. Also see: Discrete Order Quantity, Dynamic Lot Sizing

Least Unit Cost - A dynamic lot-sizing technique that adds ordering cost and inventory carrying cost for each trial lot size and divides by the number of units in the lot size, picking the lot size with the lowest unit

Definitions

cost. Also see: Discrete Order Quantity, Dynamic Lot Sizing

LesSee - A person or firm to whom a lease is granted.

Lessor - A person or firm that grants a lease.

Less-Than-Carload (LCL) - Shipment that is less than a complete rail car load.

Less-Than-Container Load (LCL) - Common term for an amount of goods to be shipped and which do not fill an entire container. Ocean rates for LCL are commonly higher on a per-unit basis than for a full container load. Thus, consolidation of several LCL loads from different places or shippers into a full container can save on costs.

Less-Than-Trailer Load - See "Less Than Container Load".

Less-Than-Truckload (LTL) - Freight from several shippers loaded onto an individual trailer. The shipment is based upon a separate rate than truckload rate. Less-than-Truckload is in contrast to Truckload, which is only one shipment from one shipper that is loaded on a tractor-trailer.

Less-Than-Truckload (LTL) Carriers - Trucking companies that consolidate and transport smaller (less than truckload) shipments of freight by utilizing a network of terminals and relay points.

Letter of credit - An international business document that assures the seller that payment will be made by the bank issuing the letter of credit upon fulfillment of the sales agreement.

Letter of Credit (LC) - Letter of agreement issued by a bank stating a foreign purchaser has established a line of credit in a seller's favour, and confirming that payment for goods will be made upon presentation of certain documents which are in agreement with terms on the letter of credit. 2. A letter addressed by a banker to a correspondent certifying that a person named therein is entitled to draw on him or his credit up to a certain sum. 3. A letter addressed by a banker to a person, to whom credit is given, authorising him to draw on the issuing bank or on a bank in his country up to a certain sum and guaranteeing to accept the drafts if duly made, also called commercial letter of credit, confirmed credit or confirmed letter of credit. 4. Letters of credit may take various forms, represent various undertakings for various purposes and be subject to different conditions.

Leverage - Taking something small and exploding it. Can be financial or technological.

Liability - Maximum amount for which a carrier is normally responsible in connection with loss or damage of cargo while in transit or storage.

License Plate - A bar code identifying a pallet or quantity of product.

Life Cycle Cost - In cost accounting, a product's life cycle is the period that starts with the initial product conceptualization and ends with the withdrawal of the product from the marketplace and final disposition. A product life cycle is characterized by certain defined stages, including research, development, introduction, maturity, decline, and abandonment. Life cycle cost is the accumulated costs incurred by a product during these stages.

LIFO - see Last In, First Out

Lift truck - Vehicles used to lift, move, stack, rack, or otherwise manipulate loads. Material handling people use a lot of terms to describe lift trucks, some terms describe specific types of vehicles, others are slang terms or trade names that people often mistakenly use to describe trucks. Terms include industrial truck, forklift, reach truck, motorized pallet trucks, turret trucks, counterbalanced forklift, walkie, rider, walkie rider, walkie stacker, straddle lift, side loader, order pickers, high lift, cherry picker, Jeep, Towmotor, Yale, Crown, Hyster, Raymond, Clark, Drexel.

Lift Van - A wooden or plywood container used mainly on overseas removals. Built specifically to transport household goods.

Lift-Gate - Power lift on the rear of a trailer or straight van used to move heavy objects to or from a trailer's level floor.

Lighter - A flat-bottomed boat designed for cross-harbor or inland waterway freight transfer.

Line - (1) A specific physical space for the manufacture of a product that in a flow shop layout is represented by a straight line. In actuality, this may be a series of pieces of equipment connected by piping or conveyor systems.(2) A type of manufacturing process used to produce a narrow range of standard items with identical or highly similar designs. Production volumes are high, production and material handling equipment is specialized, and all products typically pass through the same sequence of operations. Also see: Assembly Line

Line functions - The decision-making areas associated with daily operations. Logistics line functions include traffic management, inventory control, order processing, warehousing, and packaging.

Line Haul - Marine portion of a vessel's route covering the greatest distance, usually across an ocean (e.g. Singapore-Los Angeles).

Line Item - A specific and unique single detailed record associated to a product for a project or work order.

Line Scrap - Value of raw materials and work-in-process inventory scrapped as a result of improper processing or assembly, as a percentage of total value of production at standard cost.

Line-Haul (L/H) - Basic transportation charges for moving freight. Excludes "accessorial", pickup and delivery charges.

Line-haul shipment - A shipment that moves between cities and distances over 100 to 150 miles.

Liner Service - International water carriers that provide service on fixed routes on published schedules.

Link - The transportation method used to connect the nodes (plants, warehouses) in a logistics system.

Linked Distributed Systems - Independent computer systems, owned by independent organizations, linked in a manner to allow direct updates to be made to one system by another. For example, a customer's computer system is linked to a supplier's system, and the customer can create orders or releases directly in the supplier's system.

Little Inch - A federally built pipeline constructed during World War II that connected Corpus Christi and Houston, Texas.

Live - A situation in which the equipment operator stays with the trailer or boxcar while it is being loaded or unloaded.

LLP - see Lead Logistics Partner

LLP - see Lead Logistics Provider

LNG Carrier - Liquified Natural Gas Carrier.

Load Date Spread - Agreed-upon period within which pickup of a shipment is to take place.

Load factor - A measure of operating efficiency used by air carriers to determine the percentage of a plane's capacity that is utilized, or the number of passengers divided by the total number of seats.

DEFINITIONS

Load Tender (Pick-Up Request) - The offering of cargo to be loaded by a carrier.

Load Tendering - The practice of providing a carrier with detailed information and negotiated pricing (the tender) prior to scheduling pickup. This practice can help assure contract compliance and facilitate automated payments (self billing).

Loading allowance - A reduced rate offered to shippers and/or consignees who load and/or unload LTL or AQ shipments.

Local Area Network (LAN) - A data communications network spanning a limited geographical area, usually a few miles at most, providing communications between computers and peripheral devices.

Local Delivery - Movement of product from warehouse facility to the final destination.

Local Pick-Up - Movement of product from origin to a warehouse facility.

Local Rate - A rate published between two locations served by one carrier.

Local service carriers - An air carrier classification of carriers that operate between areas of lesser and major population centers. These carriers feed passengers into the major cities to

Locational determinant - The factors that determine the location of a facility. For industrial facilities, the determinants include logistics.

Locator System - Locator systems are inventory-tracking systems that allow you to assign specific physical locations to your inventory to facilitate greater tracking and the ability to store product randomly. Location functionality in software can range from a simple text field attached to an item that notes a single location, to systems that allow multiple locations per item and track inventory quantities by location. Warehouse management systems (WMS) take locator systems to the next level by adding functionality to direct the movement between locations.

Logbook - A daily record of the hours an interstate driver spends driving, off, duty, sleeping in the berth, or on duty but not driving.

Logistic Straps - Nylon straps used to tie off tiers in a trailer.

Logistic Track - Metal track inside a trailer onto which logistic straps are hooked.

Logistics - The management of freight and information throughout the total supply chain from the original raw material source to the ultimate consumer of the finished product, encompasing factories, assembly and packing plants, warehouses, distribution centres and retail outlets. Also known as stevedore.

Logistics Channel - The network of supply chain participants engaged in storage, handling, transfer, transportation, and communications functions that contribute to the efficient flow of goods.

Logistics Data Interchange (LDI) - An integrated computerized system that electronically transmits logistics information computer to computer.

Logistics Management - As defined by the Council of Supply Chain Management Professionals (CSCMP): "Logistics management is that part of supply chain management that plans, implements, and controls the efficient, effective forward and reverse flow and storage of goods, services, and related information between the point of origin and the point of consumption in order to meet customers' requirements. Logistics management activities typically include inbound and outbound transportation management, fleet management, warehousing, materials handling, order fulfillment, logistics network design, inventory management, supply/demand planning, and management of third party logistics services providers. To varying degrees, the logistics function also includes sourcing and procurement, production planning and scheduling, packaging and assembly, and customer service. It is involved in all levels of planning and execution-- strategic, operational, and tactical. Logistics management is an integrating function which coordinates and optimizes all logistics activities, as well as integrates logistics activities with other functions, including marketing, sales, manufacturing, finance, and information technology."

Long ton - Equals 2,240 pounds.

Longshoreman - Worker who loads and unloads a ship. Terminal operator who is designed to facilitate the operation of loading and discharging vessels, as well as other terminal activities.

Lot Control - A set of procedures (e.g., assigning unique batch numbers and tracking each batch) used to maintain lot integrity from raw materials, from the supplier through manufacturing to consumers.

Lot Number - See Batch Number

Lot size - The quantity of goods purchased or produced in anticipation of use or sale in the future.

Lot Sized System - See Fixed Reorder Quantity Inventory Model

Lot-for-Lot - A lot-sizing technique that generates planned orders in quantities equal to the net requirements in each period. Also see: Discrete Order Quantity

LT - Long Ton.1 Long Ton = 2,240 lbs

LTL - see Less-Than-Trailer Load

LTL - see Less-Than-Truckload

Lumping - A term applied to a person who assists a motor carrier owner-operator in the loading and unloading of property: quite commonly used in the food industry

Lumpy demand - See Discontinuous Demand

M

M2M - see Machine-to-Machine interface

Machine Downtimes - Time during which a machine cannot be utilized. Machine downtimes may occur during breakdowns, maintenance, changeovers, etc.

Machine-to-Machine interface (M2M) - A term describing the process whereby machines are remotely monitored for status and problems reported and resolved automatically or maintenance scheduled by the monitoring systems.

Macro environment - The environment external to a business including technological, economic, natural, and regulatory forces that marketing efforts cannot control.

Mainframe - A term sometimes generically used to refer to an organization's central computer system. Specifically the largest class of computer systems manufactured.

Maintenance, Repair, and Operating supplies (MRO) - Items used in support of general operations and maintenance such as maintenance supplies, spare parts, and consumables used in the manufacturing process and supporting operations.

Major carrier - A for-hire certificated air carrier that has annual operating revenues of $1 billion or more: the carrier usually operates between major population centers.

Make-or-buy decision - The act of deciding whether to produce an item internally or buy it from an outside supplier. Factors to consider in the decision include costs, capacity availability, proprietary and/or specialized knowledge, quality considerations, skill requirements, volume, and timing.

DEFINITIONS

Make-to-Order (MTO) - A manufacturing process strategy where the trigger to begin manufacture of a product is an actual customer order or release, rather than a market forecast. For Make-to-Order products, more than 20% of the valueadded takes place after the receipt of the order or release, and all necessary design and process documentation is available at time of order receipt.

Make-to-Stock (MTS) - A manufacturing process strategy where finished product is continually held in plant or warehouse inventory to fulfill expected incoming orders or releases based on a forecast.

Manifest - Entire listing of all cargo on board a vessel as required by the relevant local authorities e.g. customs. Same as cargo manifest.

Manufacture Cycle Time - The average time between commencement and completion of a manufacturing process, as it applies to make-to-stock products. Calculation: [Average

Manufacturer's Representative - One who sells goods for several firms but does not take title to them.

Manufacturing Calendar - A calendar used in inventory and production planning functions that consecutively numbers only the working days so that the component and work order scheduling may be done based on the actual number of workdays available. Synonyms: M-Day Calendar, Planning Calendar, Production Calendar, Shop Calendar.

Manufacturing Capital Asset Value - The asset value of the "Manufacturing fixed assets" after allowance for depreciation. Examples of equipment are SMT placement machines, conveyors, Auto guided vehicles, robot cells, testers, X-ray solder machines, Burn-in chambers, Logic testers, Auto packing equipment, PLC station controllers, Scanning equipment, PWB magazines.

Manufacturing Execution Systems (MES) - Programs and systems that participate in shop floor control, including programmed logic controllers and process control computers for direct and supervisory control of manufacturing equipment; process information systems that gather historical performance information, then generate reports; graphical displays; and alarms that inform operations personnel what is going on in the plant currently and a very short history into the past. Quality control information is also gathered and a laboratory information management system may be part of this configuration to tie process conditions to the quality data that are generated. Thereby, cause-and-effect relationships can be determined. The quality data at times affect the control parameters that are used to meet product specifications either dynamically or off line.

Manufacturing Lead Time - The total time required to manufacture an item, exclusive of lower level purchasing lead time. For make-to-order products, it is the length of time between the release of an order to the production process and shipment to the final customer. For make-to-stock products, it is the length of time between the release of an order to the production process and receipt into finished goods inventory. Included here are order preparation time, queue time, setup time, run time, move time, inspection time, and put-away time. Synonyms: Manufacturing Cycle Time. Also see: Lead Time

Manufacturing Resource Planning (MRP-II) - A method for the effective planning of all resources of a manufacturing company. Ideally, it addresses operational planning in units, financial planning in dollars, and has a simulation capability to answer what-if questions. It is made up of a variety of processes, each linked together: business planning, production planning, master production scheduling, material requirements planning, capacity requirements

101

planning, and the execution support systems for capacity and material. Output from these systems is integrated with financial reports such as the business plan, purchase commitment report, shipping budget, and inventory projections in dollars. Manufacturing resource planning is a direct outgrowth and extension of closed-loop MRP.

Mapping - An MRP system is intended to simultaneously meet 3 objectives:

Marginal Cost -

Marine insurance - Ensure materials and products are available for production and delivery to customers.

Maritime Administration - Maintain the lowest possible level of inventory.

Market Demand - Plan manufacturing activities, delivery schedules and purchasing activities.

Market dominance - In transportation rating this refers to the absence of effective competition for railroads from other carriers and modes for the traffic to which the rate applies. The Staggers Act stated that market dominance does not exist if the rate is below the revenue-to-variable-cost ratio of 160% in 1981 and 170% in 1983

Market Segment - A group of potential customers sharing some measurable characteristics based on demographics, psychographics, lifestyle, geography, benefits, etc.

Market-Positioned Warehouse - Warehouse positioned to replenish customer inventory assortments and to afford maximum inbound transport consolidation economies from inventory origin points with relatively short-haul local delivery.

Marking - Letters, numbers, and other symbols placed on cargo packages to make easy identification.

Marks and Numbers - The identifying details on or of a package or the actual markings that appear on the packages.

Marquis Partners - Key strategic relationships. This has emerged as perhaps the key competitive advantage and barrier to entry of e-marketplaces. Get the big players in the fold first, offering equity if necessary.

Marshaller or Marshalling Agent - This is a service unique to international trade and relates to an individual or firm that specializes in one or more of the activities preceding Main Carriage, such as consolidation, packing, marking, sorting of merchandise, inspection, storage, etc. References state that Marshaling Agent, Consolidation Agent and Freight Forwarder all have the same meaning.

Mass Customization - The creation of a high-volume product with large variety so that a customer may specify his or her exact model out of a large volume of possible end items while manufacturing cost is low because of the large volume. An example is a personal computer order in which the customer may specify processor speed, memory size, hard disk size and speed, removable storage device characteristics, and many other options when PCs are assembled on one line and at low cost.

Master Air Waybill (MAWB) - The air waybill of lading that provides data on a consolidated shipment of goods. The consolidator is shown as the shipper.

Master pack - A large box that is used to pack a number of smaller boxes or containers. Aids in protecting the smaller cartons or packages and reduces the number of cartons to be handled during the material handling process.

Master Production Schedule (MPS) - The master level or top level schedule used to set the production plan in a manufacturing facility.

Definitions

Material Acquisition Costs - One of the elements comprising a company's total supply-chain management costs. These costs consist of the following: (1) New Product Release Phase-In and Maintenance: This includes costs associated with releasing new products to the field, maintaining released products, assigning product ID, defining configurations and packaging, publishing availability schedules, release letters and updates, and maintaining product databases. (2) Create Customer Order: This includes costs associated with creating and pricing configurations to order and preparing customer order documents. (3) Order Entry and Maintenance: This includes costs associated with maintaining the customer database, credit check, accepting new orders, and adding them to the order system as well as later order modifications. (4) Contract/Program and Channel Management: This includes costs related to contract negotiation, monitoring progress, and reporting against the customer's contract, including administration of performance or warranty related issues. (5) Installation Planning: This includes costs associated with installation engineering, scheduling and modification, handling cancellations, and planning the installation. (6) Order Fulfillment: This includes costs associated with order processing, inventory allocation, ordering from internal or external suppliers, shipment scheduling, order status reporting, and shipment initiation. (7) Distribution: This includes costs associated with warehouse space and management, finished goods receiving and stocking, processing shipments, picking and consolidating, selecting carrier, and staging products/systems. (8) Transportation, Outbound Freight and Duties: This includes costs associated with all company paid freight duties from point-of-manufacture to end-customer or channel. (9) Installation: This includes costs associated with verification of site preparation, installation, certification, and authorization of billing. (10) Customer Invoicing/Accounting: This includes costs associated with invoicing, processing customer payments, and verification of customer receipt.

Material Index - The ratio of the sum of localized raw material weights to the weight of the finished product.

Material Requirements Planning (MRP) - A set of techniques that uses bill of material data, inventory data, and the master production schedule to calculate requirements for materials. It is a software based production planning and inventory control system used to manage manufacturing processes. Although it is not common nowadays, it is possible to conduct the MRP calculation by hand as well.

Material Safety Data Sheet (MSDS) - A document that is part of the materials information system and accompanies the product. Prepared by the manufacturer, the MSDS provides information regarding the safety and chemical properties and the long-term storage, handling, and disposal of the product. Among other factors, the MSDS describes the hazardous components of a product; how to treat leaks, spills, and fires; and how to treat improper human contact with the product. Also see: Hazardous Materials

Materials Handling - The physical handling of products and materials between procurement and shipping.

Materials Management - Inbound logistics from suppliers through the production process. The movement and management of materials and products from procurement through production.

Materials planning - The materials management function that attempts to coordinate the supply of materials with the demand for materials.

Matrix Organizational Structure - An organizational structure in which two (or more) channels of command, budget responsibility, and performance measurement exist simultaneously. For example, both product and functional forms of organization could be implemented simultaneously, that is, the product and functional managers have equal authority and employees report to both managers.

MAWB - see Master Air Waybill

MAX - The lowest inventory quantity that is desired at a ship to location or selling location. This quantity will over-ride the forecast number if the forecast climbs above the MAX. Maximum stock

Maximum Inventory - The planned maximum allowable inventory for an item based on its planned lot size and target safety stock.

Maximum Order Quantity - An order quantity modifier applied after the lot size has been calculated, that limits the order quantity to a pre-established maximum.

m-Commerce - Mobile commerce applications involve using a mobile phone to carry out financial transactions. This usually means making a payment for goods or transferring funds electronically. Transferring money between accounts and paying for purchases are electronic commerce applications. An emerging application, electronic commerce has been facilitated by developments in other areas in the mobile world, such as dual slot phones and other smarter terminals and more standardized protocols, which allow greater interactivity and therefore more sophisticate services.

M-Day Calendar - See Manufacturing Calendar

Mean - The arithmetic average of a group of values. Synonym: arithmetic mean.

Measurement ton - Equals 40 cubic feet; used in water transportation rate making.

Median - The middle value in a set of measured values when the items are arranged in order of magnitude. If there is no single middle value, the median is the mean of the two middle values.

Merchant Haulage - Inland transportation performed by an inland carrier contracted by and for the account of the shipper or consignee.

Merge In Transit - A logistics management tool that allows you to stage the simultaneous delivery of shipments from a variety of origin points.

Merger - The combination of two or more carriers into one company for the ownership, management, and operation of the properties previously operated on a separate basis.

MES - see Manufacturing Execution Systems

Message - The EDIFACT term for a transaction set. A message is the collection of data, organized in segments, exchanged by trading partners engaged in EDI. Typically, a message is an electronic version of a document associated with a common business transaction, such as a purchase order or shipping notice. A message begins with a message header segment, which identifies the start of the message (e.g., the series of characters representing one purchase order). The message header segment also carries the message type code, which identifies the business transaction type. EDIFACT's message header segment is called UNH; in ANSI X12 protocol, the message header is called ST. A message ends with a message trailer segment, which signals the end of the message (e.g., the end of one purchase order). EDIFACT's message trailer is labeled UNT; the ANSI X12 message trailer is referred to as SE.

Meta Tag - An optional HTML tag that is used to specify information about a web document. Some search engines use "spiders" to index web pages. These spiders read the information contained within a page's META tag. So in theory, an HTML or web page author has the ability to control how their site is indexed by search engines and how and when it will "come up" on a user's search. The META tag can also be used to specify an HTTP or URL address for the page to "jump" to after a certain amount of time.

This is known as Client-Pull. What this means, is a web page author can control the amount of time a web page is up on the screen as well as where the browser will go next.

Metrics - See Performance Measures

Micro-land bridge - An intermodal movement in which the shipment is moved from a foreign country to the U.S. by water and then moved across the U.S. by railroad to an interior, nonport city, or vice versa for exports from a nonport city.

Mileage allowance - An allowance based upon distance and given by railroads to shippers using private rail cars.

Mileage rate - A rate based upon the number of miles the commodity is shipped.

Milk run - A regular route for pickup of mixed loads from several suppliers. For example, instead of each of five suppliers sending a truckload per week to meet the weekly needs of the customer, one truck visits each of the suppliers on a daily basis before delivering to the customer's plant. Five truckloads per week are still shipped, but each truckload contains the daily requirement from each supplier. Also see: Consolidation

Min Max System - A type of order point replenishment system where the "min" (minimum) is the order point, and the "max" (maximum) is the "order up to" inventory level. The order quantity is variable and is the result of the max minus the available and on-order inventory. An order is recommended when the sum of the available and on-order inventory is at or below the min.

Mini-land Bridge - An intermodal movement in which the shipment is moved from a foreign country to the U.S. by water and then moved across the U.S. by railroad to a destination that is a port city, or vice versa for exports from a U.S. port city.

Minimum Charge - Least charge for which a shipment will be handled.

Minimum Truckload Weight - Least weight at which a shipment is handled at a Truckload (TL) rate.

Minimum weight - (1) The shipment weight specified by the carrier's tariff as the minimum weight required to use the TL or CL rate; the rate discount volume. 2. Specified minimum-weight basis on which shipment charges will be assessed (1,000 lbs.). If a shipment weighs less, it still will be charged at a 1,000-lb. rate.

Misguided Capacity Plans - Plans or forecasts for capacity utilization, which are based on inaccurate assumptions or input data.

Mission Critical - Is any equipment, asset, process, or item that is required for a customer to maintain operations.

Mixed loads - The movement of both regulated and exempt commodities in the same vehicle at the same time.

Mixed Shipment - Shipment consisting of items described in and rated under two or more rate items within a tariff.

MLB - An abbreviation for Mini Land Bridge Containers moving from a foreign country by vessel, and then sent to an inland point in the U.S. or elsewhere by land transportation (rail or truck). See also Land Bridge.

Modal split - The relative use made of the modes of transportation; the statistics used include ton-miles, passenger-miles, and revenue.

Mode - See Transportation Mode

Mother Vessel - Main ocean vessel in a liner service designated to move containers from set origin points to set destination ports/points on a regular basis.

Move Management - Customized and standard relocation services to meet the customer needs for availability, asset protection, data protection, and time constraints.

Move ticket - A document used to move inventory within a facility. Warehouse management systems use move tickets to direct and track material movements. In a paperless environment the electronic version of a move ticket is often called a task or a trip.

MPS - see Master Production Schedule

MRO - see Maintenance, Repair, and Operating supplies

MRP - see Material Requirements Planning

MRP-II - see Manufacturing Resource Planning

MSDS - see Material Safety Data Sheet

MSI Plessey - This barcode is a variable length barcode that can encode up to 15 numeric digits. Checksum generation is dependent on the value of the checksum parameter. The following table indicates the value of the checksum property and the type of checksum created. Setting, Description, 0, one modulus 10 checksum, 1, two modulus 10 checksums, 2, one modulus 11 checksum/one modulus 10 checksum.

MT - Metric Ton. 1 MT = 2,204.62lbs or 35.314 cft.

MTO - see Make-to-Order

MTS - see Make-to-Stock

Multi-Currency - The ability to process orders using a variety of currencies for pricing and billing.

Multi-destination - A single shipment that includes multiple deliveries at separate destination locations.

Multinational company - A company that both produces and markets products in different countries.

Multi-origin - A single shipment that includes multiple pick-ups at separate origin locations.

Multiple-car rate - A railroad rate that is lower for shipping more than one carload rather than just one carload at a time.

Multi-Skilled - Pertaining to individuals who are certified to perform a variety of tasks.

N

National carrier - A for-hire certificated air carrier that has annual operating revenues of $75 million to $1 billion; the carrier usually operates between major population centers and areas of lesser population.

National Industrial Traffic League - An association representing the interests of shippers and receivers in matters of transportation policy and regulation.

National Motor Bus Operators Organization - An industry association representing common and charter bus firms; now known as the American Bus Association.

National Motor Freight Classification (NMFC) - A tariff, which contains descriptions and classifications of commodities and rules for domestic movement by motor carriers in the U.S.

National Railroad Corporation - Also known as Amtrak, the corporation established by the Rail Passenger Service Act of 1970 to operate most of the United States' rail passenger service.

National Stock Number (NSN) - The individual identification number assigned to an item to permit inventory management in the federal supply system.

DEFINITIONS

Nationalization - Public ownership, financing, and operation of a business entity.

NCV - see No Customs Value

Negotiable Bill of Lading - Something that can be negotiated, transferred or assigned from one person to another in return for equivalent value by being delivered either with endorsement (as of an instrument to order) or without endorsement (as of an instrument to bearer) so that the title passes to the transferee who is not prejudiced in his rights by any defect or flaw in the title of prior parties nor by personal defenses available to prior parties among themselves provided in both cases that the transferee is a bona fide holder without notice e.g. bills of lading, bills of exchange, promissory notes, and cheques that are payable to bearer or order are negotiable instruments, as are also, in some jurisdictions, some other instruments (as bonds, some forms of stock) i.e. negotiable paper/negotiable securities. "Negotiable" used analogously for "transferable" - see also negotiability/transferability.

Negotiating Bank - Bank where a shipper negotiates documents or where documents are first presented, usually at country of origin. Also, often referred to as the advising bank.

Nested - Three or more different sizes of the same item or commodity which must be enclosed, each smaller piece within the next larger piece, or three or more of the items must be placed one within the other so that the top item does not project above the lower item by more than 1/3 of its height. Nested Solid: Three or more of items must be placed on or inside the other, so that the external side surfaces of the top item is in contact with the internal side surfaces of the item below, and the top item does not project above the next lower item by more than 1/2 inch.

Net Asset Turns - The number of times you replenish your net assets in your annual sales cycle. A measure of how quickly assets are used to generate sales. Calculation: Total Product Revenue / Total Net Assets

Net Assets - Total Net assets are calculated as Total Assets - Total Liabilities; where: The total assets are made up of fixed assets (plant, machinery and equipment) and current assets which is the total of stock, debtors and cash (also includes A/R, inventory, prepaid assets, deferred assets, intangibles and goodwill). The total liabilities are made up in much the same way of long-term liabilities and current liabilities (includes A/P, accrued expenses, deferred liabilities).

Net Change MRP - An approach in which the material requirements plan is continually retained in the computer. Whenever a change is needed in requirements, open order inventory status, or bill of material, a partial explosion and netting is made for only those parts affected by the change. Antonym: Regeneration MRP.

Net Requirements - In MRP, the net requirements for a part or an assembly are derived as a result of applying gross requirements and allocations against inventory on hand, scheduled receipts, and safety stock. Net requirements, lot-sized and offset for lead time, become planned orders.

Net Weight - The total weight of a shipment less the weight of pallets, containers or straps.

Neutral Body - Investigating body designated by conference carriers to ensure that all regulations and rules are adhered to.

New Product Introduction (NPI) - The process used to develop products that are new to the sales portfolio of a company.

NMFC - see National Motor Freight Classification

No Customs Value (NCV) - Indicates cargo or goods have no value per a customer's assessment.

107

No Location (No Loc) - An item that has been received for which the warehouse has no previously established storage slot.

Node - A fixed point in a firm's logistics system where goods come to rest; includes plants, warehouses, supply sources, and markets.

NOE - Not Otherwise Enumerated

Non Vessel Operating Common Carrier (NVOCC) - A firm who issues bills of lading for carriage of goods on vessels that are not owned or operated by them. NVOCCs usually act as consolidators, accepting less-than-containerload shipments and consolidating them into full container loads.

Non-Asset-Based Third Party Providers - Third party providers who generally do not own assets, such as transportation and/or warehouse equipment.

Noncertified carrier - A for-hire air carrier that is exempt from economic regulation.

Nonconformity - Failure to fulfill a specified requirement. See: blemish, defect, imperfection.

Non-Durable goods - Goods whose serviceability is generally limited to a period of less than three years (such as perishable goods and semidurable goods).

Non-Negotiable Bill of Lading - A document not made out "to order", but being a receipt and evidence of the contract of carriage, but which is not a document of title, e.g. a waybill and, in some jurisdictions (such as the USA), a (straight) consigned bill of lading.

NOPAT - Net operating profit after tax.
NOS - Not Otherwise Stated.

Notify Party - Company/person who appears on the bill of lading or waybill to be notified when the cargo arrives at destination. Could be different from the consignee, but is often the actual receiver of the goods. A notify party has no particular rights (beyond the notification) under the bill of lading or waybill.

NPI - see New Product Introduction

NSN - see National Stock Number

NVOCC - see Non Vessel Operating Common Carrier

Object Linking and Embedding (OLE) - An object system created by Microsoft. OLE lets an author invoke different editor components to create a compound document.

OBL - Original bill of lading. See also Negotiable Bill of Lading.

Obsolete Inventory - Inventory for which there is no forecast demand expected. A condition of being out of date. A loss of value occasioned by new developments that place the older property at a competitive disadvantage.

OCP - see Overland Common Port

OEE - see Overall Equipment Effectiveness

OEM - see Original Equipment Manufacturer

Offshore - Utilizing an outsourcing service provider (manufacturer or business process) located in a country other than where the purchasing enterprise is located.

OLE - see Object Linking and Embedding
OMT, ORT, DMT - Origin Motor Terminal, Origin Rail Terminal, Destination Motor Terminal. Location designated by a motor/rail carrier at origin/destination points

where, the motor carrier or his authorised agent assembles, holds or stores an ocean carrier's containers and chassis; where loaded containers are received from shippers or their agents; where empty containers are delivered to shippers or their agents.

On Deck Stowage - Cargo stowed on the deck of the vessel.

On Order - The amount of goods that has yet to arrive at a location or retail store. This includes all open purchase orders including, but not limited to, orders in transit, orders being picked, and orders being processed through customer service.

On Time In Full (OTIF) - Sales order delivery performance measure which can be expressed as a target, say, of achieving 98% of orders delivered in full, no part shipments, on the requested date.

On-Carriage - The carriage of goods (containers) by any mode of transport to the place of delivery after discharge from the ocean vessel (main means of transport) at the port (place) of discharge.

On-Demand - Pertaining to work performed when demand is present. Typically used to describe products which are manufactured or assembled only when a customer order is placed.

One Piece Flow - Moving parts through a process in batches of one

One-Way Networks - The advantages generally live with either the seller or buyer, but not both. B2C websites are one-way networks.

On-Hand Balance - The quantity shown in the inventory records as being physically in stock.

Online - A computer term which describes activities performed using computer systems.

On-line receiving - A system in which computer terminals are available at each receiving bay and operators enter items into the system as they are unloaded.

On-Time Performance - The proportion of time that a transit system adheres to its published schedule times within stated tolerances.

Open Rates - Rates established for each individual carrier. These rates are listed in a tariff list but may differ according to carrier.

Open-to-Buy - A control technique used in aggregate inventory management in which authorizations to purchase are made without being committed to specific suppliers. These authorizations are often reviewed by management using such measures as commodity in dollars and by time period.

Open-to-Receive - Authorization to receive goods, such as a blanket release, firm purchase order item, or supplier schedule.

Operating ratio - A measure of operation efficiency defined as (Operating expenses / Operating revenues) x 100

Operational Performance Measurements - (1) In traditional management, performance measurements related to machine, worker, or department efficiency or utilization. These performance measurements are usually poorly correlated with organizational performance.2) In theory of constraints, performance measurements that link causally to organizational performance measurements. Throughput, inventory, and operating expense are examples. Also see: Performance Measures

Optimization - The process of making something as good or as effective as possible with given resources and constraints.

Option - A choice that must be made by the customer or company when customizing the end product. In many companies, the term option means a mandatory choice from a limited selection.

Glossary of Terms in Logistics & Shipping

Optional Replenishment Model - A form of independent demand item management model in which a review of inventory on hand plus on order is made at fixed intervals. If the actual quantity is lower than some predetermined threshold, a reorder is placed for a quantity M x, where M is the maximum allowable inventory and x is the current inventory quantity. The reorder point, R, may be deterministic or stochastic, and in either instance is large enough to cover the maximum expected demand during the review interval plus the replenishment lead time. The optional replenishment model is sometimes called a hybrid system because it combines certain aspects of the fixed reorder cycle inventory model and the fixed reorder quantity inventory model. Also see: Fixed Reorder Cycle Inventory Model, Fixed Reorder Quantity Inventory Model, Hybrid Inventory System, Independent Demand Item Management Models

Order - A request for goods or services that is provided by telephone, fax, EDI transmission or via e-mail transmission.

Order Batching - Practice of compiling and collecting orders before they are sent in to the manufacturer.

Order Complete Manufacture to Customer Receipt of Order - Average lead time from when an order is ready for shipment to customer receipt of order, including the following sub-elements: pick/pack time, preparation for shipment, total transit time for all components to consolidation point, consolidation, queue time, and additional transit time to customer receipt. (An element of Order Fulfillment Lead-Time). Note: Determined separately for Make-to-Order, Configure/Package-to-Order, Engineer-to-Order and Make-to-Stock products.

Order Consolidation Profile - The activities associated with filling a customer order by bringing together in one physical place all of the line items ordered by the customer. Some of these may come directly from the production line others may be picked from stock.

Order Cycle - The time and process involved from the placement of an order to the receipt of the shipment.

Order Cycle Time - The time required completing a given process including the placement of an order until receipt of order. The overall process includes many sub-processes such as order entry, inspection, preparation, and shipping.

Order Entry and Scheduling - The process of receiving orders from the customer and entering them into a company's order processing system. Orders can be received through phone, fax, or electronic media. Activities may include "technically" examining orders to ensure an orderable configuration and provide accurate price, checking the customer's credit and accepting payment (optionally), identifying and reserving inventory (both on hand and scheduled), and committing and scheduling a delivery date.

Order Entry Complete to Start Manufacture - Average lead-time from completion of customer order to the time manufacturing begins, including the following sub-elements: order wait time, engineering and design time. (An element of Order Fulfillment Lead-Time). Note: Determined separately for Make-to-Order, Configure/Package-to-Order, and Engineer-to-Order products. Does not apply to Make-to-Stock products.

Order Fill - A measure of the number of orders processed without the need to back order, expressed as a percentage of all orders processed in the distribution center (dc) or warehouse.

Order Fulfillment Lead Times - Average, consistently achieved lead-time from customer order origination to customer order receipt, for a particular manufacturing process strategy (Make-to-Stock, Make-to-Order, Configure/Package-to-Order,

DEFINITIONS

Engineer to- Order). Excess lead-time created by orders placed in advance of typical lead times (Blanket Orders, Annual Contracts, Volume Purchase Agreements, etc.), is excluded. (An element of Total Supply Chain Response Time) Calculation: Total average lead time from [Customer signature/authorization to order receipt] + [Order receipt to completion of order entry] + [Completion of order entry to start manufacture] + [Start manufacture to complete manufacture] + [Complete manufacture to customer receipt of order] + [Customer receipt of order to installation complete] Note: The elements of order fulfillment lead time are additive. Not all elements apply to all manufacturing process strategies. For example, for Make-to-Stock products, the lead-time from Start manufacture to complete manufacture equals 0.

Order Interval - The time period between the placement of orders.

Order Level System - See Fixed Reorder Cycle Inventory Model

Order Management - The planning, directing, monitoring, and controlling of the processes related to customer orders, manufacturing orders, and purchase orders. Regarding customer orders, order management includes order promising, order entry, order pick, pack and ship, billing, and reconciliation of the customer account. Regarding manufacturing orders, order management includes order release, routing, manufacture, monitoring, and receipt into stores or finished goods inventories. Regarding purchasing orders, order management includes order placement, monitoring, receiving, acceptance, and payment of supplier.

Order Management Costs - One of the elements comprising a company's total supply-chain management costs. These costs consist of the following: (1) New Product Release Phase-In and Maintenance: This includes costs associated with releasing new products to the field, maintaining released products, assigning product ID, defining configurations and packaging, publishing availability schedules, release letters and updates, and maintaining product databases. (2) Create Customer Order: This includes costs associated with creating and pricing configurations to order and preparing customer order documents. (3) Order Entry and Maintenance: This includes costs associated with maintaining the customer database, credit check, accepting new orders, and adding them to the order system as well as later order modifications. (4) Contract/Program and Channel Management: This includes costs related to contract negotiation, monitoring progress, and reporting against the customer's contract, including administration of performance or warranty related issues. (5) Installation Planning: This includes costs associated with installation engineering, scheduling and modification, handling cancellations, and planning the installation. (6) Order Fulfillment: This includes costs associated with order processing, inventory allocation, ordering from internal or external suppliers, shipment scheduling, order status reporting, and shipment initiation. (7) Distribution: This includes costs associated with warehouse space and management, finished goods receiving and stocking, processing shipments, picking and consolidating, selecting carrier, and staging products/systems. (8) Transportation, Outbound Freight and Duties: This includes costs associated with all company paid freight duties from point-of-manufacture to end-customer or channel. (9) Installation: This includes costs associated with verification of site preparation, installation, certification, and authorization of billing. (10) Customer Invoicing/Accounting: This includes costs associated with invoicing, processing customer payments, and verification of customer receipt.

Order Picking - Selecting or "picking" the required quantity of specific products for movement to a packaging area (usually in response to one or more shipping orders) and documenting that the material was moved from one location to shipping. Also see:

Glossary of Terms in Logistics & Shipping

Batch Picking, Discrete Order Picking, Zone Picking

Order Point Order Quantity System - The inventory method that places an order for a lot whenever the quantity on hand is reduced to a predetermined level known as the order point. Also see: Fixed Reorder Quantity Inventory Model, Hybrid system

Order Processing - Activities associated with filling customer orders.

Order Promising - The process of making a delivery commitment, i.e., answering the question, When can you ship? For make-to-order products, this usually involves a check of uncommitted material and availability of capacity, often as represented by the master schedule available-to-promise. Also see: Available-to-Promise

Order Receipt to Order Entry Complete - Average lead-time from receipt of a customer order to the time that order entry is complete, including the following sub-elements: order revalidation, product configuration check, credit check, and order scheduling. Note: Determined separately for Make-to-Order, Configure/Package-to-Order, Engineer-to-Order, and Make-to-Stock products.

Order Tracking - The order status is monitored on the progress of the order from pickup to the final delivery.

Order-to-cash - An intertrading partner business process of taking the customer's order, picking the product at the warehouse, shipping the product through logistics, receiving the product at the customer's site, and flowing the cash from the customer's payment to the general ledgers of the respective trading partners.

Organizational transparency - Refers to virtual organizations in which all the functions of an organization are carried out but are not under the total control of a single company.

Origin - The location where a shipment begins its movement.

Original Equipment Manufacturer (OEM) - A manufacturer that buys and incorporates another supplier's products into its own products. Also, products supplied to the original equipment manufacturer or sold as part of an assembly. For example, an engine may be sold to an OEM for use as that company's power source for its generator units.

OS&D - see Over, Short, and Damaged

OTIF - see On Time In Full

Out of Gauge - Cargo which exceeds the internal dimensions of the container in width, length or height.

Out Of Stock - The state of not having inventory at a location and available for distribution or for sell to the consumer (zero inventory).

Out of Stocks - See Stock Outs

Outbound - Export shipments.

Outbound Consolidation - Consolidation of a number of small shipments for various customers into a larger load. The large load is then shipped to a location near the customers where it is broken down and then the small shipments are distributed to the customers. This can reduce overall shipping charges where many small packet or parcel shipments are handled each day. Also see: Break Bulk

Outbound Logistics - The process related to the movement and storage of products from the end of the production line to the end user.

Outlier - A data point that differs significantly from other data for a similar phenomenon. For example, if the average sales for a product were 10 units per month, and one month the product had sales of 500

DEFINITIONS

units, this sales point might be considered an outlier. Also see: Abnormal Demand

Outpartnering - The process of involving the supplier in a close partnership with the firm and its operations management system. Outpartnering is characterized by close working relationships between buyers and suppliers, high levels of trust, mutual respect, and emphasis on joint problem solving and cooperation. With outpartnering, the supplier is viewed not as an alternative source of goods and services (as observed under outsourcing) but rather as a source of knowledge, expertise, and complementary core competencies. Outpartnering is typically found during the early stages of the product life cycle when dealing with products that are viewed as critical to the strategic survival of the firm. Also see: Customer-Supplier Partnership

Outport - Destination port, other than a base port, to which rates apply but which may be subject to additional outport arbitraries.

Outsource - To utilize a third-party provider to perform services previously performed in-house. Examples include manufacturing of products and call center/customer support.

Outsourced Cost of Goods Sold - Operations performed on raw material outside of the responding entity's organization that would typically be considered internal to the entity's manufacturing cycle. Outsourced cost of goods sold captures the value of all outsourced activities that roll up as cost of goods sold. Some examples of commonly outsourced areas are assembly by subcontract houses, test, metal finishing or painting, and specialized assembly process.

Over Landed - (1) Cargo volume count more than originally shipped. 2. Cargo taken beyond original port of discharge.

Over, Short, and Damaged (OS&D) - Excess, shortage or damaged items are included in a report issued at the warehouse. Used to file a claim with a carrier.

Overall Equipment Effectiveness (OEE) - A measure of overall equipment effectiveness that takes into account machine availability & performance as well as output quality.

Overland Common Port (OCP) - A special rate concession made by shipping lines, rail carriers and truckers serving the U.S. West Coast for export and import traffic, intended to benefit midwest shippers and importers by equalising rates to and from other coastal areas, and offering these midwest companies a comparable alternative. The steamship companies lower their rates and the inland carriers pick up the terminal charges, which consist of handling charges, wharfage charges and car loading or unloading charges. OCP rates apply to cargo shipped from or consigned to the states of: North Dakota, South Dakota, Nebraska, Colorado, New Mexico and all states east thereof. OCP rates in Canada apply to the provinces of: Manitoba, Ontario and Quebec.

Over-the-road - A motor carrier operation that reflects long-distance, intercity moves; the opposite of local operations.

Owner-operator - A trucking operation in which the opener of the truck is also the driver.

P & D - Pickup and delivery.

P2P - (1) See Peer to Peer 2. See Path to Profitability

Package to Order - A production environment in which a good or service can be packaged after receipt of a customer order. The item is common across many different customers; packaging determines the end product.

Packaging - Materials used to protect a shipment when in transit or in storage at a warehouse facility. Protective packaging is often inside a carton or individual box.

Packing - Protecting individual items either by placing them in cardboard boxes or by securing them in bundles or packages with wrapping material.

Packing and Marking - The activities of packing for safe shipping and unitizing one or more items of an order, placing them into an appropriate container, and marking and labeling the container with customer shipping destination data, as well as other information that may be required.

Packing List - List showing merchandise packed and all particulars. Normally prepared by shipper but not required by carriers. Copy is sent to consignee to help verify shipment received. The physical equivalent of the electronic Advanced Ship Notice (ASN).

Pad Wrap - A service provided by moving companies and specific carriers that eliminates packaging material by wrapping product in padded "blankets". This will protect the goods during transit, usually on "air ride" vans. See Blanket Wrap.

Pallet - The platform which cartons are stacked on and then used for shipment or movement as a group. Used to support cargo and ease movement by forklifts. Pallets may be made of wood or composite materials.

Pallet Ticket - A label to track pallet-sized quantities of end items produced to identify the specific sublot with specifications determined by periodic sampling and analysis during production.

Pallet wrapping machine - A machine that wraps a pallet's contents in stretch-wrap to ensure safe shipment.

Parcel Shipment - Small packages like those typically handled by providers such as UPS and FedEx.

Pareto - A means of sorting data for example. For example, number of quality faults by frequency of occurrence. An analysis that compares cumulative percentages of the rank ordering of costs, cost drivers, profits or other attributes to determine whether a minority of elements have a disproportionate impact. Another example, identifying that 20 percent of a set of independent variables is responsible for 80 percent of the effect. Also see: 80/20 Rule

Part Period Balancing (PPB) - In forecasting, a dynamic lot-sizing technique that uses the same logic as the least total cost method, but adds a routine called look ahead/look back. When the look ahead/look back feature is used, a lot quantity is calculated, and before it is firmed up, the next or the previous period's demands are evaluated to determine whether it would be economical to include them in the current lot. Also see: Discrete Order Quantity, Dynamic lot sizing.

Part standardization - A program for planned elimination of superficial, accidental, and deliberate differences between similar parts in the interest of reducing part and supplier proliferation. A typical goal of part standardization is to reduce costs by reducing the number of parts that the company needs to manage.

Partlow Chart - A chart that indicates the temperature reading in a reefer container.

Partnerships and Alliances - Shippers and providers who enter into agreements designed to benefit both parties.

Passenger-mile - A measure of output for passenger transportation; it reflects the number of passengers transported and the distance traveled; a multiplication of passengers hauled and distance traveled.

Password - A private code required to gain access to a computer, an application program, or service.

Definitions

Path to Profitability (P2P) - The step-by-step model to generate earnings.

Pay-on-Use - Pay-on-Use is a process where payment is initiated by product consumption, i.e., consignment stock based on withdrawal of product from inventory. This process is popular with many European companies.

Payroll - Total of all fully burdened labor costs, including wage, fringe, benefits, overtime, bonus, and profit sharing.

PBIT - see Profit Before Interest and Tax

PDA - see Personal Digital Assistant

PDCA - see Plan-Do-Check-Action

Peak demand - The time period during which the quantity demanded is greater than during any other comparable time period.

Peer to Peer (P2P) - A computer networking environment which allows individual computers to share resources and data without passing through an intermediate network server.

Pegged Requirement - An MRP component requirement that shows the next-level parent item (or customer order) as the source of the demand.

Pegging - A technique in which a ERP system traces demand for a product by date, quantity, and warehouse location.

Per Diem - (1) The rate of payment for use by one railroad of the cars of another. (2) A daily rate of reimbursement for expenses.

Percent of Fill - Number of lines or quantity actually shipped as a percent of the original order. Synonym: Customer Service Ratio.

Perfect Order - The definition of a perfect order is one which meets all of the following criteria: Delivered complete, with all items on the order in the quantity requested Delivered on time to customer's request date, using the customer's definition of on-time delivery Delivered with complete and accurate documentation supporting the order, including packing slips, bills of lading, and invoices Delivered in perfect condition with the correct configuration, customer ready, without damage, and faultlessly installed (as applicable)

Performance and Event Management Systems - The systems that report on the key measurements in the supply chain : inventory days of supply, delivery performance, order cycle times, capacity use, etc. Using this information to identify causal relationships to suggest actions in line with the business goals.

Performance Measurement Program - A performance measurement program goes beyond just having performance metrics in place. Many companies do not realize the full benefit of their performance metrics because they often do not have all of the necessary elements in place that support their metrics. Also see: Performance Measures, Dashboard, Scorecard, Key Performance Indicator Typical characteristics of a good performance measurement program include the following: &

Performance Measures - Indicators of the work performed and the results achieved in an activity, process, or organizational unit. Performance measures should be both non-financial and financial. Performance measures enable periodic comparisons and benchmarking. For example, a common performance measure for a distribution center is % of order fill rate. Also see: Performance Measurement Program Attributes of good performance measurement include the following: (1) Measures only what is important: The measure focuses on key aspects of process performance (2) Can be collected economically: Processes and activities are designed to easily capture the relevant information (3) Are visible: The measure and its causal effects are readily available to everyone who is measured (4) Is easy to understand: The measure conveys at a glance what it is measuring and how it is derived (5) Is process oriented: The measure makes the proper trade-offs among utilization, productivity and performance (6) Is defined and mutually understood. The measure has been defined and mutually understood by all key parties (internal and external) (7) Facilitates trust: The measure validates the participation among various parties and discourages "game playing" (8) Are usable: The measure is used to show progress and not just data that is "collected". Indicated performance vs data

Period Order Quantity - A lot-sizing technique under which the lot size is equal to the net requirements for a given number of periods, e.g., weeks into the future. The number of periods to order is variable, each order size equalizing the holding costs and the ordering costs for the interval. Also see: Discrete Order Quantity, Dynamic Lot Sizing

Periodic Review System - See Fixed Reorder Cycle Inventory Model

Permit - A grant of authority to operate as a contract carrier

Perpetual Inventory - An inventory record keeping system where each transaction in and out is recorded and a new balance is computed.

Personal Digital Assistant (PDA) - A computer term for a handheld device that combines computing, telephone/fax, and networking features. PDA examples include the Palm and Pocket PC devices. A typical PDA can function as a cellular phone, fax sender, and personal organizer. Unlike portable computers, most PDAs are pen-based, using a stylus rather than a keyboard for input. This means that they also incorporate handwriting recognition features. Some PDAs can also react to voice input by using voice recognition technologies. Some PDAs and networking software allow companies to use PDAs in their warehouses to support wireless transaction processing and inquiries.

Personal discrimination - Charging different rates to shippers with similar transportation characteristics, or vice versa.

Phantom Bill of Material - A bill-of-material coding and structuring technique used primarily for transient (nonstocked) subassemblies. For the transient item, lead time is set to zero and the order quantity to lot-for-lot. A phantom bill of material represents an item that is physically built, but rarely stocked, before being used in the next step or level of manufacturing. This permits MRP logic to drive requirements straight through (blowthrough) the phantom item to its components, but the MRP system usually retains its ability to net against any occasional inventories of the item. This technique also facilitates the use of common bills of material for engineering and manufacturing. Synonym: Pseudo Bill of Material. Also see: blowthrough

Physical Distribution - All logistics activities from the production line to the final user, including traffic, packaging, materials handling, warehousing, order entry, customer service, inventory control etc.

Physical Inventory - The process of actual counting all items on-hand at a given time in a facility.

Physical supply - The movement and storage functions associated with raw materials from supply sources to the manufacturing facility.

Pick List - A list of items to be picked from stock in order to fill an order.

Pick on Receipt - Product is receipted and picked in one operation (movement); therefore the product never actually touches the ground within the warehouse. It is unloaded from one vehicle and re-loaded on an outbound vehicle. Related to Cross Docking.

Pick/Pack - Picking of product from inventory and packing into shipment containers.

Pick-and-Drop - Operation that normally consists of one over-the-road van operator alternating between two trailers. He transports and delivers one trailer while another is being loaded.

Pick-by-Light - A laser identifies the bin for the next item in the rack; when the picker completes the pick, the bar code is scanned and the system then points the laser at the next bin.

Picking - The operations involved in pulling products from storage areas to complete a customer order.

Picking by Aisle - A method where picking all needed items in an aisle regardless of the items' ultimate destination; the items must be sorted later.

Picking by Source - A method where pickers successively pick all items going to a particular destination regardless of the aisle in which each item is located.

Pick-to-carton - Pick-to-carton logic uses item dimensions/weights to select the shipping carton prior to the order picking process. Items are then picked directly into the shipping carton.

Pick-to-clear - A method often used in warehouse management systems that directs picking to the locations with the smallest quantities on hand.

Pick-to-light - Pick-to light systems consist of lights and LED displays for each pick location. The system uses software to light the next pick and display the quantity to pick.

Pick-to-trailer - Order-picking method where the order picker transports the materials directly from the pick location to the trailer without any interim checking or staging steps.

Pick-Up Order - A document authorizing a service provider the authority to pick up cargo or equipment from a specific location.

Pier - A structure built away from land and extending some distance over water, often used for docking boats. Also known as a wharf.

Piggyback - Terminology used to describe a truck trailer being transported on a railroad flatcar.

Pilferage - Cargo stolen from the container, warehouse or terminal.

Pin lock - A hard piece of iron, formed to fit on a trailer's pin, that locks in place with a key to prevent an unauthorized person from moving the trailer.

Place utility - A value created in a product by changing its location. Transportation creates place utility.

Plaintext - Data before it has been encrypted or after it has been decrypted, e.g., an ASCII text file.

Plan Deliver - The development and establishment of courses of action over specified time periods that represent a projected appropriation of supply resources to meet delivery requirements.

Plan Make - The development and establishment of courses of action over specified time periods that represent a projected appropriation of production resources to meet production requirements.

Plan Source - The development and establishment of courses of action over specified time periods that represent a projected appropriation of material resources to meet supply chain requirements.

Plan Stability - The difference between planned production and actual production, as a percentage of planned production. Calculation: [(Sum of Monthly Production Plans) + (Sum of the absolute value of the difference between planned and actual)]/[Sum of Monthly Production Plans] Note: Base Production Plan is the three month removed plan

Plan-Do-Check-Action (PDCA) - In quality management, a four-step process for quality improvement. In the first step, a plan to effect improvement is developed. In the second step, the plan is carried out, preferably on a small scale. In the third step, the effects of the plan are observed. In the last step, the results are studied to determine what was learned and what can be predicted. The plan-do-check-act cycle is sometimes referred to as the Shewhart cycle and as the Deming circle. Synonyms: Shewhart Cycle. Also see: Deming Circle

Planned Date - The date an operation such as a pickup or delivery of an order is planned to occur.

Planned Order - A suggested order quantity, release date, and due date created by the planning system's logic when it encounters net requirements in processing MRP. In some cases, it can also be created by a master scheduling module. Planned orders are created by the computer, exist only within the computer, and may be changed or deleted by the computer during subsequent processing if conditions change. Planned orders at one level will be exploded into gross requirements for components at the next level. Planned orders, along with released orders, serve as input to capacity requirements planning to show the total capacity requirements by work center in future time periods. Also see: Planning Time Fence, Firm Planned Order

Planned Receipt - An anticipated receipt against an open purchase order or open production order.

Planning Bill - See Planning Bill of Material

Planning Bill of Material - An artificial grouping of items or events in bill-of-material format used to facilitate master scheduling and material planning. It may include the historical average of demand expressed as a percentage of total demand for all options within a feature or for a specific end item within a product family and is used as the quantity per in the planning bill of material. Synonym: Planning Bill. Also see: Hedge Inventory, Production Forecast, Pseudo Bill of Material

Planning Calendar - See Manufacturing Calendar

Planning Fence - See Planning Time Fence

Planning Horizon - The amount of time a plan extends into the future. For a master schedule, this is normally set to cover a minimum of cumulative lead time plus time for lot sizing low-level components and for capacity changes of primary work centers or of key suppliers. For longer term plans the planning horizon must be long enough to permit any needed additions to capacity. Also see: Cumulative Lead Time, Planning Time Fence

Planning Time Fence - A point in time denoted in the planning horizon of the master scheduling process that marks a boundary inside of which changes to the schedule may adversely affect component schedules, capacity plans, customer deliveries, and cost. Outside the planning time fence, customer orders may be booked and changes to the master schedule can be made within the constraints of the production plan. Changes inside the planning time fence must be made manually by the master scheduler. Synonym: Planning Fence. Also see: Cumulative Lead Time, Demand Time Fence, Firm Planned Order, Planned Order, Planning Horizon, Time Fence.

Planogram - The end result of analyzing the sales data of an item or group of items to determine the best arrangement of products on a store shelf. The process determines which shelf your top-selling product should be displayed on, the number of facings it gets, and what best to surround it with. It results in

DEFINITIONS

graphical picture or map of the allotted shelf space along with a specification of the facing and deep.

Plant Finished Goods - Finished goods inventory that are held at the end manufacturing location.

Plimsoll Mark - Depth to which a vessel may safely load. Identified by a circle on the vessel's side with a vertical line through and a number of small horizontal lines showing the max depth for summer and winter.

PM - see Preventative Maintenance

PO - see Purchase Order

POD - Abbreviation for:(1) Port of Discharge; (2) Port of Destination; (3) Proof of Delivery:

Point Of Sale (POS) - The time and place at which a sale occurs, such as a cash register in a retail operation, or the order confirmation screen in an on-line session. Supply chain partners are interested in capturing data at the POS, because it is a true record of the sale rather than being derived from other information such as inventory movement. Also a national network of merchant terminals, at which customers can use client cards and personal security codes to make purchases. Transactions are directed against client deposit accounts. POS terminals are sophisticated cryptographic devices, with complex key management processes. POS standards draw on ABM network experiences and possess extremely stringent security requirements.

Point of Sale Information - Price and quantity data from retail locations as sales transactions occur.

Point-of-Purchase (POP) - A retail sales term referring to the area where a sale occurs, such as the checkout counter. POP is also used to refer to the displays and other sales promotion tools located at a checkout counter.

Point-of-use inventory - Material used in production processes that is physically stored where it is consumed.

Poka Yoke (mistake-proof) - The application of simple techniques that prevent process quality failure. A mechanism that either prevents a mistake from being made or makes the mistake obvious at a glance.

Police powers - The United States constitutionally granted right or the states to establish regulations to protect the health and welfare of its citizens; truck weight, speed, length, and height laws are examples.

Pooling - A shipping term for the practice of combining shipment from multiple shippers into a truckload in order to reduce shipping charges.

POP - see Point-of-Purchase

Port & Terminal Service Charge (PTSC) - South Europe Conference [SEAC] charge incurred when the shipper is not able to deliver cargo directly alongside the vessel. The carrier may assess its expenses in moving cargo from the shipper's point of delivery to the vessel.

Port authority - A state or local government that owns, operates, or otherwise provides wharf, dock, and other terminal investments at ports.

Portal - Websites that serve as starting points to other destinations or activities on the Internet. Initially thought of as a "home base" type of web page, portals attempt to provide all Internet needs in one location. Portals commonly provide services such as e-mail, online chat forums, shopping, searching, content, and news feeds.

POS - see Point Of Sale

Positioning - The moving of empty equipment from surplus areas to deficit areas.

119

Possession utility - The value created by marketing's effort to increase the desire to possess a good or benefit from a service.

Post-Deduct Inventory Transaction Processing - A method of inventory bookkeeping where the book (computer) inventory of components is reduced after issue. When compared to a real-time process, this approach has the disadvantage of a built-in differential between the book record and what is physically in stock. Consumption can be based on recorded actual use, or calculated using finished quantity received times the standard BOM quantity (backflush). Also see: Backflush

POSTNET - The POSTNET barcode is used on envelopes and postcards that are sent through the U.S. Postal Service. This barcode is placed in the lower right-hand corner of the envelope.

Postponement - The delay of final activities (i.e., assembly, production, packaging, etc.) until the latest possible time. A strategy used to eliminate excess inventory in the form of finished goods which may be packaged in a variety of configurations.

PPB - see Part Period Balancing

Pre-Deduct Inventory Transaction Processing - A method of inventory bookkeeping where the book (computer) inventory of components is reduced before issue, at the time a scheduled receipt for their parents or assemblies is created via a bill-of-material explosion. When compared to a real-time process, this approach has the disadvantage of a built-in differential between the book record and what is physically in stock.

Predictive maintenance - Practices that seek to prevent unscheduled machinery downtime by collecting and analyzing data on equipment conditions. The analysis is then used to predict time-to-failure, plan maintenance, and restore machinery to good operating condition. Predictive maintenance systems typically measure parameters on machine operations, such as vibration, heat, pressure, noise, and lubricant condition. In conjunction with computerized maintenance management systems (CMMS), predictive maintenance enables repair-work orders to be released automatically, repair-parts inventories checked, or routine maintenance scheduled.

Pre-Expediting - The function of following up on open orders before the scheduled delivery date, to ensure the timely delivery of materials in the specified quantity.

Prepaid - A freight term, which indicates that charges are to be paid by the shipper. Prepaid shipping charges may be added to the customer invoice, or the cost may be bundled into the pricing for the product.

Present Value - Today's value of future cash flows, discounted at an appropriate rate.

Preventative Maintenance (PM) - Regularly scheduled maintenance activities performed in order to reduce or eliminate unscheduled equipment failures and downtime.

Price Erosion - What causes old-line executives to break out in a cold sweat? No question about it; traditional business models are threatened by the market efficiencies of B2B. When prices begin to plummet, the margin structures of older industries are also threatened. Price Look-Up (PLU)

Primage - A charge paid by shippers to ship agents for services provided by the agent in Turkish and Greek ports, generally for loading activities conducted by port stevedores. It is not an actual contractual term so the obligation to pay does not depend on its inclusion in the bill of lading. Turkey: 3% on Total Ocean Freight including all surcharges and intermodal charges. Greece: 3% Piraeus, 5% Salonika (except on cargo originating in Bulgaria).

DEFINITIONS

Primary highways - Highways that connect lesser populated cities with major cities.

Primary Manufacturing Strategy - Your company's dominant manufacturing strategy. The Primary Manufacturing Strategy generally accounts for 80-plus % of a company's product volume. According to a study by Pittiglio Rabin Todd & McGrath (PRTM), approximately 73% of all companies use a make-to-stock strategy.

Primary-business test - A test used by the ICC to determine if a trucking operation is bona fide private transportation; the private trucking operation must be incidental to and in the furtherance of the primary business of the firm.

PRIME QR - Product Replenishment and Inventory Management Edge for Quick Response.

Private carrier - A carrier that provides transportation service to the firm and that owns or leases the vehicles and does not charge a fee. Private motor carriers may haul at a fee for wholly-owned subsidiaries.

Private Label - Products that are designed, produced, controlled by, and which carry the name of the store or a name owned by the store; also known as a store brand or dealer brand. An example would be Wal-Mart's "Sam's Choice" products.

Private Warehouse - A company-owned warehouse.

Pro Number - Any progressive or serialized number applied for identification of freight bills, bills of lading, etc.

Proactive - The strategy of understanding issues before they become apparent and presenting the solution as a benefit to the customer, etc.

Process - A series of time-based activities that are linked to complete a specific output.

Process Benchmarking - Benchmarking a process (such as the pick, pack, and ship process) against organizations known to be the best in class in this process. Process benchmarking is usually conducted on firms outside of the organization's industry. Also see: Benchmarking, Best-in-Class, Competitive Benchmarking

Process capability - Refers to the ability of the process to produce parts that conform to (engineering) specifications. Process capability relates to the inherent variability of a process that is in a state of statistical control. See also CP or CPK.

Process Improvement - Designs or activities, which improve quality or reduce costs, often through the elimination of waste or non-value-added tasks.

Process Manufacturing - Production that adds value by mixing, separating, forming, and/or performing chemical reactions. It may be done in a batch, continuous, or mixed batch/continuous mode. Products in this manufacturing group include: foods, petrochemicals, bottling, chemicals, etc. Process manufacturing frequently generates co-products and by-products as an outcome in addition to the primary product being manufactured. An example would be the manufacture of petroleum products, where multiple grades of lubricants and fuels are produced from a single run as well as non-usable by-products such as sludge.

Process technology - The technology used by a particular business or manufacturing process, using the Internet for communication purposes rather than mail, telephones, EDI, or faxes for example.

Process Yield - The resulting output from a process. An example would be a quantity of finished product output from manufacturing processes.

Procurement - The business functions of procurement planning, purchasing, inventory control, traffic, receiving, incoming

121

inspection, and salvage operations. Synonym: Purchasing.

Procurement Services Provider (PSP) - A services firm that integrates procurement technologies with product, sourcing, and supply management expertise, to provide outsourced procurement solutions. A PSP serves as an extension of an organization's existing procurement infrastructure, managing the processes and spending categories and procurement processes that the organization feels it has opportunities for improvement but lacks the internal expertise to manage effectively.

Product - An item that has been or is being produced.

Product Characteristics - All of the elements that define a product's character, such as size, shape, weight, etc.

Product Configurator - A system, generally rule-based, to be used in design-to-order, engineer-to-order, or make-to-order environments where numerous product variations exist. Product configurators perform intelligent modeling of the part or product attributes and often create solid models, drawings, bills of material, and cost estimates that can be integrated into CAD/CAM and MRP II systems as well as sales order entry systems.

Product Description - The user's detailed description of the product.

Product Family - A group of products with similar characteristics, often used in production planning (or sales and operations planning).

Product line segmentation - Separating a product line into items having similar characteristics, purposes, or manufacturing requirements.

Product modularity - An approach used to design products that can be assembled from a family of modules. Using the modular approach, many configurations of a product can be assembled from one set of modules.

Product serviceability - The ease with which a product can be serviced for maintenance or repair purposes.

Product technology - The technology used in the development of a product, analogue technology versus digital technological in the case of telephones for example.

Production Calendar - See Manufacturing Calendar

Production Capacity - Measure of how much production volume may be experienced over a set period of time.

Production Forecast - A projected level of customer demand for a feature (option, accessory, etc.) of a make-to-order or an assemble-to-order product. Used in two-level master scheduling, it is calculated by netting customer backlog against an overall family or product line master production schedule and then factoring this product's available-to-promise by the option percentage in a planning bill of material. Also see: Assemble-to-Order, Planning Bill of Material, Two-Level Master Schedule

Production Line - A series of pieces of equipment dedicated to the manufacture of a specific number of products or families.

Production Planning and Scheduling - The systems that enable creation of detailed optimized plans and schedules taking into account the resource, material, and dependency constraints to meet the deadlines.

Production-Related Material - Production-related materials are those items classified as material purchases and included in Cost of Goods Sold as raw material purchases.

Productivity - A measure of efficiency of resource utilization; defined as the sum of the outputs divided by the sum of the inputs.

DEFINITIONS

Profit - (1) Gross profit - earning from an ongoing business after direct costs of goods sold have been deducted from sales revenue for a given period.(2) Operating profit - earnings or income after all expenses (selling, administrative, depreciation) have been deducted from gross profit.(3) Net profit - earnings or income after adjusting for miscellaneous income and expenses (patent royalties, interest, capital gains) and tax from operating profit. Synonym: Income.

Profit Before Interest and Tax (PBIT) - The financial profit generated prior to the deduction of taxes and interest due on loans. Also called operating profit.

Profit ratio - The percentage of profit to sales--that is, profit divided by sales.

Profitability Analysis - The analysis of profit derived from cost objects with the view to improve or optimize profitability. Multiple views may be analyzed, such as market segment, customer, distribution channel, product families, products, technologies, platforms, regions, manufacturing capacity, etc.

Profitable to Promise - This is effectively a promise to deliver a certain order on agreed terms, including price and delivery. Profitable-to-Promise (PTP) is the logical evolution of Available-to-Promise (ATP) and Capable-to-Promise (CTP). While the first two are necessary for profitability, they are not sufficient. For enterprises to survive in a competitive environment, profit optimization is a vital technology.

Prohibited Items - Items the carrier will not handle, such as explosives, flammables and other hazardous materials.

Project - A specific scope of business that includes detailed locations and required pick-up and delivery instructions. Coordination with the services may require a pre-arranged outside installation crew.

Project Management - A disciplined process in which an individual or team of individuals provides all planning, management, design and coordination for a large customer project. See Supportive Project Management.

Promotion - The act of selling a product at a reduced price, or a buy one - get one free offer, for the purpose of increasing sales.

Proof of Delivery (POD) - Information supplied by the carrier containing the name of the person who signed for the shipment, the time and date of delivery, and other shipment delivery related information. POD is also sometimes used to refer to the process of printing materials just prior to shipment.

Proportional rate - A rate lower than the regular rate for shipments that have prior or subsequent moves; used to overcome competitive disadvantages of combination rates.

Protocol - Communication standards that determine message content and format, enabling uniformity of transmissions.

Pseudo Bill of Materials - See Phantom Bill of Materials

PSP - see Procurement Services Provider

PTI - Pre-Trip Inspection. (Typically the shipping line's inspection of reefer containers prior to release to the shipper for stuffing/loading).

PTSC - see Port & Terminal Service Charge

Public warehouse - A business that provides short or long-term storage to a variety of businesses usually on a month-to-month basis. A public warehouse will generally use their own equipment and staff however agreements may be made where the client either buys or subsidizes equipment. Public warehouse fees are usually a combination of storage fees (per pallet or actual square footage) and transaction fees (inbound and outbound). Public warehouses are most often used to supplement space requirements of a private warehouse. See also Contract warehouse and 3PL.

Public warehouse receipt - The basic document issued by a public warehouse manager that is the receipt for the goods given to the warehouse manager. The receipt can be either negotiable or nonnegotiable.

Pull or Pull-through distribution - Supply-chain action initiated by the customer. Traditionally, the supply chain was pushed; manufacturers produced goods and "pushed" them through the supply chain, and the customer had no control. In a pull environment, a customer's purchase sends replenishment information back through the supply chain from retailer to distributor to manufacturer, so goods are "pulled" through the supply chain.

Pull Signal - A signal from a using operation that triggers the issue of raw material.

Purchase Order (PO) - The purchaser's authorization used to formalize a purchase transaction with a supplier. The physical form or electronic transaction a buyer uses when placing order for merchandise. 2. Common grouping of orders for goods/services. Several SKU categories may be listed on one purchase order. Most customers group their orders in a particular way to facilitate distribution at the other end. For example, one purchase order for an apparel importer might encompass 2 dozen green sweaters and 2 dozen red sweaters. If those P.O.s originated from the same store, it is simple for the store to put all items under that P.O. onto the right truck.

Purchase price discount - A pricing structure in which the seller offers a lower price if the buyer purchases a larger quantity.

Purchasing - The functions associated with buying the goods and services required by the firm.

Pure raw material - A raw material that does not lose weight in processing

Push back rack - Utilizing wheels in the rack structure, this rack system allows palletized goods and materials to be stored by being pushed up a gently graded ramp. Stored materials are allowed to flow down the ramp to the aisle. This rack configuration allows for deep storage on each rack level.

Push Distribution - The process of building product and pushing it into the distribution channel without receiving any information regarding requirements. Also see: Pull or Pull-Through Distribution

Push Technology - Webcasting (push technology) is the prearranged updating of news, weather, or other selected information on a computer user's desktop interface through periodic and generally unobtrusive transmission over the World Wide Web (including the use of the Web protocol on Intranet). Webcasting uses so-called push technology in which the Web server ostensibly "pushes" information to the user rather than waiting until the user specifically requests it.

Put Away - Removing the material from the dock (or other location of receipt), transporting the material to a storage area, placing that material in a staging area, and then moving it to a specific location and recording the movement and identification of the location where the material has been placed.

Put-to-light - A method that uses lights to direct the placement of materials. Most often used in batch picking to designate the tote to place picked item into.

Q

QFD - see Quality Function Deployment

QR - see Quick Response

Qualifier - A data element, which identifies or defines a related element, set of elements or a segment. The qualifier contains a code from a list of approved codes.

Qualitative Forecasting Techniques - In forecasting, an approach that is based on intuitive or judgmental evaluation. It is used generally when data are scarce, not available, or no longer relevant. Common types of qualitative techniques include: personal insight, sales force estimates, panel consensus, market research, visionary forecasting, and the Delphi method. Examples include developing long-range projections and new product introduction.

Quality - Conformance to requirements or fitness for use. Quality can be defined through five principal approaches: (1) Transcendent quality is an ideal, a condition of excellence. (2) Product-based quality is based on a product attribute. (3) Userbased quality is fitness for use. (4) Manufacturing-based quality is conformance to requirements. (5) Value-based quality is the degree of excellence at an acceptable price. Also, quality has two major components: (a) quality of conformance--quality is defined by the absence of defects, and (b) quality of design--quality is measured by the degree of customer satisfaction with a product's characteristics and features.

Quality Circle - In quality management, a small group of people who normally work as a unit and meet frequently to uncover and solve problems concerning the quality of items produced, process capability, or process control. Also see: Small Group Improvement activity

Quality control - The management function that attempts to ensure that the foods or services manufactured or purchased meet the product or service specifications

Quality Function Deployment (QFD) - A structured method for translating user requirements into detailed design specifications using a continual stream of \'d4what-how' matrices. QFD links the needs of the customer with design, development, engineering, manufacturing, and service functions. It helps organizations seek out both spoken and unspoken needs, translate these into actions and designs, and focus various business functions toward achieving this common goal.

Quantitative Forecasting Techniques - An approach to forecasting where historical demand data is used to project future demand. Extrinsic and intrinsic techniques are typically used. Also see: Extrinsic Forecasting Method, Intrinsic Forecasting Method

Quantity Based Order System - See Fixed Reorder Quantity Inventory Model

Quarantine - In quality management, the setting aside of items from availability for use or sale until all required quality tests have been performed and conformance certified.

Quay - A pier, wharf or other structure built along a shore for landing, loading and unloading boats or ships.

Quick Response (QR) - A strategy widely adopted by general merchandise and soft lines retailers and manufacturers to reduce retail out-of-stocks, forced markdowns and operating expenses. These goals are accomplished through shipping accuracy and reduced response time. QR is a partnership strategy in which suppliers and retailers work together to respond more rapidly to the consumer by sharing point-of-sale scan data, enabling both to forecast replenishment needs. 2. A consumer-driven system of replenishment in which high-quality products and accurate information flow through a paperless system between all distribution points from the manufacturing line to the retail checkout counter. Distributors, carriers and suppliers act as trading partners and focus on improving the total supply system.

Quick Response Program - A system of linking final retail sales with production and shipping schedules back through the chain of supply; employs point-of-sale scanning and electronic data interchange, and may use direct shipment from a factory to a retailer.

Quitclaim - A legal instrument used to release one person's right, title or interest to another without providing a guarantee or warranty of title.

Rack - A storage device for handling material in pallets. A rack usually provides storage for pallets arranged in vertical sections with one or more pallets to a tier. Some racks accommodate more than one-pallet-deep storage. Some racks are static, meaning that the rack contents remain in a fixed position until physically moved. Some racks are designed with a sloped shelf to allow products to "flow" down as product in the front is removed. Replenishment of product on a flow rack may be from the rear, or the front in a "push back" manner.

Racking - A function performed by a rack-jobber, a full-function intermediary who performs all regular warehousing functions and some retail functions, typically stocking a display rack. Also a definition that is applied to the hardware which is used to build racks.

Radio Frequency (RF) - A form of wireless communications that lets users relay information via electromagnetic energy waves from a terminal to a base station, which is linked in turn to a host computer. The terminals can be place at a fixed station, mounted on a forklift truck, or carried in the worker's hand. The base station contains a transmitter and receiver for communication with the terminals. RF systems use either narrow-band or spread-spectrum transmissions. Narrow-band data transmissions move along a single limited radio frequency, while spread-spectrum transmissions move across several different frequencies. When combined with a bar-code system for identifying inventory items, a radio-frequency system can relay data instantly, thus updating inventory records in so-called "real time."

Radio Frequency Identificatrion (RFID) - Radio Frequency IDentification is a method of remotely storing and retrieving data using devices called RFID tags/transponders. An RFID tag is a small object, such as an adhesive sticker, that can be attached to or incorporated into a product. RFID tags contain antennas to enable them to receive and respond to radio-frequency queries from an RFID transceiver.

Railhead - Location for loading and unloading containers at railroad terminal.

Ramp Rate - A statement which quantifies how quickly you grow or expand an operation Growth trajectory. Can refer to sales, profits or margins.

Random-Location Storage - A storage technique in which parts are placed in any space that is empty when they arrive at the storeroom. Although this random method requires the use of a locator file to identify part locations, it often requires less storage space than a fixed-location storage method. Also see: Fixed-Location Storage

Rate Agreement - Group of carriers who discuss rates and common problems with options to file independent tariffs.

Rate basis number - The distance between two rate basis points.

Rate basis point - The major shipping point in a local area; all points in the local area are considered to be the rate basis point.

DEFINITIONS

Rate bureau - A group of carriers that get together to establish joint rates, to divide joint revenues and claim liabilities, and the publish tariffs. Rate bureaus have published single line rates, which were prohibited in 1984.

Rate-Based Scheduling - A method for scheduling and producing based on a periodic rate, e.g., daily, weekly, or monthly. This method has traditionally been applied to high-volume and process industries. The concept has recently been applied within job shops using cellular layouts and mixed-model level schedules where the production rate is matched to the selling rate.

Rationing - The allocation of product among customers during periods of short supply. When price is used to allocate product, it is allocated to those willing to pay the most.

Raw Materials (RM) - Crude or processed material that can be converted by manufacturing, processing, or combination into a new and useful product.

Real-Time - The processing of data in a business application as it happens - as contrasted with storing data for input at a later time (batch processing).

Reasonable rate - A rate that is high enough to cover the carrier's cost but not too high to enable the carrier to realize monopolistic profits.

Recapture Clause - A provision of the 1920 Transportation Act that provided for self-help financing for railroads. Railroads that earned more than the prescribed return contributed one-half of the excess to the fund from which the ICC made loans to less profitable railroads. The Recapture Clause was repealed in 1933.

Received for Shipment Bill of Lading - Can be issued on the carrier's actual receipt or taking custody of goods, if requested goods are not yet necessarily loaded on board a vessel or other conveyance. This form of bill of lading would usually be switched to an on board bill of lading or added as an on board notation upon the actual loading of goods on board a vessel or other conveyance.

Receiving - The function encompassing the physical receipt of material, the inspection of the incoming shipment for conformance with the purchase order (quantity and damage), the identification and delivery to destination, and the preparation of receiving reports.

Receiving Dock - Distribution center (dc) location where the actual physical receipt of the goods from the carrier occurs.

Receiving Report - Documentation completed by a warehouse to confirm the receipt of product into inventory.

Reconsignment - A carrier service that permits changing the destination and/or consignee after the shipment has reached its originally billed destination and paying the through rate from origin to final destination.

Reed-Bulwinkle Act - Legalized joint rate making by common carriers through rate bureaus; extended antitrust immunity to carriers participating in a rate bureau.

Reefer - A term used for refrigerated vehicles.

Reengineering - (1) A fundamental rethinking and radical redesign of business processes to achieve dramatic improvements in performance. 2. A term used to describe the process of making (usually) significant and major revisions or modifications to business processes. 3. An approach to improving business operations through reinventing, reevaluating, redesigning and redoing. 4. Also called Business Process Reengineering.

Re-engineering - An approach to improving business operations through reinventing, reevaluating, redesigning and redoing.

Glossary of Terms in Logistics & Shipping

Refrigerated Carriers - Truckload Carriers (TC) that provide service to keep perishables good refrigerated. While the food industry typically uses this type of carrier, museums, personal art collections, antique and fragile hospitality items also require a temperature-regulated trailer.

Regeneration MRP - An MRP processing approach where the master production schedule is totally reexploded down through all bills of material, to maintain valid priorities. New requirements and planned orders are completely recalculated or "regenerated" at that time.

Regional carrier - A for-hire air carrier, usually certificated, that has annual operating revenues of less than $74 million; the carrier usually operates within a particular region of the country.

Register Ton - A unit of interior capacity of ships. 1 Register Ton = 100 cubic feet or 2,832 cubic metres. Also known as vessel ton.

Regular-route carrier - A motor carrier that is authorized to provide service over designated routes.

Relay - Marine shipment that is transferred to its ultimate destination port after having been shipped to an intermediate point.

Relay terminal - A motor carrier terminal designed to facilitate the substitution of one driver for another who has driven the maximum hours permitted.

Released-value rates - Rates based upon the value of the shipment; the maximum carrier liability for damage is less than the full value, and in return the carrier offers a lower rate.

Release-to-Start Manufacturing - Average time from order release to manufacturing to the start of the production process. This cycle time may typically be required to support activities such as material movement and line changeovers.

Reliability - A carrier selection criterion that considers the variation in carrier transit time; the consistency of the transit time provided.

Reorder point - A predetermined inventory level that triggers the need to place an order. This minimum level provides inventory to meet anticipated demand during the time it takes to receive the order.

REP - see Request for Proposal

Reparation - The ICC could require railroads to repay users the difference between the rate charged and the maximum rate permitted when the ICC found the rate to be unreasonable or too high.

Re-plan Cycle - Time between the initial creation of a regenerated forecast and the time its impact is incorporated into the Master

Replenishment - The process of moving or re-supplying inventory from a reserve (or upstream) storage location to a primary (or downstream) storage or picking location, or to another mode of storage in which picking is performed.

REQ - see Request for Quote

Request for Information (RFI) - A document used to solicit information about vendors, products, and services prior to a formal RFQ/RFP process.

Request for Proposal (RFP) - A document, which provides information concerning needs and requirements for a manufacturer. This document is created in order to solicit proposals from potential suppliers. For, example, a computer manufacturer may use a RFP to solicit proposals from suppliers of third party logistics services.

DEFINITIONS

Request for Quote (RFQ) - A document used to solicit vendor responses when a product has been selected and price quotations are needed from several vendors.

Resellers - Organizations intermediate in the manufacturing and distribution process, such as wholesalers and retailers.

Resource Driver - In cost accounting, the best single quantitative measure of the frequency and intensity of demands placed on a resource by other resources, activities, or cost objects. It is used to assign resource costs to activities, and cost objects, or to other resources.

Resources - Economic elements applied or used in the performance of activities or to directly support cost objects. They include people, materials, supplies, equipment, technologies and facilities. Also see: Resource Driver, Capacity

RET - see Rich Text Format

Retailer - A business that takes title to products and resells them to final consumers. Examples include Wal-Mart, Best Buy, and Safeway, but also include the many smaller independent stores.

Return Cargo - Cargo to be returned to original place of receipt.

Return Disposal Costs - The costs associated with disposing or recycling products that have been returned due to End-of-Life or Obsolescence.

Return Goods Handling - The process involved with returning goods from the customer to the manufacturer. Products can be returned because of performance problems or simply because the customer doesn't like the product.

Return Material Authorization (RMA) - A number usually produced to recognize and give authorization for a defective good to be returned to a distribution center or manufacturer. The RMA number often acts as an order form for the work required in repair situations. See Return Product Authorization.

Return of Investment (ROI) - (1) A calculation that determines the length of time when an asset, process, or service provides a profit or pay for said investment to a customer. (2) A financial measure of the relative return from an investment, usually expressed as a percentage of earnings produced by an asset to the amount invested in the asset.

Return on Assets (ROA) - Financial measure calculated by dividing profit by assets.

Return on Net Assets - Financial measure calculated by dividing profit by assets net of depreciation.

Return on owner's equity (ROF) - The net income divided by average owner's equity.

Return on Sales - Financial measure calculated by dividing profit by sales.

Return Product Authorization (RPA) - Also called Return Material or Goods Authorization. A form generally required with a Warranty/Return, which helps the company identify the original product, and the reason for return. The RPA number often acts as an order form for the work required in repair situations, or as a reference for credit approval.

Return to Vendor (RTV) - Material that has been rejected by the customer or the buyer's inspection department and is awaiting shipment back to the supplier for repair or replacement.

Returns Inventory Costs - The costs associated with managing inventory, returned for any of the following reasons: repair, refurbish, excess, obsolescence, End-of-Life, ecological conformance, and demonstration. Includes all applicable elements of the Level 2 component Inventory Carrying Cost of Total Supply Chain Management Cost

Returns Material Acquisition, Finance, Planning and IT Costs - The costs associated with acquiring the defective products and materials for repair or refurbishing items, plus any Finance, Planning and Information Technology cost to support Return Activity.. Includes all applicable elements of the Level 2 components Material Acquisition Cost (acquiring materials for repairs), Supply Chain Related Finance and Planning Costs and Supply Chain IT Costs of Total Supply Chain Management Cost.

Returns Order Management Costs - The costs associated with managing Return Product Authorizations (RPA). Includes all applicable elements of the Level 2 component Order Management Cost of Total Supply Chain Management Cost. See Order Management Costs.

Returns Processing Cost - The total cost to process repairs, refurbished, excess, obsolete, and End-of-Life products including diagnosing problems, and replacing products. Includes the costs of logistics support, materials, centralized functions, troubleshooting service requests, on-site diagnosis and repair, external repair, and miscellaneous. These costs are broken into Returns Order Management, Returns Inventory Carrying, Returns Material Acquisition, Finance, Planning, IT, Disposal and Warranty Costs.

Returns To Scale - A defining characteristic of B2B. Bigger is better. It's what creates the winner takes all quality of most B2B hubs. It also places a premium on being first to market and first to achieve critical mass.

Revenue Ton - Number of tonnes which freight is paid for per ton.

Reverse Auction - A type of auction where suppliers bid to sell products to a buyer (e.g. retailer). As bidding continues, the prices decline (opposite of a regular auction, where buyers are bidding to buy products).

Reverse Engineering - A process whereby competitors' products are disassembled & analyzed for evidence of the use of better processes, components & technologies

Reverse Logistics - Reverse Logistics is a rather general term. In its broadest sense, reverse logistics stands for all operations related to the reuse of products and materials. The management of these operations can be referred to as Product Recovery Management (PRM). PRM is concerned with the care of products and materials after they have been used. Some of these activities are, to some extent, similar to those occurring in the case of internal returns of defective items due to unreliable production processes. Reverse logistics refers however to all logistics activities the collection, disassembly and processing of used products, product parts and/or materials in order to ensure a sustainable (environmentally-friendly) recovery.

RF - see Radio Frequency

RFI - see Request for Information

RFID - see Radio Frequency Identificatrion

RFP - See Request for Proposal

RFQ - See Request for Quote
RGA - Return Goods Authorization. See: Return Material Authorization

Rich Media - An Internet advertising term for a Web page ad that uses advanced technology such as streaming video, downloaded applet (programs) that interact instantly with the user, and ads that change when the user's mouse passes over it.

DEFINITIONS

Rich Text Format (RTF) - A method of encoding text formatting and document structure using the ASCII character set. By convention, RTF files have an .rtf filename extension.

Rigging - Specialized equipment, such as cranes, heavy-duty forklifts and other tools that are necessary to move heavy and complex items.

Right of eminent domain - A concept that permits the purchase of land needed for transportation right-of-way in a court of law; used by railroads and pipelines.

Risk pooling - The process of reducing the risk among customers by pooling stock in centralized warehouses. Statistically speaking, when one customer demands a lot of a particular product, another customer demands only a little of the same product. The total inventory to maintain the customer service level is smaller, on average, with a centralized warehouse because the risk of a product stockout is pooled across all the customers.

RM - see Raw Materials

RMA - see Return Material Authorization

RO - see Return of Investment

ROA - see Return on Assets

ROF - see Return on owner's equity

ROI - see Return on investment

Roll on-roll-off (RO-RO) - A type of ship designed to permit cargo to be driven on at origin and off at destination; used extensively for the movement of automobiles.

Roll-out - Referring to new store fixtures that are to be distributed throughout the country from one or more origin's.

Root Cause Analysis - Analytical methods to determine the core problem(s) of an organization, process, product, market, etc.

RosettaNet - Consortium of major Information Technology, Electronic Components, Semiconductor Manufacturing, Telecommunications and Logistics companies working to create and implement industry-wide, open e-business process standards. These standards form a common e-business language, aligning processes between supply chain partners on a global basis. RosettaNet is a subsidiary of the Uniform Code Council

Routing Accuracy - When specified activities conform to administrative specifications, and specified resource consumptions (both man and machine) are detailed according to administrative specifications and are within ten percent of actual requirements.

Routing or Routing Guide - (1) Process of determining how shipment will move between origin and destination. Routing information includes designation of carrier(s) involved, actual route of carrier, and estimated time enroute.(2) Right of shipper to determine carriers, routes and points for transfer shipments.(3) In manufacturing this is the document which defines a process of steps used to manufacture and/or assemble a product.

RPA - see Return Product Authorization

RTF - See Rich Text Format

RTV - see Return to Vendor

Rule of eight - Before the Motor Carrier Act of 1980, contract carriers requesting authority were restricted to eight shippers under contract. The number of shippers has been deleted as a consideration for granting a contract carrier permit.

Rule of rate making - A regulatory provision directing the regulatory agencies to consider the earnings necessary for a carrier to provide adequate transportation.

— S —

S&OP - See Sales and Operations Planning.

Safety Stock (SS) - The inventory a company holds above normal needs as a buffer against delays in receipt of supply or changes in customer demand.

Salable Goods - A part or assembly authorized for sale to final customers through the marketing function.

Sales and Operations Planning (S&OP) - A strategic planning process that reconciles conflicting business objectives and plans future supply chain actions. S&OP Planning usually involves various business functions such as sales, operations and finance to agree on a single plan/forecast that can be used to drive the entire business.

Sales Mix - The proportion of individual product-type sales volumes that make up the total sales volume.

Sales Plan - A time-phased statement of expected customer orders anticipated to be received (incoming sales, not outgoing shipments) for each major product family or item. It represents sales and marketing management's commitment to take all reasonable steps necessary to achieve this level of actual customer orders. The sales plan is a necessary input to the production planning process (or sales and operations planning process). It is expressed in units identical to those used for the production plan (as well as in sales dollars). Also see: Aggregate planning, Production Planning, Sales and Operations Planning

Sales Planning - The process of determining the overall sales plan to best support customer needs and operations capabilities while meeting general business objectives of profitability, productivity, competitive customer lead times, and so on, as expressed in the overall business plan. Also see: Production Planning, Sales and Operations Planning

Salvage material - Unused material that has a market value and can be sold.

Saw-Tooth Diagram - A quantity-versus-time graphic representation of the order point/order quantity inventory system showing inventory being received and then used up and reordered.

SBT - See Scan-Based Trading

Scalability - (1) How quickly and efficiently a company can ramp up to meet demand. See also uptime production flexibility.(2) How well a solution to some problem will work when the size of the problem increases. The economies to scale don't really kick in until you reach the critical mass, then revenues start to increase exponentially.

Scan - A computer term referring to the action of scanning bar codes or RF tags.

Scan-Based Trading (SBT) - Scan-based trading is a method of using Point of Sale data from scanners and retail checkout to initiate invoicing between a manufacturer and retailer, as well as generate re-supply orders.

Scanlon Plan - A system of group incentives on a companywide or plantwide basis that sets up one measure that reflects the results of all efforts. The Scanlon plan originated in the 1930's by Joe Scanlon and MIT. The universal standard is the ratio of labor costs to sales value added by production. If there is an increase in production sales value with no change in labor costs, productivity has increased while unit cost has decreased.

SCE - see Supply Chain Execution

DEFINITIONS

SCEM - see Supply Chain Event Management

Scenario Planning - A form of planning in which likely sets of relevant circumstances are identified in advance, and used to assess the impact of alternative actions.

SCI - see Supply Chain Integration

SCM - see Supply Chain Management

SCOR - see Supply Chain Operations Reference Model

Scorecard - A performance measurement tool used to capture a summary of the key performance indicators (KPIs)/metrics of a company. Metrics dashboards/scorecards should be easy to read and usually have "red, yellow, green" indicators to flag when the company is not meeting its targets for its metrics. Ideally, a dashboard/scorecard should be cross-functional in nature and include both financial and non-financial measures. In addition, scorecards should be reviewed regularly at least on a monthly basis and weekly in key functions such as manufacturing and distribution where activities are critical to the success of a company. The dashboard/scorecards philosophy can also be applied to external supply chain partners such as suppliers to ensure that suppliers' objectives and practices align. Synonym: Dashboard.

Scrap material - Unusable material that has no market value.

Seasonality - A repetitive pattern of demand from year to year (or other repeating time interval) with some periods considerably higher than others. Seasonality explains the fluctuation in demand for various recreational products which are used during different seasons. Also see: Base Series

Seawaybill - A type of bill of lading used for port-to-port or combined transport carriage. A waybill is identical to a negotiable bill of lading except that it is not a document of title. There are no originals issued for this type of document. In some jurisdictions, such as the USA, a waybill is deemed the equivalent of a (straight) consigned bill of lading. See also Waybill.

Secondary highways - Highways that serve primarily rural areas.

Secure Electronic Transaction (SET) - In e-commerce, a system for guaranteeing the security of financial transactions conducted over the Internet.

Segmentation - The process of dividing into separate pieces or segments. Customer or market segmentation is the process of dividing a company's customer base or markets into different segments that share similar characteristics.

Self Billing - A transportation industry strategy which prescribes that a carrier will accept payment based on the tender document provided by the shipper.

Self Correcting - A computer term for an online process that validates data and won't allow the data to enter the system unless all errors are corrected.

Sell In - Units which are sold to retail stores by the manufacturer or distributor for re-sale to consumers. The period of time in a Product Life Cycle where the manufacture works with it's resellers to market and build inventory for sale. Also see: Sell Through

Sell Through - Units sold from retail stores to customers. The point in a Product Life Cycle where initial consumption rates are developed and demand established. Also see: Sell In

Selling, General and Administrative (SG&A) Expenses - Includes marketing, communication, customer service, sales salaries and commissions, occupancy expenses, unallocated overhead, etc. Excludes interest on debt, domestic or foreign income taxes, depreciation and amortization, extraordinary items, equity gains or losses,

133

gain or loss from discontinued operations and extraordinary items.

Separable cost - A cost that can be directly assignable to a particular segment of the business.

Serial Number - A unique number assigned for identification to a single piece that will never be repeated for similar pieces. Serial numbers are usually applied by the manufacturer but can be applied at other points, including by the distributor or wholesaler. Serial numbers can be used to support traceability and warranty programs.

Service Agreement - Private contracts between one or more carriers and one or more shippers to transport cargo between specified points under terms and conditions of carriage agreed and listed in the contract. It often allows for particular rates based on volume over a specified period of time. Also commonly known as a service contract.

Service Level - A measure (usually expressed as a percentage) of satisfying demand through inventory or by the current production schedule in time to satisfy the customer's requested delivery dates and quantities.

Service Oriented Architecture (SOA) - Provides a blueprint for services-based, enterprise-scale business solutions that are adaptable, flexible, and open, for lower total cost of ownership. Applications can be created on top of existing enterprise applications following the Service Oriented Architecture blueprint to increase the value of those systems and extend automation to new processes.

Service Parts Revenue - The sum of the value of sales made to external customers and the transfer price valuation of sales within the company of repair or replacement parts and supplies, net of all discounts, coupons, allowances, and rebates.

Service Provider - A preferred company that has been contracted to provide transportation, warehousing, packing or installation services. Also known as an agent.

SET - see Secure Electronic Transaction

Set Point - Specific temperature that a refrigerated container has been set to keep. Ideally, the set point and the actual temperature should be identical throughout the voyage.

Setup costs - The costs incurred in staging the production line to produce a different item

Shared Services - Consolidation of a company's back-office processes to form a spinout (or a separate "shared services" unit, to be run like a separate business), providing services to the parent company and, sometimes, to external customers. Shared services typically lower overall cost due to the consolidation, and may improve support as a result of focus.

Shareholder Value - Combination of profitability (revenue and costs) and invested capital (working capital and fixed capital).

Shelf life - The amount of time an item may be held in inventory before it becomes unusable. Shelf life is a consideration for food and drugs which deteriorate over time, and for high tech products which become obsolete quickly.

Shewhart Cycle - See Plan-Do-Check-Action

Shingo's Seven Wastes - Shigeo Shingo, a pioneer in the Japanese Just-in-Time philosophy, identified seven barriers to improving manufacturing. They are the waste of overproduction, waste of waiting, waste of transportation, waste of stocks, waste of motion, waste of making defects, and waste of the processing itself.

Ship agent - A liner company or tramp ship operator representative who facilitates ship arrival, clearance, loading and unloading, and fee payment while at a specific port.

DEFINITIONS

Ship broker - A firm that serves as a go-between for the tramp ship owner and the chartering consignor or consignee.

Shipper - (1) Person who consigns something (e.g. the goods of an individual shipment). (2). Legal entity or person named on the bill of lading or waybill as shipper and/or who (or in whose name or on whose behalf) a contract of carriage has been concluded with a carrier. (3). Also known as consignor.

Shipper Packed - Contents of containers as loaded (stuffed), stowed (packed/braced), weighed and/or counted by or for the shipper, usually a CY load.

Shipper's agent - A firm that acts primarily to match up small shipments, especially single-traffic piggyback loads to permit use of twin-trailer piggyback rates.

Shipper's association - A nonprofit, cooperative consolidator and distributor of shipments owned or shipped by member firms; acts in much the same was as for-profit freight forwarders.

Shipper's Load & Count (SL&C) - Shipments loaded and sealed by shippers and not checked or verified by the carriers.

Shipping - The function that performs the tasks for outgoing shipments. It can include packaging, marking, weighing, and loading a shipment.

Shipping Lane - A predetermined, mapped route on the ocean that commercial vessels tend to follow between ports. This helps ships avoid hazardous areas. In general transportation, the logical route between the point of shipment and the point of delivery used to analyze the volume of shipment between two points.

Shipping Manifest - A document that lists items, piece count, total weight and the destinations that is included in a shipment. A manifest usually covers an entire load regardless of whether the load is to be delivered to a single destination or many destinations.

Shipping Order - Equivalent of booking and contract of carriage evidencing the agreement to transport goods.

Ship's Chandlers - Suppliers of various items to the vessel.

Shop Calendar - See Manufacturing Calendar

Shop Floor Production Control Systems - The systems that assign priority to each shop order, maintaining work-in-process quantity information, providing actual output data for capacity control purposes and providing quantity by location by shop order for work-in-process inventory and accounting purposes.

Short Landed - Cargo volume count (at delivery destination) less than originally shipped.

Short Shipment - Piece of freight missing from shipment as stipulated by documents on hand.

Short Shipped - Cargo missing a vessel that it was originally intended for.

Shortage - When the quantity received is less than that shown on the waybill.

Short-haul discrimination - Charging more for a shorter haul than for a longer haul over the same route, in the same direction, and for the same commodity.

Shrink Wrap - A layer of plastic film encasing a palletized load of merchandise.

Shrinkage - Reductions of actual quantities of items in stock, in process, or in transit. The loss may be caused by scrap, theft, deterioration, evaporation, etc.

SIC - see Standard Industrial Classification

Glossary of terms in Logistics & Shipping

Sigma - A Greek letter commonly used to designate the standard deviation of a population.

Simulation - A mathematical technique for testing the performance of a system due to uncertain inputs and/or uncertain system configuration options. Simulation produces probability distributions for the behavior (outputs) of a system. A company may build a simulation model of its build plan process to evaluate the performance of the build plan under multiple scenarios on product demand.

Single source leasing - Leasing both the truck and driver from one source.

Single sourcing - When an organization deliberately chooses to use one supplier to provide a product or service, even though there are other suppliers available.

Single-Period Inventory Models - Inventory models used to define economical or profit maximizing lot-size quantities when an item is ordered or produced only once, e.g., newspapers, calendars, tax guides, greeting cards, or periodicals, while facing uncertain demands.

SIT - see Storage in Transit

Six-Sigma Quality - A term used generally to indicate that a process is well controlled, i.e., tolerance limits are \'b16 sigma \{3.4 defects per million events) from the centerline in a control chart. The term is usually associated with Motorola, which named one of its key operational initiatives Six-Sigma Quality.

Skills Matrix - A visible means of displaying people's skill levels in various tasks. Used in a team environment to identify the skills required by the team and which team members have those skills.

SKU - see Stock Keeping Unit

SL&C - see Shipper's Load & Count

Sleeper team - The use or two drivers to operate a truck equipped with a sleeper berth; while one driver sleeps in the berth to accumulate the mandatory off-duty time, the other driver operates the vehicle.

Slip seat operation - A term used to describe a motor carrier relay terminal operation where one driver is substituted for another who has accumulated the maximum driving time hours.

Slip sheet - Similar to a pallet, the slip sheet, which is made of cardboard or plastic, is used to facilitate movement of unitized loads.

Slot Charter - A carrier's chartering of slots/spaces on other carrier's vessels.

Slotting - Placement of products within a warehouse facility, increasing picking efficiency and reducing warehouse-handling costs through optimizing product location and balancing the workload.

Slurry - Dry commodities that are made into a liquid form by the addition of water or other fluids to permit movement by pipeline.

Small Group Improvement Activity - An organizational technique for involving employees in continuous improvement activities. Also see: Quality Circle

SMART - see Specific, Measurable, Achievable, Realistic, Time-Based

Smart and Secure Trade Lanes (SST) - Private initiative of the Strategic Council on Security Technology, an assembly of executives from port operators, major logistics technology providers, transportation consultancies, and former generals and public officials. Aims to enhance the safety, security and efficiency of cargo containers and their contents moving through the global supply chain into U.S. ports.

Smart label - A label that has an RFID tag integrated into it.

SMDG - User Group for Shipping Lines and Container Terminals. SMDG develops and promotes UN/EDIFACT EDI messages for the maritime industry and is an official Pan European User Group recognised by the UN/EDIFACT Board.

SOA - see Service Oriented Architecture

Society of Logistics Engineers - A professional association engaged in the advancement of logistics technology and management.

Sole sourcing - When there is only one supplier for a product or service, and no alternate suppliers are available.

SOP - see Standard Operationg Procedure

Sortation - Separating items (parcels, boxes, cartons, parts, etc.) according to their intended destination within a plant or for transit.

SOW - see Statement of Work

Spam - A computer industry term referring to the Act of sending identical and irrelevant postings to many different newsgroups or mailing lists. Usually this posting is something that has nothing to do with the particular topic of a newsgroup or of no real interest to the person on the mailing list.

SPC - see Statistical Process Control

Special Customs Invoice - An official form usually required by U.S. Customs if the rate of duty is based upon the value, and the value of the shipment exceeds USD 500. This document is usually prepared by the foreign exporter or his forwarder and is used by customs in determining the value of the shipment. The exporter or his agent must attest to the authenticity of the data furnished.

Special Rate - Rate established for a specified commodity for a specific period of time.

Special-commodities carrier - A common carrier trucking company that has authority to haul a special commodity; there are 16 special commodities, such as household goods, petroleum products, and hazardous materials.

Special-commodity warehouses - A warehouse that is used to store products that require unique types of facilities, such as grain (elevator), liquid (tank), and tobacco (barn).

Specific, Measurable, Achievable, Realistic, Time-Based (SMART) - A shorthand description of a way of setting goals and targets for individuals and teams.

Splash Page - A "first" or "front" page that you often see on some websites, usually containing a "click-through" logo or message, or a fancy Flash presentation, announcing that you have arrived. The main content and navigation on the site lie "behind" this page (a.k.a. the homepage or "welcome page").

Split case order picking - A process used to fill orders for quantities less than a full case thereby requiring ordered items to be picked from a case or some similar container.

Split Delivery - A method by which a larger quantity is ordered on a purchase order to secure a lower price, but delivery is divided into smaller quantities and spread out over several dates to control inventory investment, save storage space, etc.

Spot - To move a trailer or boxcar into place for loading or unloading.

Spot Demand - Demand, having a short lead time that is difficult to estimate. Usually supply for this demand is provided at a premium price. An example of spot demand would be when there's a spiked demand for building materials as a result of a hurricane.

Spur track - A railroad track that connects a company's plant or warehouse with the railroad's track; the cost of the spur track and its maintenance is borne by the user.

SRT - see Scan-Based Trading

SS - Steamship.

SST - see Smart and Secure Trade Lanes

ST - 1 Short Ton = 2 000 lbs.

Stable Demand - Products for which demand does not fluctuate widely at specific points during the year.

Staff functions - The support activities of planning and analysis provided to assist line managers with daily operations. Logistics staff functions include location analysis, system design, cost analysis, and planning.

Staging - (1) Pulling material for an order from inventory before the material is required. Staging is a means to ensure that all required materials are and will be available for use at time of assembly. The downside to staging is that it creates additional WIP inventory and reduces flexibility.(2) Placing trailers. Also see: Accumulation Bin

Stakeholders - People with a vested interest in a company, including managers, employees, stockholders, customers, suppliers, and others.

Standard Components - Components (parts) of a product, for which there is an abundance of suppliers. Not difficult to produce. An example would be a power cord for a computer.

Standard Cost Accounting System - A cost accounting system that uses cost units determined before production for estimating the cost of an order or product. For management control purposes, the standards are compared to actual costs, and variances are computed.

Standard Deviation/Variance - Measures of dispersion for a probability distribution. The variance is the average squared difference of a distribution from the distribution's mean (average) value. The standard deviation is defined mathematically as the square root of the variance, and is thereby expressed in the same units as the random variable that's described by the probability distribution. A distribution that varies widely about its mean value will have a larger standard deviation/variance than a distribution with less variation about its mean value.

Standard Industrial Classification (SIC) - Classification codes that are used to categorize companies into industry groupings.

Standard Operationg Procedure (SOP) - Instructions and methods used for a specific process or situation. They document the normal or accepted methodology and help form the basis for conformance evaluation

Standing Order - See Blanket Purchase Order

Start Manufacture to Order Complete Manufacture - Average lead-time from the time manufacturing begins to the time end products are ready for shipment, including the following sub-elements: order configuration verification, production scheduling, time to release order to manufacturing or distribution, and build or configure time. (An element of Order Fulfillment Lead Time) Note: Determined separately for Make-to-Order, Configure/Package-to-Order, and Engineer-to-Order products. Does not apply to Make-to-Stock products.

Statement of Work (SOW) - A description of products to be supplied under a contract. A good practice is for companies to have SOWs in place with their trading partners especially for all top suppliers. In projection management, the first project planning document that should be prepared. It describes the purpose, history, deliverables, and measurable success indicators for a project. It captures the support required from the customer and identifies contingency plans for events that could throw the project off course. Because the project must be sold to management, staff, and review groups, the statement of work should be a persuasive document.

Statistical Process Control (SPC) - A visual means of measuring and plotting process and product variation. Results are used to adjust variables and maintain product quality.

STC - Abbreviation for Said To Contain.

Steamship conferences - Collective rate-making bodies for liner water carriers.

Stevedore - Terminal operator who is designated to facilitate the operation of loading and discharging vessels and various terminal activities. Also known as longshoreman.

Stickering - Placing customer-specific stickers on boxes of product. An example would be where Wal-Mart has a request for their own product codes to be applied to retail boxes prior to shipment.

Stochastic Models - Models where uncertainty is explicitly considered in the analysis.

Stock Keeping Unit (SKU) - A category of unit with unique combination of form, fit, and function (i.e. unique components held in stock). To illustrate: If two items are indistinguishable to the customer, or if any distinguishing characteristics visible to the customer are not important to the customer, so that the customer believes the two items to be the same, these two items are part of the same SKU. As a further illustration consider a computer company that allows customers to configure a product from a standard catalogue components, choosing from three keyboards, three monitors, and three CPUs. Customers may also individually buy keyboards, monitors, and CPUs. If the stock were held at the configuration component level, the company would have nine SKUs. If the company stocks at the component level, as well as at the configured product level, the company would have 36 SKUs. (9 component SKUs + 3*3*3 configured product SKUs. If as part of a promotional campaign the company also specially packaged the products, the company would have a total of 72 SKUs.

Stock Out - A term used to refer to a situation where no stock was available to fill a request from a customer or production order during a pick operation. Stock outs can be costly, including the profit lost for not having the item available for sale, lost goodwill, substitutions. Also referred to Out of Stock (OOS)

Stockchase - Moving shipments through regular channels at an accelerated rate; to take extraordinary action because of an increase in relative priority. Synonym: Expediting.

Stockless purchasing - A practice whereby the buyer negotiates a price for the purchases of annual requirements of MRO items and the seller holds inventory until the buyer places an order for individual items.

Stockout cost - The opportunity cost associated with not having sufficient supply to meet demand.

Storage Charge - Charge for goods held in storage facilities (warehouses) under a fixed agreement for periods of time, and which is not included in other arrangement.

Storage in Transit (SIT) - The temporary warehousing of goods. Items will be inventoried at the assigned warehouse and transported upon request. Additional charges will apply.

Store-Door Delivery - Movement of goods to the consignee's place of business, customarily applied to movement by truck.

Stores - The function associated with the storage and issuing of items that are frequently used.

Glossary of terms in Logistics & Shipping

Straight Truck - Power unit and cargo box permanently attached as a single, non-articulated unit.

Strategic Alliance - Business relationship in which two or more independent organizations cooperate and willingly modify their business objectives and practices to help achieve long-term goals and objectives. Also see: Marquis Partners

Strategic planning - Looking one to five years into the future and designing a logistical system (or systems) to meet the needs of the various businesses in which a company is involved.

Strategic Sourcing - The process of determining long-term supply requirements, finding sources to fulfill those needs, selecting suppliers to provide the services, negotiating the purchase agreements and managing the suppliers' performance. Focuses on developing the most effective relationships with the right suppliers, to ensure that the right price is paid and that lifetime product costs are minimized. It also assesses whether services or processes would provide better value if they were outsourced to specialist organizations.

Strategic variables - The variables that effect change in the environment and logistics strategy. The major strategic variables include economics, population, energy, and government.

Strategy - A specific action to achieve an objective.

Stratification - The process of arranging markets or customers within segments into different levels based on a classification scheme.

Stratified price levels - Setting product prices at different levels based upon approved and legal justifications. Offering reduced prices for larger volumes of a product is often justified based on lower handling and transportation costs for example.

Stripping - Also known as unstuffing. Physical removal of goods from the (carrier's) container(s).

Subcontracting - Sending production work outside to another manufacturer. This can involve specialized operations such as plating metals, or complete functional operations. Also see: Outsource

Sub-Optimization - Decisions or activities in a part made at the expense of the whole. An example of sub-optimization is where a manufacturing unit schedules production to benefit its cost structure without regard to customer requirements or the effect on other business units.

Substitutability - The ability of a buyer to substitute the products of different sellers.

Sunk Cost - (1) The unrecovered balance of an investment. It is a cost, already paid, that is not relevant to the decision concerning the future that is being made. Capital already invested that for some reason cannot be retrieved. (2) A past cost that has no relevance with respect to future receipts and disbursements of a facility undergoing an economic study. This concept implies that since a past outlay is the same regardless of the alternative selected, it should not influence the choice between alternatives.

Supplemental carrier - A for-hire air carrier subject to economic regulations; the carrier has no time schedule or designated route; service is provided under a charter or contract per plane per trip.

Supplier - (1) A provider of goods or services. Also see: Vendor (2) A seller with whom the buyer does business, as opposed to vendor, which is a generic term referring to all sellers in the marketplace.

Supplier Certification - Certification procedures verifying that a supplier operates, maintains, improves, and documents effective procedures that relate to the customer's requirements. Such requirements can include cost, quality, delivery, flexibility, maintenance, safety, and ISO quality and environmental standards.

Supplier-Owned Inventory - A variant of Vendor-Managed Inventory and Consignment Inventory. In this case the supplier manages the inventory, and owns the stock close to or at the customer location until the point of consumption or usage by the customer.

Supply Chain - (1) Starting with unprocessed raw materials and ending with the final customer using the finished goods, the supply chain links many companies together. (2) The material and informational interchanges in the logistical process stretching from acquisition of raw materials to delivery of finished products to the end user. All vendors, service providers and customers are links in the supply chain. (3) The global network used to deliver products and services from raw materials to end customers through an engineered flow of information, physical distribution, and cash. (4) The material and informational interchanges in the logistical process, reaching from acquisition of raw materials to delivery of finished products to the end user. All vendors, service providers, and customers are links in the supply chain.

Supply chain community - One supply chain consisting of the particular trading partners (including the final customer) for a given product or service. The physical flows, information flows, and financial flows within a supply chain community have both forward and reverse flows.

Supply Chain Design - The determination of how to structure a supply chain. Design decisions include the selection of partners, the location and capacity of warehouse and production facilities, the products, the modes of transportation, and supporting information systems.

Supply Chain Event Management (SCEM) - SCEM is an application that supports control processes for managing events within and between companies. It consists of integrated software functionality that supports five business processes: monitor, notify, simulate, control and measure supply chain activities.

Supply Chain Execution (SCE) - The ability to move the final product out of the warehouse door.

Supply Chain Integration (SCI) - Likely to become a key competitive advantage of selected e-marketplaces. Similar concept to the Back-End Integration, but with greater emphasis on the moving of goods and services.

Supply Chain Inventory Visibility - Software applications that permit monitoring events across a supply chain. These systems track and trace inventory globally on a line-item level and notify the user of significant deviations from plans. Companies are provided with realistic estimates of when material will arrive.

Supply chain management - The practice of the following set of principles: Create net value with supply chain management, build a competitive infrastructure, leverage worldwide logistics, synchronize supply with demand, and measure performance globally.

Supply Chain Management (SCM) - "Supply Chain Management encompasses the planning and management of all activities involved in sourcing and procurement, conversion, and all logistics management activities. Importantly, it also includes coordination and collaboration with channel partners, which can be suppliers, intermediaries, third-party service providers, and customers. In essence, supply chain management integrates supply and demand management within and across companies. Supply Chain Management is an integrating function with primary responsibility for linking major business functions and business processes within and across companies into a cohesive and high-performing business model. It includes all of the logistics management activities noted above, as well as manufacturing operations, and it drives coordination of processes and activities with and across marketing, sales, product design, finance and information technology."

Supply Chain Network Design Systems - The systems employed in optimizing the relationships among the various elements of the supply chain manufacturing plants, distribution centers, points-of-sale, as well as raw materials, relationships among product families, and other factors-to synchronize supply chains at a strategic level.

Supply Chain Operations Reference Model (SCOR) - This is the model developed by the Supply-Chain Council SCC and is built around six major processes: plan, source, make, deliver, return and enable. The aim of the SCOR is to provide a standardized method of measuring supply chain performance and to use a common set of metrics to benchmark against other organizations.

Supply Chain resiliency - A term describing the level of hardening of the supply chain against disasters.

Supply Chain Strategic Planning - The process of analyzing, evaluating, and defining supply chain strategies.

Supply Chain Strategy Planning - The process of process of analyzing, evaluating, defining supply chain strategies, including network design, manufacturing and transportation strategy and inventory policy.

Supply Chain Vulnerability - Of equal importance to Variability, Velocity and Volume in the elements of the Supply Chain. The term evaluates the supply chain based on the level of acceptance of the five steps of disaster logistics being planning, detection, mitigation, response and recovery.

Supply Chain-Related Finance and Planning Cost Element - One of the elements comprising a company's total supply-chain management costs. These costs consist of the following: (1) Supply-Chain Finance Costs: Costs associated with paying invoices, auditing physical counts, performing inventory accounting, and collecting accounts receivable. Does NOT include customer invoicing/ accounting costs (see Order Management Costs). (2) Demand/Supply Planning Costs: Costs associated with forecasting, developing finished goods, intermediate, subassembly or end item inventory plans, and coordinating Demand/Supply

Supply Chain-Related IT Costs - Information Technology (IT) costs (in US dollars) associated with major supply-chain management processes as described below. These costs should include: Development costs (costs incurred in process reengineering, planning, software development, installation, implementation, and training associated with new and/or upgraded architecture, infrastructure, and systems to support the described supply-chain management processes), Execution costs (operating costs to support supply-chain process users, including computer and network operations, EDI and telecommunications services, and amortization/depreciation of hardware, Maintenance costs (costs incurred in problem resolution, troubleshooting, repair, and routine maintenance associated with installed hardware and software for described supply-chain management processes. Include costs associated with data base administration, systems configuration control, release planning and management.

Supply Planning - The process of identifying, prioritizing, and aggregating, as a whole with constituent parts, all sources of supply that are required and add value in the supply chain of a product or service at the appropriate level, horizon and interval.

Supply Planning Systems - The process of identifying, prioritizing, and aggregating, as a whole with constituent parts, all sources of supply that are required and add value in the supply chain of a product or service at the appropriate level, horizon and interval.

Supply Warehouse - A warehouse that stores raw materials. Goods from different suppliers are picked, sorted, staged, or sequenced at the warehouse to assemble plant orders.

Support Costs - Costs of activities not directly associated with producing or delivering products or services. Examples are the costs of information systems, process engineering and purchasing. Also see: Indirect Cost

Supportive Project Management - Managing specific activities for relocating existing customer environments into the new locations, including management of all vendors in the de-installation and re-installation of their equipment; managing/providing the transportation for the overall effort; managing the documentation (site assessment, transportation schedules, implementation plan, and so on); and providing on-site supervision for each relocation phase. See Project Management.

Surcharge - An add-on charge to the applicable charges; motor carriers have a fuel surcharge, and railroads can apply a surcharge to any joint rate that does not yield 110% of variable cost.

Surrogate [item] Driver - A substitute for the ideal driver, but is closely correlated to the ideal driver, where [item] is Resource, Activity, Cost Object. A surrogate driver is used to significantly reduce the cost of measurement while not significantly reducing accuracy. For example, the number of production runs is not descriptive of the material disbursing activity, but the number of production runs may be used as an activity driver if material disbursements correlate well with the number of production runs.

Sustaining Activity - An activity that benefits an organizational unit as a whole, but not any specific cost object.

SWAS - Store-Within-A-Store.

Swing Gear - Items or equipment used during a transition period to limit downtime and increase availability during a relocation or migration event.

Switch engine - A railroad engine that is used to move rail cars short distances within a terminal and plant.

Switching company - A railroad that moves rail cars short distances; switching companies connect two mainline railroads to facilitate through movement of shipments.

SWOT - See SWOT Analysis

SWOT Analysis - An analysis of the strengths, weaknesses, opportunities, and threats of and to an organization. SWOT analysis is useful in developing strategy.

SWOT Analysis (SWOT) - a strategic planning tool used to evaluate the Strengths, Weaknesses, Opportunities, and Threats involved in a project or in a business venture. Strengths and weaknesses are internal to an organization. Opportunities and threats originate from outside the organization. A SWOT analysis, usually performed early in the project development process, helps organizations evaluate the environmental factors and internal situation facing a project.

Synchronization - The concept that all supply chain functions are integrated and interact in real time; when changes are made to one area, the effect is automatically reflected throughout the supply chain.

Syntax - The grammar or rules which define the structure of the EDI standard

System - A set of interacting elements, variables, parts, or objects that are functionally related to each other and form a coherent group.

Systems concept - A decision-making strategy that emphasizes overall system efficiency rather than the efficiency of the individual part of the system.

Tact Time - See Takt Time

Tactical Planning - The process of developing a set of tactical plans (e.g., production plan, sales plan, marketing plan, and so on). Two approaches to tactical planning exist for linking tactical plans to strategic plans--production planning and sales and operations planning. See: Sales and operational planning, strategic planning.

Tag Number - The number used in the hospitality commerce to identify a specific product that is related to the blueprints or layout plans. Required for maintaining accurate and updated inventory process.

Taguchi Method - A concept of off-line quality control methods conducted at the product and process design stages in the product development cycle. This concept, expressed by Genichi Taguchi, encompasses three phases of product design: system design, parameter design, and tolerance design. The goal is to reduce quality loss by reducing the variability of the product's characteristics during the parameter phase of product development.

Takt Time - Sets the pace of production to match the rate of customer demand and becomes the heartbeat of any lean production system. It is computed as the available production time divided by the rate of customer demand. For example, assume demand is 10,000 units per month, or 500 units per day, and planned available capacity is 420 minutes per day. The takt time = 420 minutes per day/ 500 units per day = 0.84 minutes per unit. This takt time means that a unit should be planned to exit the production system on average every 0.84 minutes.

Tally sheet - A printed form on which companies record, by making an appropriate mark, the number of items they receive or ship. In many operations, tally sheets become a part of the permanent inventory records.

Tandem - A truck that has two drive axles or a trailer that has two axles.

Tank cars - Rail cars that are designed to haul bulk liquids or gas commodities.

Tapering rate - A rate that increases with distance but not in direct proportion to the distance the commodity is shipped.

Tare Weight - The weight of a substance, obtained by deducting the weight of the empty container from the gross weight of the full container.

Target Costing - A target cost is calculated by subtracting a desired profit margin from an estimated or a market-based price to arrive at a desired production, engineering, or marketing cost. This may not be the initial production cost, but one expected to be achieved during the mature production stage. Target costing is a method used in the analysis of product design that involves estimating a target cost and then designing the product/service to meet that cost. Also see: Value Analysis

Tariff - Schedule of transportation costs.

Task interleaving - A method of combining warehouse picking and putaway. Warehouse Management Systems (WMS) use logic to direct a lift truck operator to put away a pallet en route to the next pick.

Tasks - The breakdown of the work in an activity into smaller elements.

TCO - see Total Cost of Ownership

Technical Components - Component (part) of a product for which there is a limited number of suppliers. These parts are hard to make, and require much more lead time and expertise on the part of the supplier to produce than standard components do.

Temporary authority - The ICC may grant a temporary operating authority as a common carrier for up to 270 days.

Ten Principles - A principle is a general rule, fundamental, or other statement of an observed truth. Over time certain fundamental truths of material handling have been found to exist. The "principles" of material handling are often useful in analyzing, planning and managing material handling activities and systems. At the very least they form a basic foundation upon which one can begin building expertise in material handling. These principles, that serve as a starting point to identifying potential problems and assessing need, are : Planning, Standardization, Work, Ergonomic, Unit Load, Space Utilization, System, Automation, Environment, Life Cycle Cost

Tender - The document which describes a business transaction to be performed.

Terminal delivery allowance - A reduced rate offered in return for the shipper of consignee tendering or picking up the freight at the carrier's terminal

Terms and conditions (T's & C's) - All the provisions and agreements of a contract.

TEU - see Twenty-foot Equivalent Unit

Theoretical Cycle Time - The back-to-back process time required for a single unit to complete all stages of a process without waiting, stoppage, or time lost due to error.

Theory of Constraints (TOC) - A production management theory which dictates that volume is controlled by a series of constraints related to work center capacity, component availability, finance, etc. Total throughput cannot exceed the capacity of the smallest constraint, and any inventory buffers

or excess capacity at non-related work centers is waste.

Third Party Logistics Provider (3PL) - A firm that provides one or multiple logistic related services for use by customers. They can facilitate the movement of parts and materials from suppliers to manufacturers, and finished products from manufacturers, and finished products from manufacturers to distributors and retailers. Among the services they provide are transportation, warehousing, receiving, cross docking, inventory management, packaging, and freight forwarding.

Third-Party Warehousing - The outsourcing of the warehousing function by the seller of the goods.

Three-layer framework - A basic structure and operational activity of a company; the three layers include operational systems, control and administrative management, and master planning.

Threshold - A pick-up or delivery service to the door only. No unpacking or placement of goods is performed.

Throughput - A measure of warehousing output volume (weight, number of units). Also, the total amount of units received plus the total amount of units shipped, divided by two.

Time Based Order System - See Fixed Reorder Cycle Inventory Model

Time Bucket - A number of days of data summarized into a columnar display. A weekly time bucket would contain all of the relevant data for an entire week. Weekly time buckets are considered to be the largest possible (at least in the near and medium term) to permit effective MRP.

Time Fence - A policy or guideline established to note where various restrictions or changes in operating procedures take place. For example, changes to the master

145

production schedule can be accomplished easily beyond the cumulative lead time, while changes inside the cumulative lead time become increasingly more difficult to a point where changes should be resisted. Time fences can be used to define these points.

Time utility - A value created in a product by having the product available at the time desired. Transportation and warehousing create time utility.

Time/service rate - A rail rate that is based upon transit time.

Time-Definite Services - Delivery is guaranteed on a specific day or at a certain time of the day.

Time-Stop - An additional service for product that requires a specific pick-up or delivery date and or time.

Timetables - Time schedules of departures and arrivals by origin and destination; typically used for passenger transportation by air, bus, and rail.

Time-to-Product - The total time required to receive, fill, and deliver an order for an existing product to a customer, timed from the moment that the customer places the order until the customer receives the product.

TL - see Truckload

TMS - see Transportation Management System

TOC - see Theory of Constraints

TOFC - see Trailer on a Flatcar

Ton-mile - A measure of output for freight transportation; it reflects the weight of the shipment and the distance it is hauled; a multiplication of tons hauled and distance traveled.

Total Annual Material Receipts - The dollar amount associated with all direct materials received from Jan 1 to Dec 31.

Total Annual Sales - Total Annual Sales are Total Product Revenue plus post-delivery revenues (e.g., maintenance and repair of equipment, system integration) royalties, sales of other services, spare parts revenue, and rental/lease revenues.

Total Average Inventory - Average normal use stock, plus average lead stock, plus safety stock.

Total Cost Analysis - A decision-making approach that considers minimization of total costs and recognizes the interrelationship among system variables such as transportation, warehousing, inventory, and customer service.

Total Cost Curve - (1) In cost-volume-profit (breakeven) analysis, the total cost curve is composed of total fixed and variable costs per unit multiplied by the number of units provided. Breakeven quantity occurs where the total cost curve and total sales revenue curve intersect. See: Break-even chart, Break-even point.(2) In inventory theory, the total cost curve for an inventory item is the sum of the costs of acquiring and carrying the item. Also see: Economic Order Quantity

Total Cost of Ownership (TCO) - Total cost of a computer asset throughout its lifecycle, from acquisition to disposal. TCO is the combined hard and soft costs of owning networked information assets. 'Hard' costs include items such as the purchase price of the asset, implementation fees, upgrades, maintenance contracts, support contracts, and disposal costs, license fees that may or may not be upfront or charged annually. These costs are considered 'hard costs' because they are tangible and easily accounted for.

Total Cumulative Manufacture Cycle Time - The average time between commencement of upstream processing and completion of final packaging for shipment operations as well as release approval for shipment. Do not include WIP storage time. Calculation: [Average

Total Inventory Days of Supply - Total gross value of inventory at standard cost before reserves for excess and obsolescence. Includes only inventory that is on the books and currently owned by the business entity. Future liabilities such as consignments from suppliers are not included. Calculation: [5 Point Annual Average Gross Inventory] / [Cost of Good Sold/365]

Total Make Cycle Time - The average total processing time between commencement of upstream processing and completion of all manufacturing process steps up to, but NOT including, packaging and labeling operations (i.e. from start of manufacturing to final formulated product ready for primary packaging). Do not include hold or test and release times. Calculation: [Average

Total Package and Label Cycle Time - The average total processing time between the commencement of the primary packaging and labeling steps to completion of the final packaging steps for shipment. Calculation: [Average

Total Product Revenue - The total value of sales made to external customers plus the transfer price valuation of intra-company shipments, net of all discounts, coupons, allowances, and rebates. Includes only the intra-company revenue for product transferring out of an entity, installation services if these services are sold bundled with end products, and recognized leases to customers initiated during the same period as revenue shipments, with revenue credited at the average selling price. Note: Total Product Revenue excludes post-delivery revenues (maintenance and repair of equipment, system integration), royalties, sales of other services, spare parts revenue, and rental/lease revenues.

Total Productive Maintenance (TPM) - Team based maintenance process designed to maximize machine availability and performance and product quality.

Total quality management (TQM) - A management approach in which managers constantly communicate with organizational stakeholders to emphasize the importance of continuous quality improvement.

Total Sourcing Lead Time - Cumulative lead time (total average combined inside-plant planning, supplier lead time [external or internal], receiving, handling, etc., from demand identification at the factory until the materials are available in the production facility) required to source 95% of the dollar value (per unit) of raw materials from internal and external suppliers.

Total Supply Chain Response Time - The time it takes to rebalance the entire supply chain after determining a change in market demand. Also, a measure of a supply chain's ability to change rapidly in response to marketplace changes. Calculation: [Forecast Cycle Time] + [Re-plan Cycle Time] + [Intra-Manufacturing Re-plan Cycle Time] + [Cumulative Source/Make Cycle Time] + [Order Fulfillment Lead Time]

Total Supply-Chain Management Cost - Total cost to manage order processing, acquire materials, manage inventory, and manage supply-chain finance, planning, and IT costs, as represented as a percent of revenue. Accurate assignment of IT-related cost is challenging. It can be done using Activity-Based-Costing methods, or based on more traditional approaches. Allocation based on user counts, transaction counts, or departmental headcounts are reasonable approaches. The emphasis should be on capturing all costs, whether incurred in the entity completing the survey or incurred in a supporting organization on behalf of the entity. Reasonable estimates founded in data were accepted as a means to assess overall performance. All estimates reflected fully burdened actuals inclusive of salary, benefits, space and facilities, and general and administrative allocations. Calculation: [Order

Management Costs + Material Acquisition Costs + Inventory Carrying Costs + Supply-Chain-Related Finance and Planning Costs + Total Supply-Chain-Related IT Costs] / [Total Product Revenue] (Please see individual component categories for component detail and calculations)

Total Test and Release Cycle Time - The average total test and release time for all tests, documentation reviews, and batch approval processes performed from start of manufacturing to release of final packaged product for shipment. Calculation: [Average

Toto authority - A private motor carrier receiving operating authority as a common carrier to haul freight for the public over the private carrier's backhaul; this type of authority was granted to the Toto Company in 1978

Touch Labor - The labor that adds value to the product - assemblers, welders etc. This does not include indirect resources such as material handlers (mover and stage product, mechanical and electrical technicians responsible for maintaining equipment.

TPM - see Total Productive Maintenance

TQM - see Total quality management

Traceability - (1) The attribute allowing the ongoing location of a shipment to be determined. (2) The registering and tracking of parts, processes, and materials used in production, by lot or serial number.

Tracing - (1) Determining where a shipment is during the course of a move. (2) The practice of relating resources, activities and cost objects using the drivers underlying their cost causal relationships. The purpose of tracing is to observe and understand how costs are arising in the normal course of business operations. Synonym: Assignment.

Tracking and Tracing - Monitoring and recording shipment movements from origin to destination.

Tracking Signal - The ratio of the cumulative algebraic sum of the deviations between the forecasts and the actual values to the mean absolute deviation. Used to signal when the validity of the forecasting model might be in doubt.

Tractor - Motor truck for towing a trailer.

Trading Partner - Companies that do business with each other via EDI (e.g., send and receive business documents, such as purchase orders).

Trading Partner Agreement - The written contract that spells out agreed upon terms between EDI trading partners.

Trading partners - Organizations a company does business with.

Traffic - A department or function charged with the responsibility for arranging the most economic classification and method of shipment for both incoming and outgoing materials and products.

Traffic Management - The management and controlling of transportation modes, carriers and services.

Trailer - Container to haul commodities that is mounted on wheels and pulled by a tractor.

Trailer Drops - When a driver drops off a full truck at a warehouse and picks up an empty one. See Drop.

Trailer on a Flatcar (TOFC) - A specialized form of containerization in which motor and rail transport coordinate. Synonym: Piggyback.

Tramp - An international water carrier that has no fixed route or published schedule; a tramp ship is chartered for a particular voyage or a given time period.

Transaction - A single completed transmission, e.g., transmission of an invoice over an EDI network. Analogous to usage of the term in data processing, in which a transaction can be an inquiry or a range of updates and trading transactions. The definition is important for EDI service operators, who must interpret invoices and other documents.

Transaction Set - Commonly used business transactions (e.g. purchase order, invoice, etc.) organized in a formal, structured manner, consisting of a Transaction Set header control segment, one or more Data Segments, and a Transaction Set trailer Control Data Segment.

Transaction Set ID - A three digit numerical representation that identifies a transaction set.

Transactional Acknowledgement - Specific Transaction Sets, such as the Purchase Order Acknowledgement (855), that both acknowledges receipt of an order and provides special status information such as reschedules, price changes, back order situation, etc.

Transfer Pricing - The pricing of goods or services transferred from one segment of a business to another. Transfer pricing generally includes the costs associated with performing the transfer and therefore item costs will be incrementally higher than when received through normal channels.

Transit Inventory - Inventory in transit between manufacturing and stocking locations, or between warehouses in a distributed warehousing model. Also see: In-transit Inventory

Transit privilege - A carrier service that permits the shipper to stop the shipment in transit to perform a function that changes the commodity's physical characteristics, but to pay the through rate.

Transit time - The total time that elapses from pickup to delivery of a shipment.

Translation Software - Software the converts or "translates" business application data into EDI standard formats, and vice versa.

Transmission Acknowledgment - Acknowledgment that a total transmission was received with no errors detected

Transparency - The ability to gain access to information without regard to the systems landscape or architecture. An example would be where an online customer could access a vendor's web site to place an order and receive availability information supplied by a third party outsourced manufacturer or shipment information from a third party logistics provider. See also: Visibility

Transportation - The movement of goods by method of rail, ocean, air, truck and/or pipeline.

Transportation Association of America - An association that represents the entire U.S. transportation system--carriers, users, and the public; now defunct.

Transportation Management System (TMS) - A computer program designed to provide optimized transportation management in various modes along with associated activities, including managed shipping units, labor planning and building, scheduling through inbound, outbound, intra-company shipments, documentation management, and third party logistics management. ##

Transportation method - A linear programming technique that determines the least-cost allocation of shipping goods from plants to warehouses of from warehouses to customers.

Transportation Mode - The method of transportation: rail, ocean, air, truck and pipeline.

Transportation Planning - The process of defining an integrated supply chain transportation plan and maintaining the information that characterize total supply

149

chain transportation requirements, and the management of transporters.

Transportation Planning Systems - The systems used in optimizing of assignments from plants to distribution centers, and from distribution centers to stores. The systems combine "moves" to ensure the most economical means are employed.

Transportation requirements planning (TRP) - Utilizing computer technology and information already available in MRP and DRP databases to plan transportation needs based on field demand.

Transportation Research Board - A division of the National Academy of Sciences which pertains to transportation research.

Transportation Research Forum - A professional association that provides a forum for the discussion of transportation ideas and research techniques.

Transshipment problem - A variation of the transportation method of linear programming that considers consolidating shipments to one destination and reshipping from that destination.

Travel agent - A firm that provides passenger travel information; air, rail, and steamship ticketing; and hotel reservations. The travel agent is paid a commission by the carrier and hotel.

Trend - General upward or downward movement of a variable over time such as demand for a product. Trends are used in forecasting to help anticipate changes in consumption over time.

Trend Forecasting Models - Methods for forecasting sales data when a definite upward or downward pattern exists. Models include double exponential smoothing, regression, and triple smoothing.

TRP - see Transportation requirements planning

Truckload (TL) - A shipment of freight that is loaded to a trailers maximum capacity either by bulk or maximum weight.

Truckload Lot - A truck shipment that qualifies for a lower freight rate because it meets a minimum weight and/or volume.

Trunk lines - Oil pipelines that are used for the long-distance movement of crude oil, refined oil, or other liquid products.

T's & C's - see Terms and conditions

Turnaround - In water transportation, the time it takes between the arrival of a vessel and its departure.

Turnover - (1) Typically refers to Inventory Turnover.(2) In the United Kingdom and certain other countries, turnover refers to annual sales volume. Also see: Inventory Turns

Twenty-foot Equivalent Unit (TEU) - Standard unit for counting containers of various capacities and for describing the capacities of container ships or terminals. One 20 Foot ISO container equals 1 TEU. One 40 Foot ISO container equals two TEU.

Two-bin system - An inventory ordering system in which the time to place an order for an item is indicated when the first bin is empty. The second bin contains sufficient supply until the order is received.

Two-Level Master Schedule - A master scheduling approach in which a planning bill of material is used to master schedule an end product or family, along with selected key features (options and accessories). Also see: Production Forecast

Ubiquity - A raw material that is found at all locations.

Definitions

UCC - see Uniform Code Council

UCS - see Uniform Communication Standard

UI - User Interface.

ULD - see Unit Load Device

Umbrella rate - An ICC rate-making practice that held rates to a particular level to protect the traffic of another mode.

UN/SPSC - see United Nations Standard Product and Service Code

Unbundled Payment/Remittance - The process where payment is delivered separately from its associated detail.

Uncertainty - Unknown future events that cannot be predicted quantitatively within useful limits.

Uniform Code Council (UCC) - A U.S. association that administers UCS, WINS, and VICS and provides UCS identification codes and UPCs. Also, a model set of legal rules governing commercial transmissions, such as sales, contracts, bank deposits and collections, commercial paper, and letters of credit. Individual states give legal power to the UCC by adopting its articles of law.

Uniform Communication Standard (UCS) - A set of standard transaction sets for the grocery industry that allows computer-tocomputer, paperless exchange of documents between trading partners. Using Electronic Data Interchange, UCS is a rapid, accurate and economical method of business communication; it can be used by companies of all sizes and with varying levels of technical sophistication.

Uniform Product Code (UPC) - A standard product numbering and bar coding system used by the retail industry. UPC codes are administered by the Uniform Code Council; they identify the manufacturer as well as the item, and are included on virtually all retail packaging. Also see: Uniform Code Council

Uniform Resource Locator (URL) - A string that supplies the Internet address of a website or resource on the World Wide Web, along with the protocol by which the site or resource is accessed. The most common URL type is http;//, which gives the Internet address of a web page. Some other URL types are gopher://, which gives the Internet address of a Gopher directory, and ftp:;//, which gives the network location of an FTP resource.

Uniform Warehouse Receipts Act - The act that sets forth the regulations governing public warehousing. The regulations define the legal responsibility of a warehouse manager and define the types of receipts issued.

Unit Cost - The cost associated with a single unit of product. The total cost of producing a product or service divided by the total number of units. The cost associated with a single unit of measure underlying a resource, activity, product or service. It is calculated by dividing the total cost by the measured volume. Unit cost measurement must be used with caution as it may not always be practical or relevant in all aspects of cost management.

Unit Load Device (ULD) - Any type of container or pallets used to consolidate packages of freight for mechanical handling.

Unit of Driver Measure - The common denominator between groupings of similar activities. Example: 20 hours of process time is performed in an activity center. This time equates to a number of common activities varying in process time duration. The unit of measure is a standard measure of time such as a minute or an hour.

Unit of Measure (UOM) - The unit in which the quantity of an item is managed,

151

e.g., pounds, each, box of 12, package of 20, or case of 144. Various UOMs may exist for a single item. For example, a product may be purchased in cases, stocked in boxes and issued in single units.

Unit Train - An entire, uninterrupted locomotive, car movement between an origin and destination.

United Nations Standard Product and Service Code (UN/SPSC) - developed jointly between the UN and Dun & Bradstreet (D&B). Has a five level coding structure (segment, family, class, commodity, business function) for nearly 9000 products.

United States Railway Association - The planning and funding agency for Conrail; created by the 3-R Act of 1973.

Unitization - In warehousing, the consolidation of several units into larger units for fewer handlings.

Unitize - To consolidate a number of packages into one unit; the several packages are strapped, banded, or otherwise attached together.

Unit-of-measure conversion - A conversion ratio used whenever multiple units-of-measure are used with the same item. For example, if you purchased an item in cases (meaning that your purchase order stated a number of cases rather than a number of pieces) and then stocked the item in eaches, you would require a conversion to allow your system to calculate how many eaches are represented by a quantity of cases. This way, when you received the cases, your system would automatically convert the case quantity into an each quantity.

Unplanned Order - Orders which are received that do not fit into the volumes prescribed by the plans developed from forecasts.

UOM - see Unit of Measure

UPC - see Uniform Product Code

Upcharges - Charges added to a bill, particularly a freight bill, to cover additional costs that were not envisioned when a contract was written. These might include costs related to rapidly increasing fuel charges or costs related to government mandates. See also: Accessorial Charges.

Upsell - The practice of attempting to sell a higher-value product to the customer.

Upside Production Flexibility - The number of days required to complete manufacture and delivery of an unplanned sustainable 20% increase in end product supply of the predominant product line. The one constraint that is estimated to be the principal obstacle to a 20% increase in end product supply, as represented in days, is Upside Flexibility: Principal Constraint. Upside Flexibility could affect three possible areas: direct labor availability, internal manufacturing capacity, and key components or material availability.

Upstream - Refers to the supply side of the supply chain. Upstream partners are the suppliers who provide goods and services to the organization needed to satisfy demands which originate at point of demand or use, as well as other flows such as return product movements, payments for purchases, etc. Opposite of downstream.

Urban Mass Transportation Administration - An agency of the U.S. Department of Transportation responsible for developing comprehensive mass transport systems for urban areas and for providing financial aid to transit systems.

URL - see Uniform Resource Locator

Usage Rate - Measure of demand for product per unit of time (e.g., units per month, etc.).

DEFINITIONS

V

Validation - To check whether a document is the correct type for a particular EDI system, as agreed upon by the trading partners, in order to determine whether the document is going to or coming from an authorized EDI user.

Valuation - Amount of a carrier's liability expressed by a dollar value placed on a shipment by the shipper that specifies the carrier's maximum liability in the event of a covered claim for losses or damages.

Valuation Charges - Charges to shippers who declare a value of goods higher than the value of the carriers' limits of liability.

Value Added - Increased or improved value, worth, functionality or usefulness.

Value Analysis - A method to determine how features of a product or service relate to cost, functionality, appeal and utility to a customer (i.e., engineering value analysis). Also see: Target Costing

Value Based Return (VBR) - A measure of the creation of value. It is the difference between economic profit and capital charge.

Value Chain - A series of activities, which combined, define a business process; the series of activities from manufacturers to the retail stores that define the industry supply chain.

Value Chain Analysis - A method to identify all the elements in the linkage of activities a firm relies on to secure the necessary materials and services, starting from their point of origin, to manufacture, and to distribute their products and services to an end user.

Value of Transfers - The total dollar value (for the calendar year) associated with movement of inventory from one "bucket" into another, such as raw material to work-in-process, work-in-process to finished goods, plant finished goods to field finished goods or customers, and field finished goods to customers. Value of Transfers is based on the value of inventory withdrawn from a certain category and is often approached from a costing perspective, using cost accounts.

Value Proposition - What the supply chain member offers to other members. To be truly effective, the value proposition has to be two-sided; a benefit to both buyers and sellers.

Value stream - All activities, both value added and nonvalue added, required to bring a product from raw material state into the hands of the customer, bring a customer requirement from order to delivery and bring a design from concept to launch.

Value stream mapping - A pencil and paper tool used in two stages: (1) Follow a product's production path from beginning to end and draw a visual representation of every process in the material and information flows. Then draw a future state map of how value should flow. The most important map is the future state map.

Value-Added Network (VAN) - A company that acts as a clearing-house for electronic transactions between trading partners. A third-party supplier that receives EDI transmissions from sending trading partners and holds them in a "mailbox" until retrieved by the receiving partners.

Value-Added Productivity Per Employee - Contribution made by employees to total product revenue minus the material purchases divided by total employment. Total employment is total employment for the entity being surveyed. This is the average full-time equivalent employee in all functions, including sales and marketing, distribution, manufacturing, engineering, customer service, finance, general and administrative, and other. Total employment should include contract and temporary employees on a full-time equivalent (FTE) basis. Calculation: Total Product Revenue-External Direct Material / [FTE's]

Value-Added Tax (VAT) - A fee levied on all goods and services as goods and services go through the production chain, from the raw material to final use. The amount taxed is the amount of the value in a particular step in the production chain.

Value-Adding/Nonvalue-Adding - Assessing the relative value of activities according to how they contribute to customer value or to meeting an organization's needs. The degree of contribution reflects the influence of an activity's cost driver(s).

Value-Based Management (VBM) - Satisfying customers to create shareholder wealth.

Value-of-service pricing - Pricing according to the value of the product being transported; third-degree price discrimination; demand-oriented pricing; charging what the traffic will bear.

VAN - see Value-Added Network

Van Operator - The individual(s) responsible for the operation of a tractor and for the loading, transportation and unloading of shipments. Also referred to as a driver.

Variable Cost - A cost that fluctuates with the volume or activity level of business.

VAT - see Value-Added Tax

VBM - see Value-Based Management

VBR - see Value Based Return

Velocity - (1) Rate of product movement through a warehouse (2) A term used to indicate the relative speed of all transactions, collectively, within a company's supply chain community. A MAXIMUM velocity is most desirable since it indicates higher asset turnover for stockholders, and faster order-to-delivery response for customers.

Vendor - The manufacturer or distributor of an item or product line. Also see: Supplier

Vendor Code - A unique identifier, usually a number and sometimes the company's DUNS number, assigned by a Customer for the Vendor it buys from. Example; a Grocery Store Chain buys Oreo's from Nabisco. The Grocery Store Chain, for accounting purposes, identifies Nabisco as Vendor

Vendor Owned Inventory (VOI) - See Consignment Inventory

Vendor Project Management - Coordinating the relocation of specific components from the existing location into the new site or the asset swap of specific equipment. This includes management of one or multiple vendors who may support the specified equipment via warranty or maintenance service contracts.

Vendor-Managed Inventory (VMI) - The practice of retailers making suppliers responsible for determining order size and timing, usually based on receipt of retail POS and inventory data. Its goal is to increase retail inventory turns and reduce stock outs. Its goal is to increase retail inventory turns and reduce stock outs. It may or may not involve consignment of inventory (supplier ownership of the inventory located at the customer).

Vertical Hub/Vertical Portal - Serving one specific industry. Vertical portal websites that cater to consumers within a particular industry. Similar to the term "vertical industry", these websites are industry specific, and like a portal, they make use of Internet technology by using the same kind of personalization technology. In addition to industry specific vertical portals that cater to consumers, another definition of a vertical portal is one that caters solely to other businesses.

Vertical Integration - The degree to which a firm has decided to directly produce multiple value-adding stages from raw

DEFINITIONS

material to the sale of the product to the ultimate consumer. The more steps in the sequence, the greater the vertical integration. A manufacturer that decides to begin producing parts, components, and materials that it normally purchases is said to be backward integrated. Likewise, a manufacturer that decides to take over distribution and perhaps sale to the ultimate consumer is said to be forward integrated.

VICS - Voluntary Interindustry Commerce Standards. The retail industry standards body responsible for the CPFR standard, among other things.

Viral Marketing - The concept of embedding advertising into web portals, pop-ups and as e-mail attachments to spread the word about products or services that the target audience may not otherwise have been interested in.

Virtual Corporation - The logical extension of outpartnering. With the virtual corporation, the capabilities and systems of the firm are merged with those of the suppliers, resulting in a new type of corporation where the boundaries between the suppliers' systems and those of the firm seem to disappear. The virtual corporation is dynamic in that the relationships and structures formed change according to the changing needs of the customer.

Virtual Factory - A changed transformation process most frequently found under the virtual corporation. It is a transformation process that involves merging the capabilities and capacities of the firm with those of its suppliers. Typically, the components provided by the suppliers are those that are not related to a core competency of the firm, while the components managed by the firm are related to core competencies. One advantage found in the virtual factory is that it can be restructured quickly in response to changing customer demands and needs.

Visibility - The ability to access or view pertinent data or information as it relates to logistics and the supply chain, regardless of the point in the chain where the data exists.

Vision - The shared perception of the organization's future--what the organization will achieve and a supporting philosophy. This shared vision must be supported by strategic objectives, strategies, and action plans to move it in the desired direction. Synonym: vision statement.

VMI - see Vendor-Managed Inventory

VOI - see Vendor Owned Inventory

Voice Activated or Voice Directed - Systems which guide users such as warehouse personnel via voice commands

Voice of the customer - The expressed requirements and expectations of customers relative to products or services, as documented and disseminated to the members of the providing organization.

Wagner-Whitin Algorithm - A mathematically complex, dynamic lot-sizing technique that evaluates all possible ways of ordering to cover net requirements in each period of the planning horizon to arrive at the theoretically optimum ordering strategy for the entire net requirements schedule. Also see: Discrete Order Quantity, Dynamic Lot Sizing

Walkboard - Walkway used as a bridge from the ground to a trailer's floor for loading or unloading.

Wall-to-Wall Inventory - An inventory management technique in which material enters a plant and is processed through the plant into finished goods without ever having entered a formal stock area.

WAN - see Wide Area Network

Glossary of Terms in Logistics & Shipping

Warehouse - Storage location for products. Principal warehouse activities include receipt of product, storage, shipment, and order picking.

Warehouse Management System (WMS) - The systems used in effectively managing warehouse business processes and direct warehouse activities, including receiving, putaway, picking, shipping, and inventory cycle counts. Also includes support of RF communications, allowing real-time data transfer between the system and warehouse personnel. They also maximize space and minimize material handling by automating putaway processes.

Warehousing - The activities related to receiving, storing, and shipping materials to and from production or distribution locations.

Warranty Costs - Includes materials, labor, and problem diagnosis for products returned for repair or refurbishment.

Waste - (1) In Lean and Just-in-Time, any activity that does not add value to the good or service in the eyes of the consumer.(2) A by-product of a process or task with unique characteristics requiring special management control. Waste production can usually be planned and controlled. Scrap is typically not planned and may result from the same production run as waste.

Waterway use tax - A per-gallon tax assessed barge carriers for use of the waterways.

Wave Picking - A method of selecting and sequencing picking lists to minimize the waiting time of the delivered material. Shipping orders may be picked in waves combined by a common product, common carrier or destination, and manufacturing orders in waves related to work centers.

Waybill - Document containing description of goods that are part of common carrier freight shipment. Show origin, destination, consignee/consignor, and amount charged. Copies travel with goods and are retained by originating/delivering agents. Used by carrier for internal record and control, especially during transit. Not a transportation contract.

Web - A computer term used to describe the global Internet. Synonym: World Wide Web

Web Browser - A client application that fetches and displays web pages and other World Wide Web resources to the user.

Web Services - A computer term for information processing services that are delivered by third parties using internet portals. Standardized technology communications protocols; network services as collections of communication formats or endpoints capable of exchanging messages.

Web Site - A location on the Internet.

Weight Break - The shipment volume at which point the less-than-truckload (LTL) charges equal the Truckload (TL) charges at the minimum weight.

Weight Confirmation - The practice of confirming or validating receipts or shipments based on the weight.

Weighted-Point Plan - A supplier selection and rating approach that uses the input gathered in the categorical plan approach and assigns weights to each evaluation category. A weighted sum for each supplier is obtained and a comparison made. The weights used should sum to 100% for all categories. Also see: Categorical Plan

Weight-losing raw material - A raw material that loses weight in processing

What You See Is What You Get (WYSIWYG) - An editing interface in which a file created is displayed as it will appear to an end-user.

Wholesaler - See Distributor

Wide Area Network (WAN) - A public or private data communications system for linking computers distributed over a large geographic area.

Will Call - The practice of taking orders that will be picked up at the selling facility by the buyer. An area where buyers can pick up an order at the selling facility. This practice is widely used in the service parts business.

Windows Meta File (WMF) - A vector graphics format for Windows-compatible computers used mostly or word processing clip art.

WIP - see Work-in-Process

WMF - see Windows Meta File

WMS - see Warehouse Management System

Work-in-Process (WIP) - Parts and subassemblies in the process of becoming completed finished goods. Work in process generally includes all of the material, labor and overhead charged against a production order which has not been absorbed back into inventory through receipt of completed products.

World Wide Web (WWW) - A "multimedia hyper linked database that spans the globe" and lets you browse through lots of interesting information. Unlike earlier Internet services, the 'Web' combines text, pictures, sounds, and even animations, and it lets you move around with a click of your computer mouse.

WWW - see World Wide Web

WYSIWYG - see What You See Is What You Get

X12 - The ANSI standard for interindustry electronic interchange of business transactions.

X400 - A standard that allows electronic messages to be sent from one computer to another regardless of hardware and software differences.

XML - see Extensible Markup Language

Yard Management System (YMS) - A system which is designed to facilitate and organize the coming, going and staging of trucks and trucks with trailers in the parking "yard" that serves a warehouse, distribution or manufacturing facility.

Yield - The ratio of usable output from a process to its input.

YMS - see Yard Management System

━━━━━ Z ━━━━━

Zone of rate flexibility - Railroads are permitted to raise rates by a percentage increase in the railroad cost index determined by the ICC; rates may be raised by 6% per year through 1984 and 4% thereafter.

Zone of rate freedom - Motor carriers are permitted to raise or lower rates by 10% in one year without ICC interference; if the rate change is within the zone of freedom, the rate is presumed to be reasonable.

Zone of reasonableness - A zone or limit within which air carriers are permitted to change rates without regulatory scrutiny; if the rate change is within the zone, the new rate is presumed to be reasonable.

Zone Picking - A method of subdividing a picking list by areas within a storeroom for more efficient and rapid order picking. A zone-picked order must be grouped to a single location and the separate pieces combined before delivery or must be delivered to different locations, such a work centers. Also see: Batch Picking

Zone price - The constant price of a product at all geographic locations within the zone.

Zone Skipping - For shipments via the US Postal Service, depositing mail at a facility one or more zones closer to the destination. This option would benefit customers operating in close proximity to a zone border or shipping sufficient volumes to offset additional transportation costs.

TERMS

14 Points
24/7
24/7/365
24-hour Manifest Rule (24-hour Rule)
3D Loading
3PL
4PL
5-Point Annual Average
5-S Program
80-20 Rule
A/P
A/R
Abandonment
ABB
ABC
ABC Classification
ABC Costing
ABC Inventory Control
ABC Model
ABC System
ABM
Abnormal Demand
ABP
Absorption
Absorption Costing
Acceptable Quality Level
Acceptable Sampling Plan
Acceptance Number
Acceptance Sampling
Accessibility
Accessorial
Accessorial charges
Accessory
Accountability
Accounts Payable
Accounts receivable (A/R)
Accreditation
Accredited Standards Committee

Accumulation bin
Accuracy
ACD
ACE
ACH
Acknowledgment
Acquisition Cost
ACSI
Act of God
Action Message
Action plan
Action Report
Activation
Active Inventory
Active Stock
Activity
Activity Analysis
Activity Based Budgeting
Activity Based Costing
Activity Based Costing Model
Activity Based Costing System
Activity Based Management
Activity Based Planning
Activity Dictionary
Activity Driver
Activity Level
Activity network diagram
Activity Ratio
Actual Cost System
Actual Costs
Actual Demand
Actual to Theoretical Cycle Time
Ad Valorem (Latin)
Adaptive Control
Adaptive Smoothing
Addendum
Add-Ons
Advance Material Request

GLOSSARY OF TERMS IN LOGISTICS & SHIPPING

Advanced Planning and Scheduling
Advanced Planning Systems
Advanced Shipping Notice
Advising Bank
Aftermarket
After-Sale Service
Agency tariff
Agent
Agglomeration
Aggregate Forecast
Aggregate Inventory
Aggregate Inventory Management
Aggregate Plan
Aggregate Planning
Aggregate tender rate
Aggregated Shipments
Agile manufacturing
Agility
AGVS
AI
Air cargo
Air Cargo Containers
Air Freight
Air Freight Forwarder
Air taxi
Air Transport Association of America
Air Waybill
Airport and Airway Trust Fund
Alaskan carrier
Alert
Algorithm
All Water
All-cargo carrier
Alliance
Allocated item
Allocation
Allocation Costing
Alpha release
Alternate Routing
American Customer Satisfaction Index
American National Standards Institute
American Society for Quality
American Society for Testing and Materials
American Society for Training and Development
American Society of Transportation & Logistics
American Standard Code for Information Interchange
American Trucking Association, Inc.
American Waterway Operators
Amtrak

Animated GIF
ANSI
ANSI ASC X12
ANSI Standard
Anticipated Delay Report
Anticipation Inventories
Any Quantity [AQ]
Any-quantity rate
Applicability Statement 2
Application Service Provider
Application-to-Application
Appraisal Costs
Approved Vendor List
APS
APS
AQ
AQI
AQL
Arbitrary
Army Corps of Engineers
Arrival Notice
Arrow diagram
Artificial Intelligence
Artificial Tween Decks
AS/RS
AS2
ASC
ASC X12
ASCII
ASN
ASP
ASQ
Assemble to Order
Assemble-to-order
Assembly
Assembly Line
Asset
Asset Management
Asset Swap
Asset-Based, Third Party Provider
Assignment
Association of American railroads: A railroad industry association that represents the larger U.S. railroads.
Assumed Receipt
ASTD
ASTM
ATD
ATP
ATS
Attachment
Attributes

160

TERMS

Audit
Audit Trail
Auditability
Auditing
Authentication
Authentication Key
Autodiscrimination
AutoID
Automated Call Distribution
Automated Clearinghouse
Automated Commercial Environment
Automated Guided Vehicle System
Automated Storage/Retrieval System
Automatic Relief
Automatic Rescheduling
Availability
Available Inventory
Available to Sell
Available-to-Promise
Average Annual Production Materials Related
A/P (Accounts Payable)
Average Cost per Unit
Average Inventory
Average Payment Period (for materials)
AVL
Avoidable Cost
AWB
B2B
B2C
Back Haul
Back Order
Back Scheduling
Backflush
Backhaul
Backlog Customer
Backorder
Backsourcing
BAF
Balance sheet
Balance to Ship
Balanced Scorecard
Balance-of-Stores Record
BAM
Bank Guarantee
Banker's Acceptance
Bar Code
Bar Code Scanner
Barcode
Barcode, 2-D
Barge
Barrier to Entry
Base Demand

Base Index
Base Inventory Level
Base Port
Base Rate
Base Series
Base Stock System
Baseload Demand
Basic Producer
Basing Points
Batch Control Totals
Batch Number
Batch Picking
Batch Processing
Baud
Bay
BCP
Beginning Available Balance
Benchmarking
Benefit-cost ratio
Berth
Best Practice
Best-in-Class
Beta release
Bilateral Contract
Bill of Activities
Bill of Exchange
Bill of Lading
Bill of Material
Bill of Material Accuracy
Bill of Resources
Billed Weight
Bin
Binary
Bisynchronous
Bitmap Image
Blanket Order
Blanket Purchase Order
Blanket Rate
Blanket Release
Blanket Wrap
Bleeding Edge
Blind Counts
Block diagram
Blocking bug
Blow Through
BMP
Body of knowledge
BOK
BOL
Bolero
BOM
Bonded Goods

161

GLOSSARY OF TERMS IN LOGISTICS & SHIPPING

Bonded Warehouse
Bonded Warehouse - Export
Bonded Warehouse - Import
Book Inventory
Booking
Booking Number
Bookings
Bottleneck
Bottom-up Replanning
Box Rate
Boxcar
Box-Jenkins Model
BPM
BPO
BPR
Bracing
Bracketed Recall
Branding
Breadman
Break-Bulk
Break-Even Chart
Break-Even Point
Bricks and Mortar
Broadband
Broken case
Broker
Brokerage Licence
Brokered Systems
Browser
BTS
Bucketed System
Bucketless system
Buffer
Buffer Management
Buffer Stock
Bulk area
Bulk packing
Bulk storage
Bulletin Board
Bullwhip Effect
Bundle
Bunker Adjustment Factor
Bunker Surcharge
Burn Rate
Business Activity Monitoring
Business Application
Business Continuity
Business Continuity Plan
Business Logistics
Business Performance Measurement
Business Plan
Business Process Outsourcing

Business Process Reengineering
Business Unit
Business-to-Business
Business-to-Consumer
Buyer Behavior
Byte
Caboose
Cabotage
CAD
CAE
CAF
Cage
Caged
Calculation
Call Center
CAM
Canadian Customs Invoice
Can-order Point
Capability maturity model
Capable to Promise
Capacity
Capacity Management
Capacity Planning
CAPEX
Capital
CAPP
Car supply charge
Cargo
Cargo Bays
Cargo Manifest
Carload Lot
Carmack Amendment
Carnet
Carousel
Carriage and Insurance Paid To
Carriage Paid To
Carrier
Carrier Certificate and Release Order
Carrier Liability
Carrier's Certificate
Cartage
Cartage Agent
Cartel
Case Code
Cash Conversion Cycle
Cash flow statement
Cash-to-Cash Cycle Time
Catalog Channel
Categorical Plan
Category management
Causal Forecast
Cause and Effect Diagram

TERMS

CBM
CBT
Cell
Cellular manufacturing
Center-of-Gravity Approach
Centralized authority
Centralized Dispatching
Centralized Inventory Control
Certificate of Analysis
Certificate of Compliance
Certificate of Insurance
Certificate of origin
Certificate of public convenience and necessity
Certificated carrier
Certified Supplier
CFD
CFR
CFS
CGMP
Chain of Customers
Chain reaction
Challenge and Response
Champion
Change agent
Change Management
Change Order
Changeover
Channel
Channel Charging area
Channel Conflict
Channel Partners
Channels of Distribution
Chargeable Weight
Chassis
Chock
CI
CIF
CIM
CIP
City driver
Civil Aeronautics Board
CL
Claim
Claim Tracer
Claims
Class I carrier
Class II carrier
Class III carrier
Class rate
Class Rates
Classification

Classification yard
CLCA
Clean On Board
Clearance
Clearinghouse
Cleat
Click-and-Mortar
Clip Art
Clipboard
CLM
Closed-loop corrective action
Closed-loop MRP
CMI
CMM
CMMS
COA
Coastal carriers
Codabar
Code
Code 128 Auto
Code 128A
Code 128B
Code 128C
Code 3 of 9
Code 93
Co-destiny
Codifying
COFC
COGS
Collaboration
Collaborative planning, forecasting, and replenishment
Collaborative Product Commerce
Co-Managed Inventory
Combined Lead Time
Combined Transport Bill of Lading
Commercial Invoice
Commercial zone
Committed Capability
Committee of American Steamship Lines
Commodities
Commodities clause
Commodity
Commodity Buying
Commodity Code
Commodity Procurement Strategy
Commodity Rate
Common Carrier
Common carrier duties
Common cost
Common Point
Common Tariff

163

GLOSSARY OF TERMS IN LOGISTICS & SHIPPING

Communication Protocol
Commuter
Company Culture
Company Guarantee
Comparative advantage
Competitive Advantage
Competitive Benchmarking
Competitive Bid
Complete & On-Time Delivery
Complete Manufacture to Ship Time
Compliance
Compliance Checking
Compliance Monitoring
Compliance Program
Component
Computer Aided Design
Computer Aided Engineering
Computer Aided Manufacturing
Computer Aided Process Planning
Computer Based Training
Computer Integrated Manufacturing
Computerized Maintenance Management Systems
Computerized process simulation
Computerized SPC
Concealed Damage
Concurrent engineering
Conference
Configuration
Configure/Package-to-Order
Confirmation
Confirming Order
Conformance
Conrail
Consensus
Consignee
Consignment
Consignment Inventory
Consignor
Consolidation
Consortium
Constraint
Constraint-based planning and scheduling
Consul
Consular Declaration
Consular Invoice
Consular Visa
Consumer Packaged Goods
Consumer-Centric Database
Consuming the Forecast
Container
Container Depot

Container Freight Station
Container Security Initiative
Container Service Charge
Container Stuffing List
Container Yard
Containerization
Contingency planning
Continuous Flow Distribution
Continuous Improvement
Continuous Process Improvement
Continuous Replenishment
Continuous Replenishment Planning
Continuous-flow, fixed-path equipment
Contract
Contract Administration
Contract Carrier
Contribution
Contribution Margin
Controlled Access
Conveyor
Cookie
Cooperative associations
Co-opetition
Coordinated transportation
Co-Packer
Co-product
Core Competency
Core Process
Cost Accounting
Cost Allocation
Cost and Freight
Cost Center
Cost Driver
Cost Driver Analysis
Cost Element
Cost Management
Cost of Capital
Cost of Goods Sold
Cost of lost sales
Cost trade-off
Cost Variance
Cost, Insurance and Freight
Cost-optimized
COTD
Council of Logistics Management
Council of Supply Chain Management Professionals
Country of Destination
Country of Origin
Courier service
CPC
CPFR

CPG
CPI
CPT
Crane
Credit Level
Credit Terms
Critical Data
Critical Differentiators
Critical Success Factor
Critical value analysis
CRM
Cross Docking
Cross functional
Cross Sell
Cross-Docking
Cross-Shipment
Cross-Subsidy
CRP
CSCMP
CSF
CSI
CSL
CSR
CTP
C-TPAT
Cubage
Cube
Cube Utilization
Cubed out
Cubic Foot
Cubic Space
Cumulative Available-to-Promise
Cumulative Lead Time
Cumulative Source/Make Cycle Time
Currency Adjustment Factor
Current good manufacturing practices
Customer
Customer Acquisition or Retention
Customer Driven
Customer Facing
Customer Interaction Center
Customer Order
Customer Profitability
Customer Receipt of Order to Installation Complete
Customer Relationship Management
Customer satisfaction
Customer Segmentation
Customer service
Customer Service Ratio
Customer Service Representative

Customer Signature/Authorization to Order Receipt
Customer/Order Fulfillment Process
Customer-Supplier Partnership
Customization
Customs
Customs Bounded Warehouse
Customs Broker
Customs Clearance
Customs Declaration
Customs Duties
Customs Entries
Customs House Broker
Customs Invoice
Customs Value
Customs-Trade Partnership against Terrorism
Cut-Off Time
CWT
CY
CY/CY
Cycle Count
Cycle Counting
Cycle inventory
Cycle Time
Cycle Time Reduction
Cycle Time to Process Excess Product Returns for Resale
Cycle Time to Process Obsolete and End-of-Life Product Returns for Disposal
Cycle Time to Repair or Refurbish Returns for Use
Cyclical Demand
DAF
Dangerous Goods
Dashboard
Data Communications
Data Dictionary
Data Interchange Standards Association
Data Migration/Relocation
Data Mining
Data Warehouse
Database
Date Code
Days of Supply
Days Sales Outstanding
DBR
DC
DDP
DDU
Dead on Arrival
Deadhead
Deadweight

GLOSSARY OF TERMS IN LOGISTICS & SHIPPING

Decentralized authority
Decision Support System
Decking
Declared Value
Decomposition
Dedicated carrier
Dedicated Contract Carriage
Defective goods inventory
De-Installation
Delimiters
Delivered at Frontier
Delivered Duty Paid
Delivered Duty Unpaid
Delivered Ex Quay
Delivered Ex Ship
Delivery
Delivery Appointment
Delivery Date Spread
Delivery Instructions
Delivery Order
Delivery Performance to Commit Date
Delivery Performance to Request Date
Delivery Ticket
Delivery-Duty-Paid
Delphi Method
Delta Nu Alpha
Demand Chain
Demand Chain Management
Demand creation
Demand management
Demand Planning
Demand Planning Systems
Demand Pull
Demand Supply Balancing
Demand Time Fence
Demand-Side Analysis
Deming Circle
Demographic Segmentation
Demurrage
Denied Party List
Density
Density Rate
DEQ
Deregulation
Derived Demand
DES
Design For Manufacture / Assembly
Design of Experiments
Destination
Destination-Enhanced Consolidation
Detention
Deterministic Models

DFMA
DFZ
DGI
Dial Up
Differential
Digital Signature
Dimensional Weight
Direct Channel
Direct Cost
Direct Product Profitability
Direct Production Material
Direct Retail Locations
Direct Store Delivery
Direct Transmission
Directed tasks
Direct-to-Store (DTS) Delivery
DISA
Disaster Recovery Planning
Discontinuous Demand
Discrete Available-to-Promise
Discrete Manufacturing
Discrete Order Picking
Discrete Order Quantity
Disintermediation
Dispatching
Distributed Inventory
Distribution
Distribution Center
Distribution Channel
Distribution On Demand
Distribution Planning
Distribution Requirements Planning
Distribution Resource Planning
Distribution Warehouse
Distributor
DIT
Diversion
Diversion Charge
DOA
Dock
Dock Receipt
Dock-to-Stock
Document
Documentation
DOD
DOE
Dolly
Domain
Domestic trunk line carrier
Door to Port
Door-to-Door
Dormant route

Double bottoms
Double Order Point System
Double stack
Double Stack Car
Double-pallet jack
Download
Downstream
Downtime
DPC
DPL
DPP
DPS
Draft
Drawback
Drayage
Driving time regulations
Drop
Drop Ship
DRP
DRP-II
Drum-Buffer-Rope
Dry Dock
DSD
DSO
DSS
DTD
DTF
DTP
Dual operation
Dual rate system
Dumping
Dunnage
DUNS
DUNS Number
Durable Goods
Duty
Duty Drawback
Duty Free Zone
Duty rate
Dynamic Lot Sizing
Dynamic Planning and Scheduling
Dynamic Process Control
EAI
EAN
EAN 13
EAN 8
EAN.UCC
Early Supplier Involvement
Earnings
Earnings Before Interest and Taxes
EBIT
EC

EC
ECCN
Echelon
ECO
E-Commerce
Economic Order Quantity
Economic Value Added
Economy of Scale
ECR
EDI
EDI message
EDI Standards
EDI Transmission
EDIFACT
Efficient Consumer Response
EFT
EIN
EIR
Electronic Commerce
Electronic Data Interchange
Electronic Data Interchange Association
Electronic Funds Transfer
Electronic Mail (E-Mail)
Electronic Product Code
Electronic Signature
Elkins Act
e-Logistics
E-mail
Empirical
Empowerment
Encryption
End item
End-of-Life
End-of-Life Inventory
Engineered flow of information
Engineering Change
Engineering Change Order
Engineer-to-Order
En-route
Enterprise Application Integration
Enterprise Resource Planning (ERP) System
Enterprise-Wide ABM
Enveloping
Environmentally Sensitive Engineering
EOQ
EPC
EPS
Equalisation
Equipment Interchange Receipt
Equipment Relocation
Ergonomic
Error List

GLOSSARY OF TERMS IN LOGISTICS & SHIPPING

ERS
ESI
Estimated Time of Arrival
ETA
ETD
Ethernet
Ethical standards
European Article Number
EVA
Evaluated Receipts Settlement
Ex Works
Exception
Exception Inventory
Exception Message
Exception Rate
Exception-Based Processing
Exclusive patronage agreements
Exclusive Use
Exempt Carrier
Expediting
Expert system
Explode-to-Deduct
Exponential Smoothing Forecast
Export
Export Broker
Export Compliance
Export Declaration
Export License
Export sales contract
Exporter Identification Number
Exports
Express
Extended 3 of 9
Extended Code 93
Extended Enterprise
Extended supply chain community
Extensible Markup Language
External Factory
Extra Loader
Extranet
Extrinsic Forecast
EXW
FA
FAA
Fabricator
Facilities
Failure Modes Effects Analysis
Fair return
Fair value
Fair-share Quantity Logic
FAK
FAS

FAST
Fast and Secure Trade
FB
FCA
FCL
Feature
Federal Aviation Administration
Federal Maritime Commission
Feeder
Feeder Railroad Development Program
FEU
FF&E
FFE
FFG
FGI
Field Finished Goods
Field Service
Field Service Parts
Field Warehouse
FIFO
File Transfer Protocol
Filed rate doctrine
Fill Rate
Fill Rates by Order
Final Assembly
Final Assembly Schedule
Final Destination
Finance lease
Financial responsibility
Finished Goods Inventory
Finite Forward Scheduling
Finite Scheduling
FIO
Firewall
Firm Planned Order
First In First Out
First Mover Advantage
First Pass Yield
Fixed Costs
Fixed interval inventory model
Fixed Interval Order System
Fixed Order Quantity
Fixed Order Quantity System
Fixed Overhead
Fixed Reorder Cycle Inventory Model
Fixed Reorder Quantity Inventory Model
Fixed-Location Storage
Fixed-Period Requirements
Flag of convenience
Flat
Flat Bed
Flat File

TERMS

Flatbed
Flatcar
Flexibility
Flexible Specialization
Flexible-path equipment
Float
Floating Cranes
Floor-Ready Merchandise
Flow rack
FMC
FMEA
FOB
Force Majeure
Forecast
Forecast Accuracy
Forecast Cycle
Forecasting
Foreign Trade Zone
For-hire carrier
For-Hire Carriers
Forklift Truck
Form utility
Forty-foot equivalent unit
Forwarder's Cargo Receipt
Four Party Logistics Provider
Four P's
Four Wall Inventory
Fourier Series
Free Alongside Ship
Free Carrier
Free On Board
Free Time
Freezing inventory balances
Freight
Freight Bill
Freight Bill
Freight Carriers
Freight Cashier
Freight Charge
Freight Collect
Freight Consolidation
Freight Forwarder
Freight Forwarders Institute
Freight Release
Freight-All-Kinds
FRM
Frozen Zone
FTE
FTL
FTP
FTZ
Fulfillment

Full Container Load
Full Truckload
Full Visible Capacity
Full-Service Leasing
Full-time Equivalents
Fully allocated cost
Functional Acknowledgment
Functional Group
Functional Silo
Furniture, Fixtures and Equipment
Future order
Gain Sharing
Gantry Crane
Gap analysis
Garment-on-Hanger
Gateway
Gathering lines
GBL
General commodities carrier
General Commodity
General-merchandise warehouse
Genset
GIF
Global Positioning System
Global Strategy
Global Trade Item Number
Globalization
GMP
GNP
GOH
Going-concern value
Gondola
Good manufacturing practices
Goods
Goods Received Note
Government Bill of Lading
GPS
Grandfather clause
Grandfathering
Granger laws
Graphics Interchange Format
Great Lakes carriers
GRI
Grid technique
GRN
Gross Inventory
Gross Margin
Gross National Product
Gross Weight
Groupthink
GTIN
GTM

Glossary of Terms in Logistics & Shipping

Guaranteed loans
Handling Costs
Hangertainer
Hard copy
Harmless Chemicals
Harmonised Tariff System
Harmonize Tariff Schedule of the United States
Harmonized Commodity Description & Coding System
Hawaiian carrier
HAWB
Hawthorne Effect
Hazardous Goods
Hazardous Material
Heavy Lift Charge
Hedge Inventory
Heijunka
Hierarchy of Cost Assignability
Highway Trust Fund
Highway use taxes
Hi-low
Hitchment
Holds
Home Page
Honeycombing
Hopper cars
Horizontal Play/Horizontal Hub
Hoshin Planning
Hospitality
Hostler
House Airwaybill
Household goods warehouse
HR
HS-code
HTML
HTS
HTTP
Hub
Hub airport
Human Resources
Human-machine interface
Hundredweight
Hustler
Hybrid Inventory System
Hyperlink
HyperText Markup Language
ICC
Igloos
Image Processing
IMC
IMCO
IMCO Classification
IMO
Import
Import/Export License
Importation Point
Imports
Impressions
In Bond
Inbound
Inbound Logistics
Incentive rate
include software program code or digital documents, music, videos, etc.
Income statement
INCOTERMS
Independent Action
Independent Carrier
Independent Demand Item Management Models
Independent Trading Exchange
Indirect Cost
Indirect Retail Locations
Indirect/Distributor Channel
Infinite Loading
Information System Agreement (ISA0
Information systems
Information Technology
Inherent advantage
Inland Carrier
Inland Point Intermodal
Insourcing
Installation
Insurance Certificate
Integrated Carriers
Integrated Logistics
Integrated Services Digital Network
Integrated tow barge
Intellectual Property
Interchange
Intercoastal carriers
Intercorporate hauling
Interleaved 2 of 5
Interleaving
Interline
Intermediately Positioned Warehouse
Intermittent-flow, fixed-path equipment
Intermodal
Intermodal Marketing Company
Intermodal Transport Unit
Intermodal Transportation
Internal customer
Internal Labor and Overhead

Internal water carriers
International Air Transport Association
International Civil Aeronautics Organization
International Freight Forwarders
International Procurement Organization
International Standards Organization
International Transport Implementation
  Guidelines Group
Internet
Interstate commerce
Interstate Commerce Commission
Interstate System
Intra-Manufacturing Re-plan Cycle
Intranet
In-transit Inventory
Intrastate commerce
Intrinsic Forecast Method
Inventory
Inventory Accuracy
Inventory Balance Location Accuracy
Inventory Carrying Cost
Inventory Carrying Costs
Inventory Control
Inventory Cost
Inventory Days of Supply
Inventory deployment
Inventory In Transit
Inventory Management
Inventory Planning Systems
Inventory Turnover
Inventory Turns
Inventory Velocity
Inventory, Days of
Invoice
IP
IPI
IPO
Irregular Route Carrier
IS
ISDN
ISO
ISO 14000 Series Standards
ISO 9000
Issuing Carrier
IT
ITE
Item
ITIGG
ITL
ITU
Java
Java Applet

Java applets
Java Script
Jidoka
JIT
JIT/QC
JIT-II
Job costing
JOC
Joint cost
Joint Photographic Expert Group
Joint rate
Joint Supplier Agreement
Jones Act
Journal of Commerce
JPEG
JSA
Just-in-Time
Just-in-Time II
Kaizen
Kaizen Blitz
Kanban
KD
Keiretsu
Key Custodians
Key Performance Indicator
Kitting
Knocked Down
Known Damage
Known Loss
KPI
L/H
Label Cargo
Lading
Laid-down cost
LAN
Land bridge
Land grants
Landed Cost
Lash barges
Last In, First Out
LC
LCL
LCL
LDI
Lead Logistics Partner
Lead Logistics Provider
Lead Time
Lead Time from Complete Manufacture to
  Customer Receipt
Lead Time from Order Receipt to Complete
  Manufacture
Least Total Cost

171

Glossary of terms in Logistics & Shipping

Least Unit Cost
LesSee
Lessor
Less-Than-Carload
Less-Than-Container Load
Less-Than-Trailer Load
Less-Than-Truckload
Less-Than-Truckload (LTL) Carriers
Letter of credit
Letter of Credit
Leverage
Liability
License Plate
Life Cycle Cost
LIFO
Lift truck
Lift Van
Lift-Gate
Lighter
Line
Line functions
Line Haul
Line Item
Line Scrap
Line-Haul
Line-haul shipment
Liner Service
Link
Linked Distributed Systems
Little Inch
Live
LLP
LLP
LNG Carrier
Load Date Spread
Load factor
Load Tender (Pick-Up Request)
Load Tendering
Loading allowance
Local Area Network
Local Delivery
Local Pick-Up
Local Rate
Local service carriers
Locational determinant
Locator System
Logbook
Logistic Straps
Logistic Track
Logistics
Logistics Channel
Logistics Data Interchange

Logistics Management
Long ton
Longshoreman
Lot Control
Lot Number
Lot size
Lot Sized System
Lot-for-Lot
LT
LTL
LTL
Lumping
Lumpy demand
M2M
Machine Downtimes
Machine-to-Machine interface
Macro environment
Mainframe
Maintenance, Repair, and Operating supplies
Major carrier
Make-or-buy decision
Make-to-Order
Make-to-Stock
Manifest
Manufacture Cycle Time
Manufacturer's Representative
Manufacturing Calendar
Manufacturing Capital Asset Value
Manufacturing Execution Systems
Manufacturing Lead Time
Manufacturing Resource Planning
Mapping
Marginal Cost
Marine insurance
Maritime Administration
Market Demand
Market dominance
Market Segment
Market-Positioned Warehouse
Marking
Marks and Numbers
Marquis Partners
Marshaller or Marshalling Agent
Mass Customization
Master Air Waybill
Master pack
Master Production Schedule
Material Acquisition Costs
Material Index
Material Requirements Planning
Material Safety Data Sheet
Materials Handling

Terms

Materials Management
Materials planning
Matrix Organizational Structure
MAWB
MAX
Maximum Inventory
Maximum Order Quantity
m-Commerce
M-Day Calendar
Mean
Measurement ton
Median
Merchant Haulage
Merge In Transit
Merger
MES
Message
Meta Tag
Metrics
Micro-land bridge
Mileage allowance
Mileage rate
Milk run
Min Max System
Mini-land Bridge
Minimum Charge
Minimum Truckload Weight
Minimum weight
Misguided Capacity Plans
Mission Critical
Mixed loads
Mixed Shipment
MLB
Modal split
Mode
Mother Vessel
Move Management
Move ticket
MPS
MRO
MRP
MRP-II
MSDS
MSI Plessey
MT
MTO
MTS
Multi-Currency
Multi-destination
Multinational company
Multi-origin
Multiple-car rate

Multi-Skilled
National carrier
National Industrial Traffic League
National Motor Bus Operators Organization
National Motor Freight Classification
National Railroad Corporation
National Stock Number
Nationalization
NCV
Negotiable Bill of Lading
Negotiating Bank
Nested
Net Asset Turns
Net Assets
Net Change MRP
Net Requirements
Net Weight
Neutral Body
New Product Introduction
NMFC
No Customs Value
No Location (No Loc)
Node
NOE
Non Vessel Operating Common Carrier
Non-Asset-Based Third Party Providers
Noncertified carrier
Nonconformity
Non-Durable goods
Non-Negotiable Bill of Lading
NOPAT
NOS
Notify Party
NPI
NSN
NVOCC
Object Linking and Embedding
OBL
Obsolete Inventory
OCP
OEE
OEM
Offshore
OLE
OMT, ORT, DMT
On Deck Stowage
On Order
On Time In Full
On-Carriage
On-Demand
One Piece Flow
One-Way Networks

173

Glossary of terms in Logistics & Shipping

On-Hand Balance
Online
On-line receiving
On-Time Performance
Open Rates
Open-to-Buy
Open-to-Receive
Operating ratio
Operational Performance Measurements
Optimization
Option
Optional Replenishment Model
Order
Order Batching
Order Complete Manufacture to Customer Receipt of Order
Order Consolidation Profile
Order Cycle
Order Cycle Time
Order Entry and Scheduling
Order Entry Complete to Start Manufacture
Order Fill
Order Fulfillment Lead Times
Order Interval
Order Level System
Order Management
Order Management Costs
Order Picking
Order Point Order Quantity System
Order Processing
Order Promising
Order Receipt to Order Entry Complete
Order Tracking
Order-to-cash
Organizational transparency
Origin
Original Equipment Manufacturer
OS&D
OTIF
Out of Gauge
Out Of Stock
Out of Stocks
Outbound
Outbound Consolidation
Outbound Logistics
Outlier
Outpartnering
Outport
Outsource
Outsourced Cost of Goods Sold
Over Landed
Over, Short, and Damaged

Overall Equipment Effectiveness
Overland Common Port
Over-the-road
Owner-operator
P & D
P2P
Package to Order
Packaging
Packing
Packing and Marking
Packing List
Pad Wrap
Pallet
Pallet Ticket
Pallet wrapping machine
Parcel Shipment
Pareto
Part Period Balancing
Part standardization
Partlow Chart
Partnerships and Alliances
Passenger-mile
Password
Path to Profitability
Pay-on-Use
Payroll
PBIT
PDA
PDCA
Peak demand
Peer to Peer
Pegged Requirement
Pegging
Per Diem
Percent of Fill
Perfect Order
Performance and Event Management Systems
Performance Measurement Program
Performance Measures
Period Order Quantity
Periodic Review System
Permit
Perpetual Inventory
Personal Digital Assistant
Personal discrimination
Phantom Bill of Material
Physical Distribution
Physical Inventory
Physical supply
Pick List
Pick on Receipt

TERMS

Pick/Pack
Pick-and-Drop
Pick-by-Light
Picking
Picking by Aisle
Picking by Source
Pick-to-carton
Pick-to-clear
Pick-to-light
Pick-to-trailer
Pick-Up Order
Pier
Piggyback
Pilferage
Pin lock
Place utility
Plaintext
Plan Deliver
Plan Make
Plan Source
Plan Stability
Plan-Do-Check-Action
Planned Date
Planned Order
Planned Receipt
Planning Bill
Planning Bill of Material
Planning Calendar
Planning Fence
Planning Horizon
Planning Time Fence
Planogram
Plant Finished Goods
Plimsoll Mark
PM
PO
POD
Point Of Sale
Point of Sale Information
Point-of-Purchase
Point-of-use inventory
Poka Yoke (mistake-proof)
Police powers
Pooling
POP
Port & Terminal Service Charge
Port authority
Portal
POS
Positioning
Possession utility

Post-Deduct Inventory Transaction Processing
POSTNET
Postponement
PPB
Pre-Deduct Inventory Transaction Processing
Predictive maintenance
Pre-Expediting
Prepaid
Present Value
Preventative Maintenance
Price Erosion
Primage
Primary highways
Primary Manufacturing Strategy
Primary-business test
PRIME QR
Private carrier
Private Label
Private Warehouse
Pro Number
Proactive
Process
Process Benchmarking
Process capability
Process Improvement
Process Manufacturing
Process technology
Process Yield
Procurement
Procurement Services Provider
Product
Product Characteristics
Product Configurator
Product Description
Product Family
Product line segmentation
Product modularity
Product serviceability
Product technology
Production Calendar
Production Capacity
Production Forecast
Production Line
Production Planning and Scheduling
Production-Related Material
Productivity
Profit
Profit Before Interest and Tax
Profit ratio
Profitability Analysis

Glossary of terms in Logistics & Shipping

Profitable to Promise
Prohibited Items
Project
Project Management
Promotion
Proof of Delivery
Proportional rate
Protocol
Pseudo Bill of Materials
PSP
PTI
PTSC
Public warehouse
Public warehouse receipt
Pull or Pull-through distribution
Pull Signal
Purchase Order
Purchase price discount
Purchasing
Pure raw material
Push back rack
Push Distribution
Push Technology
Put Away
Put-to-light
QFD
QR
Qualifier
Qualitative Forecasting Techniques
Quality
Quality Circle
Quality control
Quality Function Deployment
Quantitative Forecasting Techniques
Quantity Based Order System
Quarantine
Quay
Quick Response
Quick Response Program
Quitclaim
Rack
Racking
Radio Frequency
Radio Frequency Identificatrion
Railhead
Ramp Rate
Random-Location Storage
Rate Agreement
Rate basis number
Rate basis point
Rate bureau
Rate-Based Scheduling

Rationing
Raw Materials
Real-Time
Reasonable rate
Recapture Clause
Received for Shipment Bill of Lading
Receiving
Receiving Dock
Receiving Report
Reconsignment
Reed-Bulwinkle Act
Reefer
Reengineering
Re-engineering
Refrigerated Carriers
Regeneration MRP
Regional carrier
Register Ton
Regular-route carrier
Relay
Relay terminal
Released-value rates
Release-to-Start Manufacturing
Reliability
Reorder point
REP
Reparation
Re-plan Cycle
Replenishment
REQ
Request for Information
Request for Proposal
Request for Quote
Resellers
Resource Driver
Resources
RET
Retailer
Return Cargo
Return Disposal Costs
Return Goods Handling
Return Material Authorization
Return of Investment
Return on Assets
Return on Net Assets
Return on owner's equity
Return on Sales
Return Product Authorization
Return to Vendor
Returns Inventory Costs
Returns Material Acquisition, Finance, Planning and IT Costs

Terms

Returns Order Management Costs
Returns Processing Cost
Returns To Scale
Revenue Ton
Reverse Auction
Reverse Engineering
Reverse Logistics
RF
RFI
RFID
RFP
RFQ
RGA
Rich Media
Rich Text Format
Rigging
Right of eminent domain
Risk pooling
RM
RMA
RO
ROA
ROF
ROI
Roll on-roll-off
Roll-out
Root Cause Analysis
RosettaNet
Routing Accuracy
Routing or Routing Guide
RPA
RTF
RTV
Rule of eight
Rule of rate making
S&OP
Safety Stock
Salable Goods
Sales and Operations Planning
Sales Mix
Sales Plan
Sales Planning
Salvage material
Saw-Tooth Diagram
SBT
Scalability
Scan
Scan-Based Trading
Scanlon Plan
SCE
SCEM
Scenario Planning

SCI
SCM
SCOR
Scorecard
Scrap material
Seasonality
Seawaybill
Secondary highways
Secure Electronic Transaction
Segmentation
Self Billing
Self Correcting
Sell In
Sell Through
Selling, General and Administrative (SG&A) Expenses
Separable cost
Serial Number
Service Agreement
Service Level
Service Oriented Architecture
Service Parts Revenue
Service Provider
SET
Set Point
Setup costs
Shared Services
Shareholder Value
Shelf life
Shewhart Cycle
Shingo's Seven Wastes
Ship agent
Ship broker
Shipper
Shipper Packed
Shipper's agent
Shipper's association
Shipper's Load & Count
Shipping
Shipping Lane
Shipping Manifest
Shipping Order
Ship's Chandlers
Shop Calendar
Shop Floor Production Control Systems
Short Landed
Short Shipment
Short Shipped
Shortage
Short-haul discrimination
Shrink Wrap
Shrinkage

Glossary of terms in Logistics & Shipping

SIC
Sigma
Simulation
Single source leasing
Single sourcing
Single-Period Inventory Models
SIT
Six-Sigma Quality
Skills Matrix
SKU
SL&C
Sleeper team
Slip seat operation
Slip sheet
Slot Charter
Slotting
Slurry
Small Group Improvement Activity
SMART
Smart and Secure Trade Lanes
Smart label
SMDG
SOA
Society of Logistics Engineers
Sole sourcing
SOP
Sortation
SOW
Spam
SPC
Special Customs Invoice
Special Rate
Special-commodities carrier
Special-commodity warehouses
Specific, Measurable, Achievable, Realistic, Time-Based
Splash Page
Split case order picking
Split Delivery
Spot
Spot Demand
Spur track
SRT
SS
SST
ST
Stable Demand
Staff functions
Staging
Stakeholders
Standard Components
Standard Cost Accounting System

Standard Deviation/Variance
Standard Industrial Classification
Standard Operationg Procedure
Standing Order
Start Manufacture to Order Complete Manufacture
Statement of Work
Statistical Process Control
STC
Steamship conferences
Stevedore
Stickering
Stochastic Models
Stock Keeping Unit
Stock Out
Stockchase
Stockless purchasing
Stockout cost
Storage Charge
Storage in Transit
Store-Door Delivery
Stores
Straight Truck
Strategic Alliance
Strategic planning
Strategic Sourcing
Strategic variables
Strategy
Stratification
Stratified price levels
Stripping
Subcontracting
Sub-Optimization
Substitutability
Sunk Cost
Supplemental carrier
Supplier
Supplier Certification
Supplier-Owned Inventory
Supply Chain
Supply chain community
Supply Chain Design
Supply Chain Event Management
Supply Chain Execution
Supply Chain Integration
Supply Chain Inventory Visibility
Supply chain management
Supply Chain Management
Supply Chain Network Design Systems
Supply Chain Operations Reference Model
Supply Chain resiliency
Supply Chain Strategic Planning

TERMS

Supply Chain Strategy Planning
Supply Chain Vulnerability
Supply Chain-Related Finance and Planning Cost Element
Supply Chain-Related IT Costs
Supply Planning
Supply Planning Systems
Supply Warehouse
Support Costs
Supportive Project Management
Surcharge
Surrogate [item] Driver
Sustaining Activity
SWAS
Swing Gear
Switch engine
Switching company
SWOT
SWOT Analysis
SWOT Analysis
Synchronization
Syntax
System
Systems concept
Tact Time
Tactical Planning
Tag Number
Taguchi Method
Takt Time
Tally sheet
Tandem
Tank cars
Tapering rate
Tare Weight
Target Costing
Tariff
Task interleaving
Tasks
TCO
Technical Components
Temporary authority
Ten Principles
Tender
Terminal delivery allowance
Terms and conditions
TEU
Theoretical Cycle Time
Theory of Constraints
Third Party Logistics Provider
Third-Party Warehousing
Three-layer framework
Threshold

Throughput
Time Based Order System
Time Bucket
Time Fence
Time utility
Time/service rate
Time-Definite Services
Time-Stop
Timetables
Time-to-Product
TL
TMS
TOC
TOFC
Ton-mile
Total Annual Material Receipts
Total Annual Sales
Total Average Inventory
Total Cost Analysis
Total Cost Curve
Total Cost of Ownership
Total Cumulative Manufacture Cycle Time
Total Inventory Days of Supply
Total Make Cycle Time
Total Package and Label Cycle Time
Total Product Revenue
Total Productive Maintenance
Total quality management
Total Sourcing Lead Time
Total Supply Chain Response Time
Total Supply-Chain Management Cost
Total Test and Release Cycle Time
Toto authority
Touch Labor
TPM
TQM
Traceability
Tracing
Tracking and Tracing
Tracking Signal
Tractor
Trading Partner
Trading Partner Agreement
Trading partners
Traffic
Traffic Management
Trailer
Trailer Drops
Trailer on a Flatcar
Tramp
Transaction
Transaction Set

Glossary of terms in Logistics & Shipping

Transaction Set ID
Transactional Acknowledgement
Transfer Pricing
Transit Inventory
Transit privilege
Transit time
Translation Software
Transmission Acknowledgment
Transparency
Transportation
Transportation Association of America
Transportation Management System
Transportation method
Transportation Mode
Transportation Planning
Transportation Planning Systems
Transportation requirements planning
Transportation Research Board
Transportation Research Forum
Transshipment problem
Travel agent
Trend
Trend Forecasting Models
TRP
Truckload
Truckload Lot
Trunk lines
T's & C's
Turnaround
Turnover
Twenty-foot Equivalent Unit
Two-bin system
Two-Level Master Schedule
Ubiquity
UCC
UCS
UI
ULD
Umbrella rate
UN/SPSC
Unbundled Payment/Remittance
Uncertainty
Uniform Code Council
Uniform Communication Standard
Uniform Product Code
Uniform Resource Locator
Uniform Warehouse Receipts Act
Unit Cost
Unit Load Device
Unit of Driver Measure
Unit of Measure
Unit Train

United Nations Standard Product and Service Code
United States Railway Association
Unitization
Unitize
Unit-of-measure conversion
Unplanned Order
UOM
UPC
Upcharges
Upsell
Upside Production Flexibility
Upstream
Urban Mass Transportation Administration
URL
Usage Rate
Validation
Valuation
Valuation Charges
Value Added
Value Analysis
Value Based Return
Value Chain
Value Chain Analysis
Value of Transfers
Value Proposition
Value stream
Value stream mapping
Value-Added Network
Value-Added Productivity Per Employee
Value-Added Tax
Value-Adding/Nonvalue-Adding
Value-Based Management
Value-of-service pricing
VAN
Van Operator
Variable Cost
VAT
VBM
VBR
Velocity
Vendor
Vendor Code
Vendor Owned Inventory
Vendor Project Management
Vendor-Managed Inventory
Vertical Hub/Vertical Portal
Vertical Integration
VICS
Viral Marketing
Virtual Corporation
Virtual Factory

Visibility
Vision
VMI
VOI
Voice Activated or Voice Directed
Voice of the customer
Wagner-Whitin Algorithm
Walkboard
Wall-to-Wall Inventory
WAN
Warehouse
Warehouse Management System
Warehousing
Warranty Costs
Waste
Waterway use tax
Wave Picking
Waybill
Web
Web Browser
Web Services
Web Site
Weight Break
Weight Confirmation
Weighted-Point Plan
Weight-losing raw material
What You See Is What You Get
Wholesaler
Wide Area Network
Will Call
Windows Meta File
WIP
WMF
WMS
Work-in-Process
World Wide Web
WWW
WYSIWYG
X12
X400
XML
Yard Management System
Yield
YMS
Zone of rate flexibility
Zone of rate freedom
Zone of reasonableness
Zone Picking
Zone price
Zone Skipping

About the Editor

Paul Denneman (1963) received in 1991 cum laude his Master of Science Degree in Industrial Engineering & Management Sciences from the Eindhoven University of Technology. Since then Paul worked in different positions like Material & Quality-, Project-, Program-, Physical Distribution-, Business Unit- and Country Manager for companies like Kuehne + Nagel, MARC Global, Optelec, DSL Star Express and Maersk Logistics.

In 1993 Paul Denneman founded Mutatis Mutandis, logistic knowledge transfer, to make logistic knowledge more available to organizations. As from then he published a lot of articles and research reports, works as (chief) editor of handbooks in Logistics & IT, and is an often invited (APICS) logistics trainer.

In 2005 the free Internet weblog service eLogistics Trendwatch™ was developed and introduced. With visitors from over eighty countries, it seems to fill in a gap. In 2006 he started a logistics publishing company www.theKnowLedgeTransfer.com ™

Paul's main passion outside the logistics field of expertise is singing classical choir music. Of course this is done according to the same high standards as in his professional life. Paul lives in Eindhoven (the Netherlands) and has a daughter Willemijn (1999).

CPSIA information can be obtained
at www.ICGtesting.com
Printed in the USA
LVHW041620190621
690653LV00004B/417